SURVIVING
CHRONIC ILLNESS
GRACE IN THE FLAMES

'In *Surviving Chronic Illness: Grace in the Flames*, Steph Penny guides us through the choppy seas of chronic illness with the acuity of a seasoned sailor and the tenderness of a friend. Penny tells the story of her diagnosis with lupus and the constantly changing catalogue of symptoms, baring not only her body but her soul to the reader, offering us both her honest despair and genuine hope, painful doubt and joy-filled faith, plumbing the depths of her own experience in order to offer solidarity, companionship, and resources to her readers. This is one of the most generous books I've ever read.'

Jessica Kantrowitz,
author of *The Long Night*,
365 Days of Peace, and *Open Things*

'Dealing with chronic illness is A LOT and it's such a personal journey. This book presents that journey with an unexpected, but welcome, combination of humour, fact and faith. For anyone facing a difficult diagnosis or indeed on a challenging journey of self-discovery this book could be a welcome companion to let you know it can be OK despite the ups and downs.'

Charlie Bishop,
Director of MRKH Connect

'As I read this book, I felt like I'd engaged in a chat with a close friend who understood my heart, my pain, my worries and my earnest prayers. This book says all the things I've at some point thought privately and not had the courage to say out loud. It feels personal and conversational in nature, filled with heartfelt words, honest thoughts, real feelings, and an array of day-to- day challenges that I have personally experienced in living with chronic illness. This hope-filled and uplifting book captures the essence of my personal struggles in dealing with chronic illness in a way that no other book I've read has.'

Tamika Spaulding,
founder of *His Herd Ministries*,
hospital chaplain and fellow chronic illness survivor

'A great read for a unique, raw and honest perspective on living with a chronic debilitating illness. Steph adds some quirky humor and practical tips for those living with constant pain.'

Anders Halvorsen,
OAM recipient,
5 decades of lived experience with paraplegia
(and seeing God's blessing in the midst of it all)

'Hats off to Steph Penny for courageously persevering through her own pain and ill-health to produce this insightful and invaluable gem, *Surviving Chronic Illness*. With searing honesty, Steph tells it like it is for those suffering chronic illness and, in the process, gives them a voice we all need to hear. Yet she also reaches out to them with grace, understanding and compassion, sharing tested life strategies and encouraging them to see they are more than their illness. The quirky humour Steph employs throughout the book, combined with her clear, relaxed, inclusive writing style, serves to make a difficult topic much more reader-friendly, and her sincere determination to hold onto her faith in God, while still having so many unanswered questions, is both inspiring and challenging to us all.'

Jo-Anne Berthelsen,
author and speaker,
www.jo-anneberthelsen.com

'*Surviving Chronic Illness: Grace in the Flames* is a straight-talking, perspective shifting, posture of grace that is coated with the residue of Steph's tenacity, endurance, and staying power. With her boldness, authentic faith, and vulnerability, Steph reflects God's light and allows His love to shine through even in the darkest of places, as each page bears the mark of some hard-won wisdom that gives the reader a future and a hope. If you, or someone you know is struggling to find a sliver of beauty in the remnants of the ashes that chronic illness brings, this insightful book is the guide that will hold your hand and walk beside you through each and every challenge'

Wendy Parker,
Theologian, author,
and host of *The Spacious Room* podcast

'Surviving Chronic Illness is a book that will deeply resonate with anyone with long-term illness or their carers and friends. Relentlessly honest, it shatters apart the many ravaging lies told to those who suffer: that we must not have enough faith, that we should be more useful, that we are not 'claiming' our healing. There is great relief to be found in such authenticity and vulnerability. Rarely have I come across a book that digs so comprehensively and practically into every area that can affect the sick person, from loneliness to depression to how it is possible to keep worshipping God when life hurts. I found myself relaxing as Steph's poetic words of truth and assurance swept over me and took me to new places of hope where there often seems none. I warmly recommend it to everyone.'

Liz Carter,
author of *Valuable*

'Steph Penny's latest book Surviving Chronic Illness grabbed me from the word go. The author possesses a unique writing style – one that captivates her readers immediately and makes them want to keep reading. Her humorous style of writing transforms what could at times be heavy reading into what's delightful. As one who's battled chronic illness myself, I found it heartening to read her honest accounts of the struggles and challenges she faced. Christians can often feel judged when chronically ill, so what the author shares about grappling with the difficulties of faith and illness is especially encouraging. The author has a beautiful command of the language and she crafts each sentence with her unique quirky style, creating a very readable book. It's a book I highly recommend.'

Anusha Atukorala,
writer

'With regular doses of silliness, satire, pastoral sensitivity and brutal honesty, Steph Penny speaks grace to those of us affected by chronic illness. In one breath, she lampoons her condition to make us laugh, and in the next she somehow normalises and creates space for the depression, grief, and trauma that often comes with living with chronic illness. Her account of her own lived experience helps give voice to the relentlessness many of us feel, asking God 'Why haven't you healed me yet?', while showing us that meaning can still show up in tension with that mystery. As a health and pastoral professional, I think this is an incredible resource and invaluable guide to a world half our population inhabits. As a fellow "survivor", I feel deeply seen, valued, and loved.'

Krystyna Kidson,
Resident Psychologist for the
Baptist Association of NSW & ACT Churches

'Part pep-talk, part resource, part best friend lifting my chin to remember God's unceasing care, *Surviving Chronis Illness* is honest and real. Steph Penny navigates the unpredictable life of ongoing illness with authenticity and deep faith, inspiring readers in similar situations – or those who care for them – to lean on Christ with similar grit and grace.'

Penny Reeve,
award-winning author, speaker and
creator of *Dig-In Discipleship* Bible studies

'Steph doesn't dish out easy answers in this book - because there are none. But she does ask the hard questions with honesty, grace and humour - some gentle, some sharp. If you live with chronic illness, it will help you feel heard and validated. If you don't, it will open your eyes and your heart in ways that may well be life changing.'

Carolyn Bourke,
chaplain and writer

'Some books change you deep inside. This one had a profound, healing impact on me. As someone living with complex chronic illness, Steph's welcome and understanding leapt off the pages, reminding me I am seen. She shares her own story in an inspiring, captivating way without downplaying, minimising or over-spiritualising her experience. She took me on a journey I had been afraid to take alone. Through the pages, I faced my fears, my grief and my illnesses head-on as I connected with her raw honesty. I found company and grace. I felt the arms of Jesus lifting me and reassuring me I'm safe even in my questions, in the not-knowing. I found myself laughing out loud at Steph's fun humour and personality and weeping with both relief and joy as I connected with her words and God's heart. I would love everyone to read this book, not just those with a chronic illness. It will open your eyes and offer beautiful, life-giving grace and hope. It is a gift from God.'

Jenny Glazebrook,
author, speaker and chaplain

'Steph takes readers on a no-holds-barred journey into the dark depths of chronic illness and up again into a life of determined joy. Her story is gritty, humorous, and above all, genuine. Throughout it her love for God shines brightly, even as she wrestles with her faith. The hope she offers is never trite, never easy, but it is worth it.'

Emily J. Maurits,
author of *Two Sisters and a Brain Tumour*,
founder of *Called to Watch*—a resource ministry for
friends and family of those living with chronic illness
www.calledtowatch.com

'I'm so glad Steph wrote this book! I believe her raw authenticity and insights into how her life has been challenged by living with chronic pain and illness will bring practical help to others, and will help them feel understood and validated so that they know that they are not alone. I love the honesty, courage and great humour Steph brings to this topic. As someone who's been through my seasons of suffering and supported others in their struggles, I find this book resonates with me and is a great read. I pray this book will help Christ's followers better understand, care for, and love one another in suffering, grief, and deep pain.'

Jill Bell,
Senior Minister C3 church

Surviving Chronic Illness

Copyright © 2024 Steph Penny

Printed by Pegasus Media and Logistics
Cover design and internal layout by Book Whispers

ISBN
Paperback: 978-0-6450627-2-4-
Ebook: 978-0-6450627-3-1

 A catalogue record for this book is available from the National Library of Australia

Scripture quotations taken from The Holy Bible, New International Version® NIV® Copyright © 1973 1978 1984 2011 by Biblica, Inc. TM Used by permission. All rights reserved worldwide.

All quoted scriptures are from the NIV unless otherwise indicated.

Scripture quotations marked MSG are taken from THE MESSAGE, copyright © 1993, 2002, 2018 by Eugene H. Peterson. Used by permission of NavPress. All rights reserved. Represented by Tyndale House Publishers, Inc.

Scripture quotations marked (GNT) are from the Good News Translation in Today's English Version- Second Edition Copyright © 1992 by American Bible Society. Used by Permission.

Scripture quotations marked AMP are from the Amplified Bible (AMP) Copyright © 2015 by The Lockman Foundation, La Habra, CA. All rights reserved. Used by Permission. www.lockman.org.

Scripture quotations taken from the Amplified® Bible (AMPC), Copyright © 1954, 1958, 1962, 1964, 1965, 1987 by The Lockman Foundation. Used by permission. www.lockman.org.

SURVIVING
CHRONIC ILLNESS

GRACE IN THE FLAMES

STEPH PENNY

ALSO IN THE SURVIVAL SERIES:

Surviving Singledom: Or Hang in There!
Surviving Childlessness: Faith and Furbabies

For Krystyna
Who understands

CONTENTS

Acknowledgements xii

SECTION ONE STRIKING THE MATCH 1

Introduction — *My Story, the Springboard for this Book* 3
1: Knowing Me, Knowing Lupus — *Living in Lockdown* 16
2: Language and Metaphor — *I'm Sick of Labels* 37

SECTION TWO: FLARES AND FLAMES 51

3: Medicine — *A Tough Pill to Swallow* 53
4: Church — *Have You Tried Praying?* 75
5: Society — *But You Don't Look Sick* 106

SECTION THREE: BUSHFIRE! 128

6: Grief and Trauma — *I'm Not Crazy, I'm Just …
Living with Chronic Illness* 130
7: Relationships — *Sex, Singledom and Childlessness* 169
8: God — *Through Many Dangers, Toils and Snares* 181

SECTION FOUR: REGROWTH 211

    9: Phenomena — *Alternative Stories to Illness* 213
    10: Carers — *Whom I Love* 223
    11: Sanity — *Silliness and Other Survival Strategies* 235
    12: Faith — *Ambushed by Kindness* 266
    13: Inconclusions — *How Shall We Live?* 297

    Helpful Resources 311
    About the Author 313
    References 314

ACKNOWLEDGEMENTS

It takes a village to write a book.

Thanks to my editor, Nola Passmore, whose expertise and enthusiasm is unparalleled. To my beta-readers for seeing what I couldn't see. To my wonderful endorsers who championed this cause. To my designers for turning my words into an actual thing.

Special thanks to Omega Writers, especially my Sydney chapter, my 'tribe', who validate my writing at every turn.

Thanks to my church, family and friends, who insist on asking helpful questions like, 'When will your book be published?' Seriously though, your mere interest jump-starts my motivation.

To every one of my readers, especially my fellow 'lupies' and anyone living with chronic illness—thanks for taking a look at this book. It's for you.

Special thanks to my husband and furbaby—I would not be here without you.

To my Father, Emmanuel in name and presence—thank you.

Through many dangers, toils and snares
I have already come
Tis grace that brought me safe thus far
And grace will lead me home.

John Newton, *Amazing Grace*[1]

SECTION ONE
STRIKING THE MATCH

*I am in a dark cave. I can't see a thing.
I have no flashlight, no candle, not even a match.*

*There is a musty smell and the sound of dripping water coming from somewhere. It echoes in the space.
I do not know how to get out.*

I am searching, my hands outstretched before me, my feet shuffling through the dirt. I sense there is something here in the cave, waiting to be found. I do not know what it is; it might be treasure; it might be danger. But there is something here.

So I search in the dark, trying to make out the shape of things with my fingertips, trying to discover that which awaits me.

INTRODUCTION

My Story, the Springboard for this Book

I was fourteen years old when the pain started.

The saga began on the school bus. We were trundling down the highway, heading for home. The bus had emptied along the way but there were still a few kids littered about, talking, laughing, gossiping. I was sitting alone, sweating through my uniform, one of those blue-checkered crimes against humanity.

The bus was loud, bumpy and outrageously hot. The stench of petrol filled the back of the bus, where I sat in perspiration paradise. My primary mission was to get as many of the windows open as possible, as soon as the other kids vacated their seats. Each departure granted me access to the wonderful world of ventilation.

Air: that was my chief worry.

I squirmed in my seat, pulling down my dress as far as I could to minimise the effect of sweaty-legs-sticking-to-the-vinyl syndrome. That's when it happened for the first time. I felt a sharp, stabbing sensation in my back.

I didn't know it then, but my back was in bad shape. One of my legs was shorter than the other which tilted my hips, causing my spine to grow twisted. My back was always going to end up curved. It was only a matter of time.

My pain-free days were officially over.

The dominant story

I suffered from terminal outsiderness as a teenager. I never fitted in anywhere. Being diagnosed with scoliosis (curvature of the spine) did nothing to help my spectacular unpopularity. No one else suffered from health issues. Even one of my friends who had previously lived with epilepsy had been healed by God.

My friends had 'normal' interests like boyfriends. (My first boyfriend was at the ripe old age of twenty-three.) Or they were into the latest pop-song lyrics. (Which I could not memorise to save my life.) Or they dabbled in ouija boards. (Anyone else raised in a strict Christian household?)

I felt slightly less leper-like at church, and there was less let's-get-drunk talk, but still, there was no one there with health issues. The only people with bad backs were older people, like in their forties (no hard feelings, I am now in my forties, OK?) so I had no one to talk to about pain or health problems.

If the dominant story among my peers was boyfriends and alcohol, I was definitely a carrier of the alternative pain story. But it soon became my personal dominant story.

Is this normal?

In my twenties I developed other health worries, such as

constant fatigue. It was always present. I reasoned this was an effect of full-time work. After all, everyone works full-time, and everyone is tired, aren't they? This is normal.

But the fatigue persisted. Every weekend was a desperate attempt to recuperate before Monday morning rushed upon me and the exhaustion started all over again. It didn't get better, no matter what I did. I took days off. I slept in. I went on long holidays. Nothing helped. It finally dawned on me after a few years (I'm a slow learner) that this was serious.

So I told my doctor. He said, 'You're too stressed. You need to take more time off. When was the last time you had a holiday?'

'I just got back from one months' holiday.'

Is this normal?

He said nothing. But something clicked in my brain. *Wow*, I thought. *I have just been on a long holiday, yet I feel no better. Is this normal?*

I experimented with part-time hours which made a huge difference to my mental health and wellbeing, but also to my pay packet. I was single, living alone in Sydney. I simply could not afford to live on part-time pay. I spent half my time worrying about whether I could afford to eat. To cut a long story short (too late for that), part-time work was great for my health but financially unsustainable.

I returned to full-time—and exhaustion.

The plot thickens

At twenty-five I developed vocal problems. *Ah*, I thought, *I know what this is. I'm a singer. This has to be vocal nodules—* calluses on the vocal chords caused by vocal overuse or abuse. That was what the rational, reasonable part of my brain said.

The other part of my brain started screaming.

Every singer has nightmares about the dreaded nodules. They are discussed in hushed tones and accompanied by rapid signs of the cross. OK, I'm exaggerating, but many singers live in genuine fear of this harrowing fate. I can readily list famous singers who developed nodules and lost their amazing voices forever, either through surgery or by virtue of stubborn nodules that never healed. Nodules can feel like a death sentence for the singer.

I got mine checked with alacrity. I saw an Ear, Nose and Throat (ENT) specialist who squirted anaesthetic up my nose and stuck a long cord up my nose and down my throat. The cord had a tiny camera at the end so they could see my vocal chords.

It's as fun as it sounds.

He confirmed my self-diagnosis. I had singer's nodules. He referred me for speech therapy, the gold standard treatment for vocal nodules. He reassured me I could get better if I followed the therapist's prescribed exercises.

I had speech therapy for a year. If you have not had the pleasure of doing speech therapy for nodules, allow me to clue you in. First, they forbid you to sing. The rationale is: you have developed nodules because of bad singing technique, therefore you have to stop singing and get the bad technique corrected. Telling a singer to stop singing is like inviting a fish to live on land for a while. Nevertheless, I complied. They also give you a bunch of singing and breathing exercises that must be done three times a day, religiously, or you will never get better. I complied. Religiously. I was committed. I was motivated. I was their star patient.

After several months of treatment with no sign of improvement, I complained to my speech therapist. Even though I was highly motivated, I was becoming dejected at my lack of progress. 'Think about it this way,' she urged, 'you have been singing this way for a long time. You might have had these nodules for a long time. It is going to take them a long time to heal.'

OK, I thought. *Suck it up, princess. Keep going.*

On and on we went for a year. I kept raising the subject of my lack of progress. 'Remember how long you have had these nodules,' she would remind me. After a very long time, my voice gradually began to show improvement. But it was several years before I felt truly back to normal.

Meanwhile, the fatigue soared to new heights. Seriously, there were days when all I wanted was to put my head on my desk and sleep. Once again, I raised the subject with various doctors.

'You're stressed,' they advised.

'You have a weak spot,' they suggested.

'You have a virus,' they hazarded.

Apparently I had a non-stop parade of viruses marching through my system, each piggybacking on the last one.

Then the nodules came back.

The penny drops

I turned thirty-one and developed vocal nodules again. Same symptoms, same devastation. I went to a different speech therapist. I stopped singing completely. I commenced rigorous and enthusiastic vocal exercises. The speech therapist guaranteed improvement within a few weeks.

She was wrong.

The not-singing, combined with the complete absence of promised healing, was killing me. I had been singing all my life. If I could not sing, what was the point of living? It might sound silly to you. But imagine a dancer without legs. A painter without brushes. A guitar without strings. The prospect of a life without singing was pointless to me. Purposeless. Meaningless. I began thinking about ending my life. (FYI I didn't act on it or anything, but I felt hopeless, like I was never going to get better.)

Through tears and gritted teeth, I did those blessed exercises three times a day. Then I went back to the speech therapist and burst into tears.

'I'm doing all the exercises,' I wailed, 'and I'm on complete vocal rest, and there is no change. I can't go on like this. Help me!'

She was baffled. I was way past baffled. I was at the end of my rope.

Then she did the best thing. She didn't tell me to work harder. She didn't say she didn't believe me. She didn't tell me it will take a while. She sat back in her chair and thought. We sat there, gazing at the space between us, me hoping against hope she would have an answer. After several minutes, she took a breath. 'I wonder if we're missing something.'

My ears pricked up. 'Like what?'

'Well, we've been assuming these are vocal nodules. But maybe they're not. Maybe they're a cyst or something.'

'Oh…and a cyst would not respond to speech therapy, I'm guessing?'

'Correct.'

She sent me to her ENT colleague and they shoved the lovely camera up my nose and down my throat again. There I was, mouth open, trying not to gag on the camera, while my speech therapist and ENT watched a little screen on the other side of the room. They asked me to sing, and I gave them a stunning rendition of *Fever*. They made interesting noises. Then they started talking animatedly. I caught little grabs of their conversation: 'There, do you see it?'…'Oh, yeah'…'I think'…'No, you're right…'

'Excuse me,' I sang out, 'Any chance of filling me in?'

They turned. 'First of all,' said my speechie, 'Your singing technique is perfect. There is absolutely no reason for you to continue vocal rest.'

My heart leaped. 'So I can sing again?'

'Absolutely. Your singing is not the cause of the problem.'

The weight of the world lifted from my shoulders.

The ENT took over. 'Have you ever been diagnosed with an autoimmune disease?'

That one took me by surprise. 'Um, no. Why?'

He showed me the screen. 'You have something called bamboo nodules,' he said. 'They're different from normal vocal nodules. Normal nodules have symmetrical callouses, one on each side of the vocal folds. When you speak or sing, the vocal folds try to close, but they can't close completely because the callouses meet in the middle.' I nodded. I was familiar with the physiology of nodules.

He pointed to my right vocal chord on the screen. 'See how there is one nodule here, and then another one above it? That's bamboo nodules. They look like nodes on a stick of bamboo, and they aren't caused by bad singing technique.'

I let this sink in. *I have bamboo nodules. I can sing again. My technique is perfect. I can sing again. Wait, what causes bamboo nodules?* I said this last bit out loud.

'They are very rare,' mused the ENT. 'In my twenty years of practice, I have seen four or five cases of bamboo nodules. And they are always caused by autoimmune disease.'

The penny dropped.

What now?

From there I went to see the vampire—I mean, immunologist—who took more blood out of me than I knew I had. He ran every test known to humankind. He was unwilling to diagnose me with anything, even though some bloods came back positive.

My husband and I did our own research. We thought lupus was a likely culprit, but without an official diagnosis, our theory was useful only to ourselves. Then I did what every person with chronic illness should do.

> I did what every person with chronic illness should do.
>
> Get. A. Second. Opinion.

Get. A. Second. Opinion.

My second immunologist reviewed my file, ran some repeat tests, and diagnosed me with lupus. That diagnosis has since been confirmed by a rheumatologist.

Right. Got a diagnosis. Only took me eight years. Now what?

My immunologist gently broke the news that while lupus is not fatal, there is no cure and no treatment. You just 'manage' it, meaning that when you're tired, you rest, when you're in pain, you take painkillers, and when something new emerges, you go back to your immunologist.

Great plan.

Since then, I have researched this shapeshifting disease and found there is precious little information about its cause. Glandular fever is a known factor, which I have had. Women are more susceptible. Tick. One lesser-known theory concerns Adverse Childhood Experiences (ACEs) and their links to adult health outcomes, including lupus and other autoimmune conditions (see *How Childhood Trauma Affects Health Across a Lifetime*[2]). But it's hard to draw a direct link between childhood trauma and lupus.

Lupus is autoimmune, meaning the immune system has crossed wires. It misreads signals in the body and attacks healthy cells, like a police officer going rogue and shooting civilians. Lupus can attack any organ in the body at any time: heart, lungs, liver, kidneys, brain, bones, skin, blood and guts. It's a pick-and-mix disease, and it's completely unpredictable. That's why no two cases of lupus are alike.

There are certain medications frequently used by those living with lupus, but those medications are only good for certain symptoms. Most hard-core medications like immunosuppressants have devastating side effects, including mood swings, significant weight gain and psychosis. Anyone want psychosis? Um—no thanks. How about chemo? Or steroids? Yikes. For example, the only way to cure bamboo nodules is to inject steroids directly into the vocal folds. *Mentally runs into the distance, screaming*

I try to manage my symptoms as best I can. But how can I 'manage' fatigue? Have a lie-down every time I feel weak, which is all the time? I have to drag my carcass through the day, desperately trying to focus, peering at my computer through brain fog, attempting to string sentences together while resisting the urge to become an instantaneous caffeine addict.

Many symptoms cannot be 'managed'. I endure them. I survive. On a bad day, I am not living my #bestlife. I am trying to hold my eyelids open. I am trying to get up from my chair without hollering in pain. I am trying to walk without bumping into walls. I am pacing myself, knowing once I am out of energy, that's it. There is no getting that energy back. How do you pace yourself in survival mode?

Read on for half-formed answers to this and other questions.

No panacea

I have accepted, for the most part, my illness is chronic and has no specific cure. There is no panacea (apart from chocolate) for pain or fatigue or a dysfunctional immune system. This does not make it easier. I struggle on a daily basis. And even though I have good days and beautiful friends and loved ones, and even though my gratitude cup is overflowing, chronic illness sucks. It just does.

I have struggled to find books on chronic illness. Some books on cancer survival are inspiring, yet I find them oddly unsatisfying. What about illnesses that never go into remission? What about illness that make your life miserable without killing you? What about unabating pain and slow, agonising, lifelong deterioration? These questions deserve answers. Hence I am writing my own experience of chronic illness, hoping it will help others like me.

INTRODUCTION

Every flare adds fuel to my writing fire. You could say it inspires me.

I am not the only one living in pain without a panacea. Others are surviving illness like me. Perhaps you live with chronic illness, pain, fatigue, disability or mental distress. Welcome. Perhaps you, like me, have struggled to find answers and meaning in illness. Welcome to you. Perhaps you have been impacted mentally and emotionally by long-term illness. You are welcome here. And perhaps your faith has suffered because of sickness. A very special welcome to you.

As we walk through these pages, let us be here for each other. Let us hold our collective faith, optimism, despair and terror.

There is no one-size-fits-all solution within these pages. (Sorry to disappoint.) I will not provide answers because I do not have any. I will simply articulate my lived experience in the context of my Christian faith. I will share what has helped. I will give suggestions to carers, family, friends and loved ones. I will ask the too-hard questions and grapple with mysteries.

> There is no one-size-fits-all solution

I invite you to join me in the asking and grappling. Hopefully we will find good things to hold on to, like in an Easter egg hunt. Who knows what cool eggs we might find. And we will try to follow God in spite of—and because of—inordinate suffering.

If you're already feeling faint at this prospect, now might be a good time to fortify yourself with chocolate. But seriously, please do look after yourself as you move through this book. Illness is relentless and tiring, and you might feel tired reading about it. I certainly found it draining to write about it! So pace yourself, take breaks, read a little at a time. Breathe. Indulge in self-care. There are reflection spots at the end of each chapter; I encourage you to check-in with yourself to see what is surfacing or standing out as you read.

*I am standing waist-deep in open water.
I can feel the bottom beneath my feet, particles of
sand curling between my toes.*

*It is twilight; I cannot see far ahead. He is there,
standing in the deeper water, silhouetted against the
setting sun. He holds out his hand to me. I take it and he
grasps me firmly; he will not let go.*

*He wades out further into the water and our arms
stretch taut, his hand gently tugging mine. I feel a moment
of panic. Where is he taking me? How deep is the water?
What if I cannot touch the bottom?*

*He answers my silent questions with a tug of the hand,
and I follow. I am willing. I will follow him anywhere.
I just do not know where that will be.*

1
KNOWING ME, KNOWING LUPUS
Living in Lockdown

I had a heart attack.

OK, it wasn't really a heart attack. But it sure felt like one.

When the pain first started I took pills and tried lying down but the pain immediately got worse. I got up again. Even as I sat there, arms wrapped around my knees, hoping the painkillers would kick in, the task of breathing became steadily more difficult. My husband hovered nearby, concern written all over him.

'I'm taking you to hospital,' he finally said.

'It's just muscular,' I countered. 'I've taken pills for it.'

'OK, but if you're not feeling better in twenty minutes, I'm taking you in.'

'But why?' I said, playing the role of difficult patient beautifully.

'Because it could be your heart.'

I hadn't thought of that.

Twenty minutes later I reluctantly conceded defeat and we went to hospital. By the time we walked into the Emergency Department (ED), I was struggling for breath. It felt like someone had laid a slab of concrete across my chest. When they admitted me, I was hardly breathing. I was vomiting green. I could hardly speak. I was fighting for air.

They didn't know what was wrong. They gave me pills which my stomach promptly rejected. They grabbed a giant syringe and filled it with morphine. 'This can make some people feel nauseous,' they warned me, as I vomited yet again. 'Don't care,' I gasped, heroically resisting the urge to grab the needle and do the job myself. As the needle found its way home, the pain finally began to ease. Relief flooded my body as I sank back into my chair.

They got me a bed on the cardio ward with three other patients who were several decades older than me, all awaiting major heart surgery. I felt like a fraud. What's a thirtysomething doing on the cardio ward? I experimented with the mammoth task of getting out of bed, but I vomited. I contented myself with the more achievable jobs of sleeping and breathing.

The next afternoon my family visited. They prayed for me and the pain receded. It actually lessened as the prayers were spoken. I was already breathing easier. It was not completely gone but noticeably better. It was like God had joined me in that hospital bed and given me a helping hand.

The hospital never worked out what was wrong with me. In the end they diagnosed me with 'atypical chest pain', code for 'we have no idea'. I saw a specialist soon afterwards who said the most likely diagnosis was pericarditis—inflammation of the lining around the heart. No wonder it felt like a heart attack. I have not had pericarditis since, but I learned pericarditis is one of the signs of lupus. Apparently I had been living with it without knowing it. Knowing about lupus helps.

Pericarditis gave a much-needed diagnosis, and a moment in time to witness God's grace when he joined me in that hospital bed and helped me breathe a little easier.

The great chameleon

Lupus has been called the 'great chameleon' or 'great imitator' because it mimics other diseases. Take pericarditis, for example. It mimicked a heart attack. The bamboo nodules masqueraded as normal singer's nodules. Even joint pain can mimic other joint issues.

> Lupus has been called the 'great chameleon' or 'great imitator' because it mimics other diseases.

This raises a pertinent question. How do I tell which is which? How do I know if my headache is just a headache or something more serious? In my lived experience, I have had the following causes of headaches:

- Dehydration;
- Migraine;
- Gastro or food poisoning;

- Muscular tension;
- Lupus flare;
- Mal De Debarquement syndrome (chronic dizziness);
- Sleep deprivation;
- Pericarditis;
- Inappropriate Sinus Tachycardia (racing heart); and
- Temporomandibular Joint (TMJ) Disorder.

This causes problems when doctors ask me what is going on. I often don't have an answer. In addition to lupus, I live with endometriosis, scoliosis, vasculitis (inflammation of the blood vessels), osteoporosis, a temporomandibular joint (TMJ) disorder, a balance disorder, a swallowing disorder, neuropathy and undiagnosed adrenal and respiratory issues. Plus the occasional migraine. And they feed into one another, less like separate countries and more like warring tribes in one district. Every action of one tribe adversely affects every other tribe.

Lupus introduces a wildcard factor in any investigation. When I first saw my cardiologist, she said, 'You don't have any cardiac risk factors, but you do have lupus. So we should run all the tests anyway.' Doctors find my illness just as perplexing as me.

Being immunocompromised, I live with constant risk factors. (It made life fun when COVID-19 broke out.) I am only one virus away from complete disablement, one slip from a fracture, one COVID-19 contact from hospitalisation. I still wear masks everywhere even though it is not mandatory, because I am susceptible to every bug doing the rounds. I am not ruled by risk, but there are precautions I need to take.

Treatment is complex and sometimes pure guesswork. (So complex it gets its own chapter.) I often do not know what a thing is until I try medication, and if it helps, it confirms the diagnosis. This is life with the great chameleon: treatment often precedes diagnosis, not the other way around.

Some complex illnesses like lupus only get diagnosed when everything else has been ruled out. They call it a diagnosis of exclusion or elimination. Given they don't know about lupus causes, I don't know whether I caused it—and whether I am still inadvertently contributing to it!

With most illnesses, you get sick then make a full recovery. But chronic illness is not just another species of sickness; it's a different planet entirely. Society, like an alien race, struggles to grasp that. They don't comprehend 'chronic', and they can't fathom 'untreatable'. Most times, when you're sick, the doctor provides an answer and prescribes a particular pill or treatment regime. Unfortunately, most autoimmune diseases, like naughty children, refuse to fall in line. Lupus is a changeable kind of naughty child, requiring constant quick-footing and rethinking, a never-ending game of improvisation.

> Chronic illness is not just another species of sickness; it's a different planet entirely.

One thing that helps with the chameleon is proactivity. If my symptoms change, I see my doctor. If I develop new symptoms, even if only mild or nuisancesome, I tell them. I do this because I view my doctors less as gurus and more as fellow detectives in my crime-solving-esque investigation into lupus. Doctors don't know everything. Medical degrees do not necessarily give another human being better insight into my body than me. (Although living in my body does not necessarily make me an expert, either. I misread my body's signals all the time. Apparently I missed the webinar on 'How To Develop Your Illness Intuition'.)

There is more mystery in the world of medicine than we like to admit. This gives me both hope and despair. It means there are things in God's universe we are yet to discover. It also means that sometimes, despite my best efforts, I will not get answers. While that can be depressing and frustrating, there is a quiet place in my heart that simply bows her head to God and worships.

If we're not careful, our entire world can come to revolve around illness. Living with illness encourages a peculiar form of 'self-policing'. Doctors frequently ask me to describe my symptoms, so I pay attention to them. But my attention can get wrapped up in my illness, every waking moment preoccupied with what the symptoms are doing today. This feeds my dominant story of illness. Not to mention my anxiety.

Sometimes lupus is a mere nuisance, smouldering quietly, giving me, say, split nails that catch on everything. Other times it is completely disabling, flaring into wildfire, rendering me housebound. Living with lupus can be a lot like living in a COVID-19 lockdown: you can't go anywhere or do things you want to do.

If I had the chance to walk away, I would.

Rarity

Lupus is a rare disease. Less than 0.1% of the population has lupus[3]. While lupies can live rich, full lives, it can flare at any time and the consequences can be degenerative and even fatal.

When I tell someone about lupus I include a full description, otherwise they have no idea what it means. This is the trouble with rare disease. Mention the flu and people instantly know what you are talking about. When I fractured my shoulder, everyone instantly understood the diagnosis. Even pericarditis, less common, is relatively easy to explain. But how do you describe lupus? There's no reference point for a completely insane disease that hijacks your life without warning, attacks random organs and saps your will to live.

Some people have a comparison: 'Oh, my cousin had lupus.' But my brand of lupus might be different from what your cousin had, because no two versions of lupus are alike. And if you're unlucky like me, your first symptom is so rare it takes years to correctly diagnose.

On the TV show *Scrubs*, the character J.D. has a 'Zebra' moment, the doctorly urge to diagnose exotic diseases instead of ordinary ones presenting with unusual symptoms—akin to hearing hoof falls and thinking, 'Zebra' instead of 'Horse'. J.D. is instructed to instead look for the simplest medical explanation. But for me, and anyone with autoimmune disease, we are zebras. Some of us might be even rarer than that: our doctors should be thinking, 'Unicorn!'

> *our doctors should be thinking, 'Unicorn!'*

Being a zebra (or unicorn) makes it hard to get the right diagnosis and treatment. It's hard to talk to friends and family. I spend entire conversations explaining lupus. I don't want to be pitied, but I also don't want to be misunderstood.

There's one more thing rarity does. Now this might sound strange to you, or even totally wrong. All I can say is you may not understand unless you live with rare disease. But I get so sick of living with lupus that some days I would rather have cancer. In saying this, I don't want to diminish anyone's experience of cancer. I certainly don't want to minimise how cancer can force one to face their mortality, something I have not yet done. I don't have a death wish either. Every illness has its challenges and cancer is certainly nothing to sneeze at.

At the same time, cancer is common and therefore widely understood. Everyone has been touched by cancer, either firsthand or through witnessing a loved one's experience. Cancer has a known cause with a clear trajectory. Prognosis, while sometimes hard to pin down, has general parameters. I desperately want an illness with a plan. (My current treatment plan is 'Ring me if you need to'.) I want something clear-cut and easy to explain and understand. Lupus ain't it.

I am not alone in feeling this way. The below article compares chronic illness to cancer:

> Rachel was diagnosed as a teenager with myalgic encephalomyelitis, or ME, which you might know as chronic fatigue syndrome. At the time, her doctor said that she'd rather be diagnosed with a treatable cancer than with ME. And if you don't know much about chronic illness, that might seem incredibly inflammatory. Cancer is serious, and we all

know it. But chronic illness is serious too... Rachel told me she felt validated to have her illness taken seriously. And she felt like her doctor was being honest about how difficult life with chronic illness can be, even if it's not life-threatening. Many chronic illnesses are unlikely to take your life but incredibly likely to take you away from the life you love.[4]

Lupus can be just as life-changing as fatal illness. It may not take your life, but it may take the life you love.

> It may not take your life, but it may take the life you love.

Randomness

Like Jonathan Larson in *Tick, Tick...Boom!*, I am waiting for a time bomb to go off.

Because lupus is a fluctuating disease, I can regress into a non-coping, non-functioning, pain-overloaded state quite rapidly. At worst, my illness has taken me from 'Normal' to 'Call an ambulance' in the space of an hour. I don't care how resilient you are, that randomness is frightening.

It can happen anywhere and with no apparent trigger. It can happen when I lie down. It can happen after showering. It can happen before or after eating. I have no control. It's maddening.

It has struck at work. That's pretty embarrassing. Imagine going to your boss, clutching your chest, casually mentioning you need to call an ambulance. It's not my favourite look.

Once I was at an appointment and I came over feeling awful. I could hardly walk straight. There I was, having a nice, sunny Saturday, feeling as though I was about to faint. I cancelled my plans. When I got home, I collapsed on the couch and didn't move for eight hours—and felt no better at all. That's right. No progressive story. I rested yet did not recuperate.

This is how random lupus can be. It's quite rude and inconsiderate, really. Given how impossible it is to predict its movements, it is impossible to plan for things. If I knew a flare was coming, I could plan to rest, or at least clear my calendar. But lupus does not send me calendar invites. I am living in an unreliable, unpredictable, uncooperative body that simply will not do what I want it to do. It is the uncommunicative roommate, messy, violent, impossible, constantly pulling the rug from under my feet.

It is, quite literally, insanity-making.

The job interview

It would be great if illness followed the path of a job interview. First, you would get the selection criteria. The expectations would be clearly spelled out so you would know what's involved. Then, if you chose to accept your mission, you could ask clarifying questions and negotiate hours or benefits. You could request part-time hours. You could ask for perks. You could find out about overnight shifts or other hidden expectations. Oh, how I wish I could do this with chronic illness.

If someone approached me and said, 'Hey Steph, there's this great illness that I think is perfect for you. The thing is, you can't do it part-time, it costs more than you earn, and it's relentless. Oh, by the way, you'll probably wind up going a bit mad. Interested?'

I'd tell them where to stick that job offer.

In my head, the selection criteria for a job like lupus would look something like this:

The Role:

You will live with lupus 24/7 and yield complete and irrevocable control of every domain of your life.

Essential Skills:

- Experience living with any kind of chronic illness, including chronic pain and/or fatigue, will be highly regarded.
- Must be well-versed in symptomology with working knowledge of dates and timeframes of all symptoms. Knowledge of dates when medications were commenced, increased or ceased is desirable, preferably plotted in a Venn diagram.
- Must be able to converse with all types of doctors and specialists and doctor-shop as required. A partnership approach to working with medical professionals is preferred.
- High levels of adaptability, flexibility and on-the-spot improvising are required, without use of a technical manual.
- Ability to work in a high-pressure environment in a constant state of flux is a must.

- Experience in self-driven research of possible illnesses, differential diagnoses and emerging symptoms is essential.
- Must be competent in collecting scans and blood test results, maintaining a diary of doctor's appointments, completing tests in a timely manner and applying for a string of sick leave absences from work.
- Will be required to work evenings, overnights, weekends, usual business hours when you would otherwise be at your day job, and any other time at the discretion of lupus. You will be on-call at all times, regardless of other reasonable demands or prior commitments. This role carries a high risk of burnout with no additional compensation.
- Having family, friends and carers with limitless patience and adaptability is highly desirable.

NOTE: at present there is no capacity to hire a Personal Assistant.

Benefits:

None. But we can guarantee lupus will greatly reduce your quality of life and quite possibly your life expectancy. Also, this role will cost you financially, physically, mentally, emotionally, spiritually, socially and existentially.

NOTE: as funding permits, there may be unexpected random

> *bonuses such as silver linings, humorous anecdotes and glimpses of hope.*
>
> If interested in this role, please apply, but we may select you without your applying and without regard for your gender, age, socioeconomic status, education, employment, living situation, access to healthcare, social support or level of faith.
>
> Send your CV to the below email address and lupus will be in touch with you—although you may not know it until many years later.

I am certain many of these criteria could apply to a range of chronic illnesses. There may also be criteria not included here. Chronic illnesses are gifts that keep on giving.

From eight to eighty

I was full of energy as a kid.

When the pain of scoliosis hit at age fourteen, I lost my childhood. I grew up fast. I couldn't carry my schoolbag on one shoulder like other kids. This might not sound like a big deal, but I was painfully unpopular at school. Carrying a bag on both shoulders did nothing to improve my alienation. I couldn't stand on one leg for too long. I couldn't lean on one elbow or slouch against the wall. Sitting cross-legged was definitely out of the question. If I ever dared step outside the bounds of prescribed postural practice, my body rewarded me with acute stabbing sensations in the back. Sometimes it would let me off lightly, only lasting a matter of seconds. But other times the pain persisted for days on end. I paid dearly for my momentary coolness.

I was also given homework for chronic pain. Yep, in addition to schoolwork. Every morning and night, I followed a religious regime of physiotherapy stretches aimed at untwisting my twisted spine. Not one of my friends went through that.

Carrying heavy textbooks felt like corporal punishment. I inwardly raged against the injustice of being told to give up my seat on the bus for adults. *What about me? I'm living with chronic pain!* I learned responsibility while my peers were learning club dancing and proper kissing technique. I embraced it willingly enough. But it distanced me from my peers. Everyone my age seemed profoundly immature. Living with pain was lonelifying.

> Living with pain was lonelifying.

As a result of growing up fast, I related better to older people. We had more in common: I was as serious and responsible and mature as them. While this may not be totally attributable to juvenile chronic pain—I am a firstborn child, and I understand we firstborns are notorious let's-make-friends-with-older-people types—I really felt I understood them better, and they understood me better.

Not only did I leap straight from carefree childhood to responsible adulthood, I also seemed to skip the joyous part of independent adult life. I spent most of my twenties comatose from exhaustion. I never had spare reserves for anything apart from worship ministry at church. I was on a constant merry-go-round of full-time work and recovering from same.

I aged prematurely. At twenty-five, I was told I had the spine of a forty-year-old. Yay! Then, at age thirty, I spent time on a cardiac ward with people in their sixties and seventies. I felt like I was about sixty too. At forty, I was diagnosed with osteoporosis. I now have the bones of a seventy-five or eighty-year-old. Which is exactly the kind of news every forty-year-old wants to hear. Obviously.

I currently relate more to people in their seventies and eighties than my same-aged peers. When I read medical articles, it is the geriatric case-studies that ring true for me. Yes, it's sad. You may well relate.

I feel like I have gone from eight to eighty without much carefree adulthood. I didn't just grow up; I grew old. Sure, I have enjoyable moments. But every day the illness is in the back of my mind, whispering unhelpful things like, *These people don't understand you. You're eighty on the inside. Your body is eating you alive from the inside out.* Thanks, brain. Who asked you, anyway?

This is, and will continue to be, a large portion of my grief. And grief is central to chronic illness. When you lose your health, you lose your sense of control. You lose certainty and predictability. You lose the ability to make and keep plans. You lose choice. You lose the life you wanted to live.

Chronic illness means losing your sense of who you are.

Faking good, feeling bad

It is surprisingly difficult to be honest about illness.

Once I told a work colleague I felt bad. She told me, 'If you have symptoms, you should stay home.' To which I tactfully retorted, 'If I stayed home every time I had symptoms, I'd never leave the house.'

When I tell people at church how I'm feeling, they often don't know what to say. I get blank stares or stammered sympathy, and the topic changes pretty fast. While I understand their awkwardness around my illness (what do you say to someone in perpetual unwellness?), it's hard for me to be honest with them. I feel I have to take care of them if they get distressed or coach them in appropriate responses. It's exhausting to explain the great chameleon each time. Much easier to say, 'I'm fine, and you?' This then reinforces my sense of being different, outsiderly and alone.

Sometimes I look well when I'm feeling awful. Other times, I'm having a good day but others say I look like crap. (Thanks for that.) I suppose this could be true for most people. But I seem to experience it quite often, the mismatch between what others see and how I really feel. Most of the time I'm faking good but underneath I'm feeling bad and screaming for someone to notice. I know faking isn't helpful or healthy—it disrupts our hearts and minds, not to mention authentic relationships with others—but what do you do when it takes every ounce of energy just to show up at church, and thirty people ask how you are feeling?

Even around carers, I curb my neediness. I don't want to burn them out. I don't want to complain or appear high maintenance. Sometimes being sick and emotional is downright embarrassing.

I expect a lot of myself as a sick person. Apparently, I've got some 'Shoulds' around my illness and functionality:

'I should work at the same pace as everyone else.'

'I should adapt to whatever curve ball lupus throws at me and never get overwhelmed.'

'I should ask for help without feeling guilty.'

'I should be grateful for what this illness has taught me.'

'I should trust God and never question what's going on.'

Illness shackles me, but some shackles I place on myself. This is why I fake good: not just because of social awkwardness and stigma, but because I've got some badly skewed beliefs about being perfect, irrespective of illness. It horrifies me when my physical body does not line up with my idea of how I should be. So I pretend. That's no one else's fault. That's on me.

> Illness shackles me, but some shackles I place on myself.

Faking good is a skill and an art form. I have several fronts I can choose from: the brave face, the coping front, the I'm-feeling-well front, the energetic front (great for compensating for fatigue), the happy front, the polite front ('You look so well!' 'Why, thank you!' *while dying inside*), and the calm front. I've even developed my own personal code:

'I'm good today' means I'm honestly feeling well, relative to bad days.

'I'm fine' or 'Doing OK' means I'm struggling with pain, fatigue or something else.

'Not too bad' is a cry for help.

'I'm sick' means I should definitely be at home and possibly in hospital.

I have my own five-tier code for daily functioning levels. It helps me work out little things like when I should call in sick or go to hospital. It's also a tool for communicating what's going on without having to describe what's going on.

Tier 1: Can I breathe? Can I breathe without chest pain? If

I cannot breathe, I cannot function. I should stay home in bed. I should probably see a doctor and possibly go to hospital. I might need help—with everything.

Tier 2: Do I have chest pain? Any kind of chest pain, pressure or tightness needs careful evaluation, as it may quickly progress to tier 1. I might need medical help. I might need support with transport and making decisions.

Tier 3: Can I get out of bed, shower, dress and eat without significant pain? If I struggle to do any of these, I need to seriously think about calling in sick. Pain will distract me at work and problems with movement might limit driving or walking. Another limitation is dizziness; if I cannot walk without support, I am probably not fit for work.

Tier 4: Did I get enough sleep last night, and do I have the physical and mental energy for work? If not, brain fog—the feeling of wading through mental quicksand—might incapacitate me. The fatigue—the sensation of having weights tied to every single part of my body—might be debilitating. I need enough 'spoons' to work a full day and possibly shop and cook afterwards. I might need people to cut me some slack in tier 4; I will be less productive.

Tier 5: Can I bring passion and creativity to my job today? Can I be present with others, listen attentively, think laterally about problems and challenge people when needed? How flexible and adaptable can I be today? If a crisis presents itself, can I handle it?

If I pass tier 5, this is as good as I can generally hope to get. Tier 5 is a pretty good day. But I have plenty of other-tier days. I am not sure what tier 6 would look like. It's hard to imagine a level of functioning beyond tier 5. Perhaps being on holiday. But for me, even on holiday, the threat of chronic illness is still there. It never completely goes away. (And don't get me started on the stress of applying for travel insurance!)

Codes can be useful, but they can get exhausting. We need permission to be candid. So this book will be an honest place to share the impact of prolonged illness. We will not mince words. We will not be polite. (We won't be rude either, just in case non-politeness makes you nervous.) We won't dress up illness in battle or bravery narratives.

We're gonna tell it like it is.

Devastation and regrowth

I am constantly inspired by the metaphor of bushfire.

When roaring devastation has ripped through the landscape, we watch with bated breath for the first signs of regrowth to emerge. A vista of complete charcoal never stays that way. The vegetation is designed to regenerate. It needs fire, thrives on it, depends on destruction for new life to begin. Though the wait seems long, how wonderful that moment when the first sign of green breaks through.

There's a lot we can learn from the fire-ravaged tree: digging deep for water, patience and forbearance (not my favourite words, but they seem to be part of the package deal of suffering), and that even when our lives appear utterly destroyed—hope burned to a crisp, ashes scattered to the wind—we are still standing. God, in his grace, keeps bringing regrowth out of devastation.

It's like God gives us a picture of the cycle of grace in nature.

First we see black, then we see green. First we have a storm, then a rainbow. First everything dies, then it makes a comeback. Grace is all around us. Regrowth is possible. Even with the great chameleon.

We who live in a constant state of grief need that reminder.

May the Holy Spirit join us as we journey through these pages. May he grant us peace for the dangers, toils and snares. May we know his companionship in the fire and regrowth in the aftermath.

Take a moment to notice how you are feeling after the chapter, and whether anything stood out for you or resonated with you. Time for some self-care

I am surrounded by fire. I am standing in the middle of the inferno, flames leaping and dancing about me. They are taller than me, standing over me, threatening me. I hear crackling all around. The fierce heat is everywhere; there is no escape.

I spin around, looking for a way to put out the fire. But the fire swirls around me, choking me, burning my eyes, mocking me with its relentless force. And he is here too, standing in the fire. He is surrounded by heat and flames and smoke. He knows I am here; he is not leaving.

Part of me wishes he would just put the fire out. I know he can. But there is something in his posture, something in the way he stands, that tells me he is not here to take action. He is not looking at me. He is looking at something else. I cannot see what he is looking at; all I can see is fire.

Somehow I know we are both here for the same thing. I do not know what it is. Perhaps he does.

2

LANGUAGE AND METAPHOR

I'm Sick of Labels

I hate the term 'disabled'.

Some people embrace it. I applaud them. It personally makes my skin crawl. I don't want to accept what is happening to me. I don't want to resign myself to disability.

Which is why language matters. Medicine often gives us labels that are stigmatising and depressing. But the right words can give us helpful language for our experience. Medical terms don't cut the ice; pain scales fall short; but metaphor and imagery can convey our lived experience.

Let's kick off with my least favourite illness metaphors of all time.

Battlers and fighters

'She lost her battle with cancer.'

'He's fighting to stay active.'

Metaphors of aggression and violence are rife in our society. But are they helpful? Are they even accurate?

In my experience, and yours may be different, I have not 'fought' my illness. I have never stood in battle armour and faced off with lupus. I have never sparred with it, sat in a war room to strategise against it, or negotiated peace with it. Lupus simply exists.

The battling metaphor presumes I am an active participant in the war. It also assumes I have the capacity to fight. While I do have options, lupus can often overthrow these. The battling metaphor ultimately places me as the 'loser' of the battle and lupus as the 'victor'. Not a helpful mindset.

> The battling metaphor ultimately places me as the 'loser' of the battle and lupus as the 'victor'.
>
> Not a helpful mindset.

The battle metaphor also creates a dichotomy between winning and losing. But living with illness is neither winning or losing. It is living with it. In the battle metaphor, dying is 'losing', but for some of us dying is the ultimate promotion. If I ever 'lose my battle with lupus', I will consider myself the luckiest, most enviable of Christ's servants.

The very idea of fighting sounds exhausting. It's like telling someone with a broken leg to go for a run, or a person with a migraine to turn on the light, or a person with depression to cheer up. In my experience, those with chronic illness do not want to hear about fighting. Besides, fighting things like pain and fatigue can actually make them worse.

Surviving chronic illness is not a matter of willpower; if it was, we would have kicked it long ago. The language of fighting is incomplete and unsatisfactory. Or, to use a technical term, a load of old codswallop.

There must be a better alternative.

Victims and survivors

Being a 'victim' of chronic illness can be just as bad as 'fighter'.

On the one hand, we don't want the pressure of fighting all the time. But neither do we want to be labelled a victim, because even though we may be passive recipients of illness (in the sense we didn't go out looking for it), we do not want to feel weak or inept. 'Victim' can sound like we're wallowing in self-pity.

An alternative is the 'survivor' or 'warrior'. These work for some people, but even these terms have become tarnished. (And I appreciate the irony of writing about 'survivor' language in a book called *Surviving Chronic Illness*.) Some object to 'survivor' as a totalising label. We are more than mere survivors, and there is more to life than simply surviving each day. Isn't there?

The issue with labelling people in this way is we are labelling them. If a person chooses a label for themselves, like 'fighter' or 'survivor', I am OK with that. But often these labels are thrust upon us, along with 'strong' and 'brave' and 'courageous'. Aren't we allowed to collapse and feel weary and scared witless from time to time? Why should we live up to society's expectations of chronically ill and disabled people? Don't even get me started on the whole 'She's not letting her disability get her down' or 'He's not letting his illness get in the way of living his best life' crapola. Reality check: sometimes illness gets us down. I don't care how accepting you are of your illness; being sick is *no one's* idea of their best life.

Alia Joy, author of *Glorious Weakness*, puts it this most articulate way:

> We are a society that despises lack. We despise weakness and need and insufficiency...We admire pain only if it's healed, only if it's endured with perfect grace, with perfect faith, and never succumbed to in weakness, in f-bombs and rants and curses raised to the heavens.[5]

When chronically sick 'heroes' become depressed, deflated or even suicidal, society can struggle to comprehend this. That's not 'heroic' behaviour. Society wants to be inspired by us, but their spectator stance effectively distances themselves from us. They want to minimise our pain or sanitise it, making it easier for them to bear. And if we don't inspire them, they blame us: 'You need to try harder,' 'You need more faith,' 'Suicide is the coward's way out,' 'You're being selfish.' Well, I refuse to be their inspiration porn. I'm tired of the heroising of sick people. I'm no one's hero.

> *I refuse to be their inspiration porn.*

'Warrior' sounds super cool and some like to champion their cause, like advocating for a cure or working hard at rehabilitation. Some warriors get real results from treatment, and they are fortunate. For me, the term carries a similar vibe to the 'fighter' label, an expectation that I will heroically rise above every challenge and transcend my bodily illness. *Cringe*

Many chronically ill people do not feel like survivors and do not feel brave. They feel devastated by illness, their bodies and minds torn apart by disease and the treatments aimed at curing them. Perhaps if someone chose chronic illness, they might be considered brave. But for those of us who do not choose, we do not feel brave.

And don't ask me how I actually do survive. I have no idea. Survival often happens on a day-to-day level, sometimes a minute-to-minute level. I do not survive because of anything I do or because of a particular 'brave' mindset. I survive purely by the grace of God. Many of us feel this way: we are here because of God's grace. Nothing else.

People living with chronic illness may not feel like survivors. If they describe themselves in that way, great. Otherwise, let's look for terms of better fit.

Lupies and spoonies

Some people living with lupus call themselves 'lupies'. In addition to sounding super cute, this label can promote solidarity among those who live with lupus. Finding fellow lupies breaks down the isolation brought on by the rarity and chronicity of lupus.

However, I am not a big fan of describing myself by a diagnosis. I get a slightly skin-crawling sensation calling myself a 'lupie', much like if you referred to me as 'bed seventeen' in hospital. Finding our tribe is important, though, so I understand why some have embraced the lupieness. Hey, maybe we're all a little lupie!

Then there are 'spoonies'. This is a reference to the spoons theory, coined by Christine Miserandino.[6] You start each day with a set amount of metaphorical 'spoons' representing your available energy for the day, say thirty spoons per day. Each time you do something it costs a spoon.

Sometimes spoons disappear for no reason, like while I'm staring at the computer. Bam. Gone. Sometimes I start the day with fewer spoons than normal. If I wake up in pain, I'm down to fifteen spoons before I've got out of bed. If I haven't slept, I've got ten spoons total. If I am worried about anything, it's a constant drain on my spoonage. If I have a crisis at work, or a stressful conversation, or I receive bad news, I might run clean out of spoons. How do I then get home? Very slowly. I have days when I get home from work, collapse on the couch and don't move for hours.

Spoons can reduce your usable hours in a day from sixteen to three. Or zero.

I've heard of spoonies who require a spoon to pick out an outfit and another to get dressed. For such spoonies, going out is costly. Meeting up with a friend for coffee takes three to five spoons. It's expensive, but worth it. I've had days when getting a bowl out of the cupboard requires a spoon. So does getting a spoon. My worst time spoon-wise was when I had glandular fever. Having a shower took all thirty spoons. I'm no longer that bad, but some spoonies are. Rest doesn't restore their spoons. They have a permanently low spoon count.

I find spoon language helpful. I can let others know I'm running on

> *The spoons give me and others a respectful way to talk about illness without invading my privacy.*

low spoons. It's easier than saying my pain is *x* out of ten. This also makes it easier for others to check in using spoon-based language: 'Wow, you look wiped, did that phone call take all your spoons?'

The spoons give me and others a respectful way to talk about illness without invading my privacy. What a great tool.

Disability

As mentioned at the start of this chapter, some people embrace the disabled label. 'There is nothing wrong having a disability,' they cry, eager to be welcomed by society for who they are, not for who they aren't. They have a point.

One alternative term is 'differently abled', preferring a strengths-based approach. There are benefits to focusing on ability. But some people hate the term. It sounds like they have a superpower, which is not the case. They have lost their normal powers and feel the loss.

Another alternative, 'diversely bodied', has truth to it, as well as a positive invitation to be respected in diversity. But it doesn't tell the whole story. It says nothing of people's lived experience of pain, suffering and loss. Many people would rather use 'disabled', which says what it means.

Despite its popularity, 'disability' remains negatively loaded and attracts stigma, discrimination, obstacles and mistreatment. Even though discrimination based on disability is illegal, it happens. But legal and employment considerations aside, I am seriously reluctant to define myself as 'disabled'. Some of my reticence is due to stigma. Most articles about disability feature pictures of old folk, people in wheelchairs or with walkers, or a pair of bespotted, wrinkled hands.

I'm not super excited about being associated with that.

I also don't want pity. I don't want to be treated differently due to disability. I don't want people walking on eggshells around me. I've had my share of that during temporary disabilities. I would hate to live with that forever. I've seen the opposite of pity too: irritation. I've heard office gossip about *that* person being off sick again. I've received it directly from colleagues: 'If you go off sick again, my workload is going to explode.' Thanks for the unsolicited guilt trip. I'm not exactly captain of this ship, you know.

The word 'disability' can grant you access to medication, subsidies, testing, specialists, in-home care, walking aids and other equipment, home modifications, respite for carers and extra support. It can help you jump queues. It can get you a car disability sticker, making places more accessible. It can give you recognition and credibility as a patient. When I lost the ability to work in 2022, I went from reticence to wholly embracing 'disability'. I pursued insurance, accessibility and treatment. It was 'disabled' all the way. It was the most apt description for what I had lost.

'Disability' is sometimes the best fit.

Narratives of illness

Narrative Therapy is a gentle therapy that focuses on retelling the problem-saturated stories, or narratives, of our lives in helpful ways. It centres us as the expert on our own lives, separates us from the Problem, and explores how we possess the means to reduce the Problem's influence on our lives. In Narrative Therapy, there are no right or definitive answers, only questions and possibilities.[7]

In Kaethe Windgarten's excellent piece on Narrative Therapy

and illness[8], she describes various types of illness narratives based on the work of Kenneth Gergen. In particular, three types of illness narratives stood out to me:

1. Progressive. The progressive illness gets incrementally better over the course of time. Each day I feel a little better. A popular version of the progressive story centralises medicine as the hero: I took medicine, or saw a doctor, and now I am better.

2. Stability. In the stability story, the illness gets no better nor worse. I feel the same level of sickness, day in, day out, no change.

3. Regressive. By far the least popular is the regressive story where illness gets worse instead of better. Each day I go backwards, despite treatment. In the regressive story, rescue fantasies abound. I dream of the day I will wake up feeling normal, or God will heal me, or a doctor will finally nail the problem—or a miracle cure.

As Windgarten points out, progressive and stability stories receive more positive reception than regressive narratives. This favouring of progressive and stable narratives is underpinned by society's love of 'overcoming all odds' stories and the underlying belief that 'If I work hard enough, I can achieve anything'. But those of us with pervasive illness know there are some things no amount of believing or positive affirmations can change. 'Mind over matter' does not apply.

There are some things even faith does not shift. I do not say faith cannot shift them, because Jesus tells us faith can move mountains.

But I know many Christians pray and believe for healing and do not receive it. We cannot blame an absence of healing on an absence of faith. Yes, for some people, a fresh infilling of faith may help. But plenty of faithful and prayer-minded Christians do not get healed.

Churches, in particular, value the progressive story where faith or God is the central hero. 'I was sick; I prayed; and now I'm better.' I value these testimonies. Who wouldn't? But I've noticed that while improvement in symptoms is credited to God, a no-change situation or worsening condition is often blamed on the sick individual. Christians yearn for resolution, but many Christians with chronic illness do not have this testimony.

> While improvement in symptoms is credited to God, a no-change situation or worsening condition is often blamed on the sick individual.

I get positive responses to my progressive illness stories. People love hearing that I had the flu last week and now I am better. People don't mind hearing my stability illness narratives either. If they ask how I am and I say, 'About the same,' they usually reply, 'At least you're no worse.' (Like anyone would want to get worse?) The most difficult conversations are around regressive stories. People hate hearing I am worse, and church friends in particular tend to get the deer-in-headlights look, followed by the 'We need to pray for healing!' knee-jerk response. Of course, it's lovely they care about me and want to pray for me. I deeply appreciate it. I'm not sure if God will heal me, as I have received plenty of prayer before, but it certainly can't hurt.

Ultimately, these responses deftly dodge the real issue: the powerlessness of living with a seemingly all-powerful disease. Helplessness is a horrible feeling. I feel it churning in my gut and clawing at my throat, threatening to choke me. Others must feel it too. People generally avoid feeling powerless if they can help it. My loved ones cannot cope with my regressive stories, and I don't blame them. Hey, I can barely stand thinking about it myself. At the same time, I don't want to be alone in this overwhelming powerlessness.

If things get worse and I am entering that all-too-familiar state of despair, I generally do not share that with church friends (beyond asking for prayer). I do not share it at work (beyond mentioning I may go home early). I certainly don't publicise it on social media (unless it is intentionally pastoral). Instead, I share with friends who have been through difficult things. They have some listening fortitude: they can tolerate hearing about my pain and sitting with their own vulnerability at the same time. I trust them to hold my story without fixing it or giving advice. They will be there for me.

Narrative Therapy is a powerful way to rethink illness stories. I highly recommend Windgarten's article for anyone who wants to think differently about illness or get a fresh perspective on their relationship with illness.

Lived experience

I would prefer not to inflict a label on someone unless they themselves have embraced it. There's certain power in giving name to our own difficulties and naming our strengths and skills in facing those challenges. Naming ourselves and our illness stories can help us reclaim them.

But when others label us, we often feel the urge to reject it even if it's correct. That's because we are wired to reject totalisation. We don't want to feel like a single label defines us or is the sum total of our existence (like 'woman', 'teacher', 'chocoholic', etc.).

The language around illness and mental distress has moved toward 'lived experience'. Rather than describing people by their illness or diagnosis, we say that person has 'lived experience of illness'. Just like a person might have lived experience of depression or unemployment or faith. Throughout this book, I refer to us as 'living with' or 'having lived experience of' chronic illness. Illness does not define or totalise us. But we have to live alongside it. Metaphors can help with that. Why use metaphors? Pictures and analogies pick up where words leave off. I have days where words do not suffice. But give me a picture of a fire, or a cave, or a chameleon, and suddenly I understand the illness exactly, like a lightbulb switching on. (See what I did there?)

> Illness does not define or totalise us. But we have to live alongside it.

Metaphors encapsulate our lived experience. They help us find our tribe ('Oh, you've had the leg-on-fire thing too!') and articulate symptoms to doctors ('Please tell them to stop drilling inside my brain'). It's more than language: it's colours, depth and scope. With the sweeping brushstrokes of metaphor, we can paint a picture clearer than a thousand words.

I have woven metaphors throughout this book. Each image is a chance for us to breathe, pause and reflect on our lived experience. Some may connect with you more than others, and that's OK. They reflect the broad range of experience illness can bring.

Illness is more than numbers on a pain scale. Illness is a rich, lived experience, unique and yet shared by us. I hope this book gives you language and imagery that resonates with you.

Labels from God

Not all labels are bad:

God has labelled us 'redeemed'. (Isaiah 43:2)

We are 'chosen' and 'included in Christ'. (Ephesians 1:11-13)

We are 'a chosen people, a royal priesthood, a holy nation, God's special possession'. (1 Peter 2:9)

We are Christ's 'friends'. (John 15:14-15)

We are 'children of God'. (Matthew 5:9, 1 John 3:1)

We are 'loved'. (John 15:9)

We are 'citizens with God's people and also members of his household'. (Ephesians 2:19)

We are 'God's handiwork'. (Ephesians 2:10)

We are 'the body of Christ, and each one of you is a part of it'. (1 Corinthians 12:27)

We are his children, welcomed into his family through Jesus. Our identity lies not in symptoms or diagnoses, but in Christ alone. When we struggle with how others see us; when we seek medical or legal labels for treatment and funding; when we run out of words to describe ourselves and our lived experience; when we want to protest that we are more than illness, mental distress or limitations; may we remember what God has called us. Regardless of what happens to our bodies and minds or what awaits us in the future, we belong to God.

Just for today, may that label be enough.

Take a moment to notice how you are feeling after the chapter, and whether anything stood out for you or resonated with you. Time for some self-care.

SECTION TWO
FLARES AND FLAMES

I live with an unwanted roommate.
He is messy, noisy and intrudes on my space at the worst possible moments. He gives no warning and he never tells me what he is up to. He has no sensitivity, no finesse, no manners whatsoever.

This roommate comes into my room at night and stands over me, haunting my dreams, causing me to wake in pain. He has intimidated me and threatened to take my job, my relationships, my faith and my very life from me. He has a way of spreading his mess throughout the whole house.

I don't know why he wants to live with me so badly. I hate having him here. But I can't make him leave. His name is on the lease. I hope one day he will get sick of me and leave of his own accord. Or die before I do.

3

MEDICINE

A Tough Pill to Swallow

The pain was unbearable.

Actually, 'pain' does not begin to describe it. I was in agony. My left hip and leg felt like they were on fire. I was flaring and I didn't know why.

The new GP called me and I hobbled into his room with my husband, who had driven me because I was too crippled to drive myself. I told the GP about the burning pain radiating from my hip down my thigh (bursitis, for anyone playing at home), and mentioned the possibility of an autoimmune flare. The doctor made a dismissive comment about how I probably didn't have an autoimmune problem. I stared at him. 'No,' I said in firm self-advocacy, 'I have an autoimmune problem. I have been diagnosed with an autoimmune disease.'

'Which disease?'

'Lupus.'

'Ah! Lupus is easy!'

I don't know if it was the pain. I don't know if it was the doctor. But I was fed up with being minimised and dismissed. Being told lupus was 'easy' was the last straw. I laughed in his face. I stood up and, much to the surprise of the doctor and my husband, walked out the door. I went straight to the receptionist and complained, through tears, that the GP had just minimised my chronic illness. I looked back at the GP, who was standing frozen in the doorway of his room. I made an instant decision: he will never talk to another patient that way.

I strode towards him in full fiery flow and said, 'Do me a favour. If you have any other patients with chronic illnesses, don't tell them it's easy. Never do that to anyone again. OK?' And I turned my back on him and walked away. I have never been that assertive in my life.

In all fairness, this doctor did apologise to me later. But it illustrates the time, energy, pain tolerance, physical stamina, emotional reserves and mental fortitude required in seeking help for one's illness.

Doctors

Doctors are not always the most understanding or

compassionate beings on earth.

Thankfully, I managed to find a good GP after the ghastly experience at the start of this chapter. Still, even the most empathic doctors may be constrained by time, Medicare requirements (in Australia), unfamiliarity with you and your illness (not one of my doctors has heard of bamboo nodules, barring the ENT who diagnosed me), language barriers, fatigue, personal biases and lack of specialised skill and knowledge. Doctors are human too. But some can put you off doctors for life.

I have met doctors who clearly suffer from some kind of 'God complex'. They treat staff like minions. They insist on being called 'Doctor'. They use their prestige to gain access to certain privileges or kickbacks. They push drugs. They don't listen to patients. They avoid eye contact—and empathy. It is inevitable we should meet these weird creatures in our travels. But there are ways of making such encounters more palatable. The following suggestions are ideas, not advice, gleaned from my own experience.

First, do your homework. The best way to find a good GP is word-of-mouth recommendations. Don't do what I did and walk into an unknown medical centre.

Second, take a support person with you. You can compare notes with your support person and debrief afterwards. If the doctor turns out to be terrible, at least you have a witness.

Third, paper and phones are awesome for taking notes. I prepare questions or a 'shopping list' beforehand. Jot down medications, differential diagnoses, tests, plans of action, etc. I ask my GP to write stuff down and draw pictures for me. Visuals help and they're good for later research.

Fourth, trust your instincts. If you get a good vibe and feel safe and believed, that's great. But if something seems off, even if you can't pinpoint it, get out of there.

Fifth, back yourself. You are the patient, seeking a professional service. Ask and advocate for that. Speak up when you don't understand, when you have concerns or when you want alternatives. My current GP, who is great, has sent me to some terrible specialists. Every time I go back to him and give my honest feedback (so he doesn't refer anyone else to said terrible specialist), I ask for a better alternative.

Finally, ground your expectations. Doctors are not gurus (even those with God complexes!) and while they know medicine, they don't necessarily know about our bodies. They don't have all the answers. Boy, I really wish they had the answers. When I am at the end of my rope with pain or debilitating disease, any doctor's appointment looms large with promise on my calendar. I find myself pinning all my hope on that one appointment. It's not because I've forgotten God or I mistakenly believe the doctor actually is God. It's because I'm desperate. In those moments, I remind myself a doctor's consultation is merely the starting point. It may take a while to work out what's wrong, let alone find relief. So I treat my doctors' appointments as a partnership or collaboration, not a wizard-consulting session.

Even worse than the doc not having the answers is me not having the answers. Sometimes doctors ask me questions

> *Not true—lupus is the driver and I am just along for the ride!*

that I cannot answer. They assume I am the expert on my body. Not true—lupus is the driver and I am just along for the ride!

Specialists

I have met some remarkably delusional all-knowing beings in specialists' rooms.

When I had bursitis in my hip, I went to see the most unbelievable specialist, and not in a good way. After his initial poking and prodding (how I love being poked and prodded by strange men), this specialist—I swear this really happened—started talking over the top of me, saying my GP and other health professionals were wrong. I stared at him, perplexed. When I challenged him, he again talked over the top of me (a sure-fire way of losing every ounce of my respect), insisting he was the expert and everyone else was wrong.

'You need a steroid injection,' he said.

'I've had one. It did nothing.'

'Then they did it wrong. They don't know what they're doing.'

Clearly, I replied in my head, this is your *modus operandi*. You are right and everyone else is wrong. Always.

I paid $300 for that dreadful appointment. I walked out and promptly burst into tears. I was in so much pain and had hoped this specialist would have a solution. I never went back. Even though I knew he was a jerk, the whole incident was upsetting. He took my money, time and hope.

Getting a specialist appointment takes mental and emotional energy. Referral pathways are complicated, and every specialist has their own rules. Some are happy to book you in immediately, some need you to scan and email your referral first, and some want you to send them the results of every test you have ever had in your life. Some specialists only run their clinics one day a week, so when they offer you an appointment you have to take it, no matter how inconvenient. This often results in rescheduling the rest of your life to fit around it.

And specialists make mistakes that cost you. One specialist once referred me for a scan and I was told the scan technician would contact me for an appointment. So I waited for the technician. And waited. Then I followed up. They apologised profusely for the delay. Apparently they had lost my file. They. Lost. My. File.

We sorted it out in the end, but it's just one example of how a seemingly simple process can quickly run away from you. If I hadn't called them back, I might have waited indefinitely. This may sound trivial. But it was one more thing for me to track, one more thing taking up badly needed headspace.

It wouldn't be so bad if there was only one specialist in my life. But people with chronic illness often have multiple specialists. I have the following specialists:

- An immunologist (lupus stuff);
- A cardiologist (heart stuff);
- A second-opinion cardiologist (atypical heart stuff);
- An arrhythmia cardiologist (complex heart stuff);
- A pulmonary physician (lung stuff);
- A gastroenterologist (you don't wanna know);
- An upper gastrointestinal surgeon (stomach stuff);
- A gynaecologist (secret women's stuff);

- A haematologist (blood stuff);
- A maxillofacial surgeon (jaw stuff);
- A dermatologist (skin stuff);
- A nephrologist (kidney stuff);
- A neurologist (nerve and balance stuff); and
- An endocrinologist (bone and hormone stuff).

Fourteen specialists. Try working your life around that.

And they all have waitlists. I recently rang my specialist to book in and was told he had a six-month wait. That's just great. What am I supposed to do in the meantime? They put me on their cancellation list, but in the end, I waited the full six months.

In addition to seeing specialists, I get regular massage and chiropractic treatment, see my GP, take medication and do daily exercises. (Yes, I have homework. There is no day off, and no promise of retirement.) If my illness flares, it might mean anything from taking extra pills to calling an ambulance. If I go to hospital, the ED doctors know nothing of my history. (I could write a whole chapter on deciding whether symptoms warrant a trip to ED. Will they take me seriously? Will I wait eight hours to simply be discharged? Or will this be the day they finally find something?)

In the past, my illness has been even more complex. I have dealt with ENTs, speech pathologists, orthopaedic surgeons, nuclear medicine specialists, audiologists and physiotherapists. There have been stretches of weeks where I have had a medical appointment every day. As if lupus wasn't exhausting enough.

> I can get medical burnout from the constant treadmill of appointments.

I can get medical burnout from the constant treadmill of appointments, let alone burnout from constant illness. That's why my mind sometimes goes blank or the brain fog gets worse. It says, 'I've had enough of this circus. You're on your own!'

I need a Personal Assistant.

You're fired!

I don't know whether it's the effect of ageing (I'm in my forties) or maturation (without being completely mature), but my tolerance for bad doctors is at an all-time low. The more time I spend with doctors, the more I understand what good treatment is supposed to be, and the less I accept poor behaviour.

At the start of this chapter, I fired a GP for minimising my illness and pain.

I fired one specialist because he repeatedly talked over me.

I fired another specialist because he showed no interest whatsoever in my story. Just pushed a medication. I'm not swallowing that.

I fired yet another specialist who, after months of waiting, played down my pain and asked why on earth I'd come to see him. He said he couldn't help me. He tried to fire me. I fired him.

I fired a physiotherapist because even though I did the homework, I wasn't getting better. The treatment didn't fit.

It is entirely appropriate to fire your professional if they:

- Suggest questionable or contraindicated treatments;
- Don't listen to your story or concerns;
- Don't take your wellbeing seriously;

- Gaslight you—tell you it's all in your head or you're imagining or exaggerating your symptoms;
- Are too pushy;
- Are not thorough;
- Behave unprofessionally or inappropriately;
- Try to work outside their area of expertise;
- Do not know what they are talking about;
- Do not liaise with your other doctors or health professionals;
- Do not follow-up; or
- Do not understand complex or chronic illness.

We need doctors who can think outside the box, but we don't need gurus who think they know everything. We need doctors to work in partnership with us, not just as patients but as people.

Bad experiences have taught me assertiveness with doctors. I ask questions. I challenge them. I tell them when they are wrong. I set boundaries, like firing them. The first time I met my current GP, I said, 'Hi, I'm Steph, and I'm complex. I need to know that you can handle complex.'

Gauntlet. Thrown. Down.

He said, 'OK, tell me everything.'

I said, 'How much do you want to know? There's a lot.'

'All of it.'

I was impressed. My story is complicated and doctors are not always interested. Plus, I always worry I will leave out some vital ingredient, like flour in a cake, and the appointment will come out flat and tasteless. But I took the plunge with this GP and told him every little symptom, right down to the split nails. He was thoughtful. He believed me. He made suggestions and floated ideas past me. I've been seeing him ever since.

Should we fire bad doctors and keep searching for good ones? Absolutely.

> Should we fire bad doctors and keep searching for good ones?
>
> Absolutely.

Medication

OK, here we go. *Cracks knuckles*

Most medication is inadequate. Some drugs take weeks or months to kick in, and you must live with your symptoms until then. Trialling medication requires mental and emotional stamina. Some medications are amazing. But some are no good, or the side effects effectively neutralise any benefit. These are medical cul-de-sacs, where you have to u-turn and try another road.

I once took Viagra (for blood vessel problems, guys, not the other thing) and I felt so bad I nearly went to ED. The doctor recommended I stop taking it. Good call. But there was no alternative. When medication doesn't work, finding another one is like a chemical roundabout with no exit in sight.

When medication works, it's worth it. I lived with outrageous pain from endometriosis for five years. When I was finally prescribed an oral contraceptive, I went from crazy lady to normal human being. It was wonderful. We've got to celebrate these wins!

I am currently on a cocktail of meds. Some meds are all the time, some are PRN (patient's required need), some after food. I have to keep track of which ones I am taking and when. If you're human like me and occasionally forget, there are consequences.

You might feel worse. You might have side effects. The medication may not be as effective.

I often forget to fill my scripts before I run out of medication. What follows is a mad scramble through the pile of scripts for that elusive one I need in the next twenty-four hours, praying it hasn't expired or run out of repeats. It has transpired, more than once, I've had to see my GP urgently for medication I needed that night.

Some medication is multi-purpose. When I developed mental distress secondary to chronic illness (no surprise to most people reading this book), my GP prescribed anti-depressants. They helped with the depression, but they also helped with nerve pain I developed down the track. It's rare that medication is a bonus, but it happens.

Win-win.

Testing times

Fitting medical tests into a work week requires a Master's degree.

I try, as best I can, to schedule tests on my one precious day off. If I must get a test on a work day, I book it around meetings. Most of the time, this is straightforward. Some tests, however, are a pain in the proverbial.

I once underwent an MIBG scan. (I'd never heard of it either.) They inject you with radioactive iodine and scan you over two days. It's the kind of scan they do when they're looking for tumours or cancer.

Let's put a pin in the C-word for a second.

This test was particularly testing. It took several weeks just to book the blessed thing. First the receptionist told me they were not doing MIBG scans because of the pandemic. (Thanks, COVID-19.) She said they were only doing tests for cancer.

'Oh,' I said in a moment of sparkling mental clarity. 'Then you should know I'm being referred for a suspected tumour.' She fit me right in.

I went into the city for nuclear medicine tests. They injected me with iodine at 10 am and told me to come back at 3.30 pm. Out for lunch, I copped a bolt in one of my tyres. Ringing the NRMA was fun—'Please come quickly, I have to get to hospital!'—and thankfully they showed up fast. I got back in time and they made me lie on a scanning bed. They lowered a big board over me until it almost touched my nose. (I don't mind these kinds of scans. But for people who fear enclosed spaces, 'routine' testing can be very testing indeed.) I went back the next day for the second round of scans.

I had a near-panic attack on the scanning table. Not because I was anxious about the scan itself; it was the reality that today they might find something—or not. *This is it! They'll either confirm the tumour or find zip, which means back to square one.* It was the thought of starting over after nearly two years of searching that was closing up my throat.

How did I cope? I remembered I was on the right track, I knew there was a problem, I just didn't know exactly how big yet. This grounded me and kept me from panicking about the dreaded 'Square One' outcome. Beyond that, I just held on to Jesus.

They said the results would go to my doctor the following Monday. *No problem. I'll just be over here, sweating bullets.* I white-knuckled my way through that weekend. By Monday I was on a knife edge. I didn't know if the doc would call, but I kept my phone by my side. The mental treadmill had commenced.

He didn't call. By day's end, I was utterly exhausted. I journaled some of the mental merry-go-round at the time:

> I scroll on facebook but I'm looking through the screen. I am on the verge of tears most of the time. Prayer feels like a special form of agony: I don't want to talk about this anymore. I want to google it, but I don't want to read any more about it. My heart is racing and I feel warm all over. Sometimes my hands shake; sometimes my stomach trembles. I feel sick, yet I want to binge-eat chocolate instead of normal meals. I am constantly distracted by thoughts of receiving a terrifying diagnosis. I am plagued by daytime nightmares of resigning my job in tears, telling my pastors, delivering this sucker-punching news to my family. At night I sleep long and deep; when I wake, I am exhausted. Sometimes my mind unexpectedly clears and I am my normal self; the next minute, I am weeping softly and all clarity is gone, usurped by an impenetrable fog. The tide of panic tugs at my heart. I am threatened by riptides, weary from the constant swimming. I am swallowing saltwater, the sea swallowing me up. I am drowning in fear. God, rescue me. Please send a boat.

Soon after, I got sick of waiting.

'Good afternoon,' came the receptionist's cheery voice, 'How can I help you?'

'Oh, yeah, hi,' I said with forced casualness, 'I'm ringing coz I had a test recently, just wondering if you have the results?'

There was a pause. 'No, that hasn't come through yet.' I narrowly avoided the temptation to scream. 'Would you like me to chase that up for you?'

'Yes please!'

I felt like Schrodinger's cat (the unfortunate animal who, hidden in a box with a random subatomic event that may or may not occur, was deemed simultaneously dead and alive). I was both well and profoundly sick at the same time. (The cat was a thought experiment, by the way. No cats were harmed in the making of that experiment or the writing of this book.) Ultimately the news was good: no tumour. But I never got an answer to that problem. Another unsolved mystery to add to the pile. These tests can induce a state of acute vulnerability and raw terror, so if you have experienced this, you are definitely not alone.

> These tests can induce a state of acute vulnerability and raw terror.

Another time, I went in for what was supposed to be a routine scan with oral contrast. I drank the disgusting oily substance, and soon after experienced the compelling desire to vomit, along with stomach cramps and diarrhoea. I had to wait four hours for the stuff to take effect, and the minute the scan was over, I vomited everywhere. The pain was so bad they sent me to ED. After a few hours, the symptoms subsided and they sent me home. Turned out to be an allergic reaction.

And the test came back normal. After all that.

If you know someone who has undergone tests lately, ask them how they went. They might have quite a story.

Cracking codes

As seen above, mentioning 'suspected tumour' got me a test booking.

Another time, mentioning 'stroke code' got me into an MRI very quickly.

Saying 'chest pain', especially when accompanied by 'trouble breathing', will get you an impressive response from doctors. Especially when you throw in 'elevated troponin' (heart attack blood marker) for free.

Doctors use codewords too. When doctors ask if I have a history of 'anxiety', I say no. Even though I am highly anxious at times, this is a consequence of my illness, not primary anxiety. 'Anxiety' from doctors is usually their code for 'All your symptoms are in your head'.

Sometimes doctors ask if I have a 'low pain threshold'. I don't know what to say to that (surely pain is relative to oneself?) but I think it's code for 'Are you exaggerating your pain?' I say no; after all, isn't a high pain threshold a qualifying criterion for living with chronic illness?

Experience has taught me how to navigate the health system. Codes help me communicate with health professionals. I am also conscious of my appearance matching my description, because in hospital they write down how distressed you appear. (Thank you, lived experience.) If you look normal and crack jokes with staff, they write, 'Nil distress'. But if you present bent double, gasping for breath or in tears, they note that for treatment. Both verbal and non-verbal codes are important. If I say I'm short of breath and I stop several times during that sentence to gasp for air, that will tell the doctors far more than my words ever could. It is important I do not mask my symptoms or 'fake good' but let them see how bad I feel.

Sometimes raw honesty is the best code.

Money makes the MRI go round

It's *really* expensive being sick.

I went for an MRI not covered by Medicare (thanks for that) and was out of pocket more than $500. Specialised tests cost extra, especially if you need contrast or if you have not been diagnosed. Some doctors order several tests at once, making for a very expensive week. And it often feels like a giant waste of money. Scans come back negative. Medication doesn't work. I have paid hundreds of dollars for trial medications that made me worse instead of better. I have paid doctors to tell me, 'I can't help you'. It erodes my sense of humour—and my bank account.

I am in a privileged position to be able to afford these costs at present. But when I was single? No way. Even pensions and concession cards can't touch these costs. Often these people go without medical care—or go without food instead.

At times I take leave without pay because I have exhausted my paid leave. The usual leave entitlements are simply inadequate for someone with chronic illness. When I am not being paid, I am more frugal about medical costs.

It pays to shop around. Some doctors are better at bulk billing. I am happy to stay with doctors who are clearly aware of how expensive their services are and who make them more accessible. Sometimes, though, the best medical decision is to pay up. You can skip some waiting lists if you pay. I need to work full-time just to fund my sickness. Which is a full-time job.

Because my bones are disintegrating, I am currently facing surgery which is going to cost me in the vicinity of $100,000. Yup, I tried the cheaper interventions first!

As important as it is to look after money, sometimes I say, 'Stuff it' and splurge a little. Because quality of life is a thing. Occasionally I opt for takeaway dinner or a nice chocolate or a book binge over medical costs. As important as it is to stay alive, it's important to have things worth staying alive for.

> Sometimes I say, 'Stuff it' and splurge a little. Because quality of life is a thing.

Therapy

And I don't just mean the talking kind.

I get regular massages, chiropractic adjustments and physiotherapy. This helps with chronic pain, especially that cause by twisted spine. (I always knew I was a bit twisted.) While this treatment doesn't make me better—my spine will never be straight—it stops things getting worse. It's maintenance, if you will, like getting your car serviced regularly. Sure, it's disheartening to know my homework is not making me better. I would love the physio to actually cure me. At best, it's relapse prevention. But it is something within my control. Unlike illness.

Sometimes treatment isn't enough. Illness has a mind of its

own, and even if I do everything right, illness can still upend my life. A relapse is not necessarily a sign that I've messed up. It's the nature of the beast.

I've sought counselling when my illness has raged out of control and affected my mental health. How do I know when it is affecting my mental health? I have a few unmistakable signs:

- Bursting into tears;
- Feeling more irritable;
- Intolerance for interruptions;
- Worsening concentration and memory;
- Exhaustion;
- Fantasising about hiring a Chronic Illness P.A.;
- Feeling angry with myself;
- Thinking about death or dying.

Don't be surprised by that last one. Many people living with chronic pain or other conditions experience thoughts of dying. Please be assured, if you have these thoughts, you are not alone. If they persist, speak with someone you trust about them. You are too important, and your mental health is too important, to let that slide. You might have different warning signs to me, but whatever your signs look like, it's important to attend to them.

This is the counsellor bit. As good as doctors are, they do not have a lot of time to listen. As supportive as your friends and loved ones are, they may get sick of hearing about illness (an unfortunate reality of being a carer) and they may be busy with their own stuff. So having an independent person can help. They are unbiased, can give a fresh perspective and won't judge you. Plus, there are no consequences of telling your counsellor how you really feel, as they are not emotionally invested in a personal relationship with you.

Disclaimer: if you tell your counsellor you are suicidal, they may need to act on that. Your safety is paramount, so they may need to arrange extra support until the suicidal crisis is past. They also need to act on other risks of harm, including hurting others or harm to children. Apart from that, it's the counsellor's job to simply listen and help you work out your own solutions.

One favourite counsellor was a Narrative Therapist who invited me to speak about illness in ways other than problem-saturated, which is how I normally talk about illness. Narrative Therapy can be a refreshing alternative to the usual depressiveness that marks illness. (If interested, check out the Dulwich Centre, home to Narrative Therapy, at https://dulwichcentre.com.au.)

If a counsellor tries to give me advice, I walk. If they tell me my illness comes from unprocessed emotion (yep, it happened), I walk. If they suggest meditation or mindfulness, I walk. I am aware mindfulness can be helpful for many people, but I have already tried it. A lot. In the heights of pain, I don't want to tune into my body more. I actually want the opposite of mindfulness: I want total distraction! There is such a thing as too much self-awareness.

It takes time to find a counsellor of good fit. So don't be afraid to shop around.

A breath of fresh air

I broke my shoulder in 2021. I slipped on a wet floor, fell sideways and couldn't move. Such a stupid thing. While my arm was in a sling, I couldn't do anything—I needed help with eating, showering and dressing. It was kinda neat working out what I could do single-handedly, such as doing up buttons. I'm so talented.

But here's the thing. Even though I was off work, in pain and rendered useless, my mental health was the best it had been for a long time.

Are you crazy, Steph?

Nope. At least, not yet.

> *In the context of the chameleon, it was a relief to have something as simple and straightforward as a broken bone.*

In the context of the chameleon, it was a relief to have something as simple and straightforward as a broken bone. It was great to have a problem that showed up on an x-ray; typically, my tests come back normal. It was wonderful to have a problem that is widely understood: when you say 'fracture', people grasp your meaning, as opposed to 'lupus'. It was fabulous to have a condition with a known treatment, timeline and expected prognosis.

This surprised people. When my rehab provider asked about my mental health, I said, 'You'll think I'm crazy, but…my mental health is awesome. Do you know how great it is to have something which is well understood, easily treated and likely to heal?'

He got it.

I had self-efficacy in my recovery. I worked hard at the physio and regained strength fast. When you are used to feeling helpless—when you are living with a random and all-powerful illness—when you are told by specialists there's nothing they can do—doing physio homework guaranteed to produce results is a Godsend.

That's a breath of fresh air.

Perspective

Perspective is why I enjoyed the experience of a broken bone. That's why my mental health was so good. That's why I was filled with gratitude. It's also why I enjoy getting the flu. It's a known entity.

Gaining perspective does not mean we were lacking in perspective before. It doesn't mean we need a lesson. It is simply a shift that can be good for us. No, it does not make up for all we suffer. It is not compensation for being sick. It's a glimpse of kindness, a moment of respite from self-pity and pain and powerlessness. It reminds us we are not alone. It might lead us to pray for others too.

Asking God for help can shift our perspective. It can settle us as we lean on God. It can throw anxiety and depression into sharp relief. It can remind us how deep and wide and high the love of God is. God sees everything we go through: tests, appointments, medications, hospital visits and diagnoses, and he cares about all of it. He may not heal us but he is with us. We can draw on his strength, especially in chronic weakness.

Not a bad perspective.

Take a moment to notice how you are feeling after the chapter, and whether anything stood out for you or resonated with you. Time for some self-care.

*We are sailing on a boat, drifting, aimless.
We are surrounded by water, no land in sight.*

*I do not know how long we have been here. I have
lost count of the days, rocking under the blinding sun.
My throat is parched. We still have a little water,
but not nearly enough.*

*He was steering for a while, but now he sits, with
seemingly infinite patience, watching the space where sky
meets water. Perhaps he is my watchman, staring at the
horizon, waiting for the first signs of hope to appear.*

*Perhaps he will announce its arrival like a sailor
at the top of the mast, awaiting the moment
he can cry, 'Land ho'.*

4

CHURCH

Have You Tried Praying?

I walked into church feeling unwell. A friend asked how I was, and I decided to conduct an experiment in honesty.

'I'm feeling yuck.'

Her face showed concern. 'What is it? Do you know?'

'Um…I've been diagnosed with lupus.'

'Well, we need to pray for healing!'

I flinched. 'Actually, I think God has told me I won't be healed.' Her face fell. 'But,' I continued hurriedly, 'thanks for praying for me!'

Christians are, in my experience, willing to leap straight into prayer without knowing anything about my illness or what God may be doing. Sure, prayer can be helpful because sometimes God heals. I have witnessed God's healing in my own life and the lives of others. At the same time, prayer can be administered in a knee-jerk fashion. It can even be 'ambush prayer' (thanks Brian Brock for this term[9]), done without the consent of the sick person. I have been ambushed a few times, had people lay hands on me, pray for me in public, even confess sins on my behalf without my informed consent. Don't do it. It's not cool. If you feel genuinely prompted to pray a particular way, just ask. Simples.

Sometimes prayer, as good as it is, is not the most important thing. Sometimes I want practical help. Sometimes I need money. Sometimes I need to be told to get off my seat and see the doctor already.

And sometimes I just need to be heard.

The problem with prayer

As I type this, I feel reticent about problemising prayer. Prayer is a good thing. Prayer is conversation with our Father. Prayer, in our native language or other tongues, is beautiful. It can bring relief and respite to our suffering and isolation.

But I have been subjected to prayer that is prayed *at* me rather than *with* me. Some Christians seem to assume prayer is always helpful and wanted. But sometimes prayer is complicated. When illness is affecting my prayer life, it is not prayer I crave. It is empathy. It is patience. It is willingness on the part of others to sit with me and listen without judging or problem-solving my illness.

> I have been subjected to prayer that is prayed at me rather than with me.

Why is it so crucial that fellow Christians don't solve my

sickness? Because some illnesses cannot be solved. Hence 'chronic' illness. Some problems do not respond to prayer; God has other ideas. This isn't fatalism or defeatism. I'm not saying we're doomed and we should give up praying for healing. I'm being realistic about the fact that sometimes God heals, but many times he doesn't. This is part of the mystery of healing—and God.

Some Christians assume God always heals and healing is always God's will. Sometimes he doesn't and it's not. Sometimes he allows sickness. Sometimes he takes people home. Sometimes dying is a different kind of answer to prayer. God does not always heal—he still cares, though.

I don't pretend to understand this. I wish I did. It would be great to have a formula for healing, something like this:

*If you have **x** type of illness*
*For **y** number of years,*
*And pray with **z** number of people*
*For **a** amount of time*
*In **b** particular way*
Then...

YOU WILL BE HEALED!

I think the correct term for that is magic. Or sorcery.

We can't corral healings like cattle. We can't apply prayer to our pain like antiseptic. Yet many Christian responses seek to prove otherwise:

'Can I try praying for you?'

'Maybe you need more faith.'

'Have you gone to a healing service?'

'Has God shown you anything about your illness?'

'Do you need to repent of something?'

'Perhaps God has already healed you, and you just need to walk in it.'

'Ask the pastor for prayer.' (Apparently the prayers of pastors are different from the prayers of lesser, normal Christians. That was tongue-in-cheek, by the way.)

Some Christians seem to view God as a vending machine who responds to certain amounts of prayer slipped into his cosmic coin slot. Or a genie who provides wish-fulfilment to those who rub the religious lamp the right way. But God is not a vending machine. Or a genie. He's our Father.

My problem with knee-jerk praying is not just about viewing God as a pharmacy dispenser. It is about those who offer such prayer. When they are too quick to pray, it raises suspicions in my mind that they don't want to hear about my illness.

Maybe my pain is too big for them.

Maybe they can't tolerate my vulnerability or stuckness.

Maybe they can't stand testimonies without happy endings.

Yes, there may be a spiritual component to my illness. But jumping straight to a spiritual solution without hearing the rest of my story, or feeling my pain, is a form of spiritual bypassing. Coined by John Welwood in 1984, this term arose when he observed a tendency among members of his Buddhist community to over-spiritualise things as a way of escaping from or avoiding their pain. It is the 'trying to rise above the raw and messy side of our humanness before we have fully faced and made peace with it.'[10] I think the term applies just as well to our situation. Some of us have been taught by society, family and church subcultures to avoid vulnerability by jumping straight to a spiritual so-called 'solution'.

When people start praying before they've heard my story, it renders my voice and story mute. I assume, being an optimist, most people do not intend to do that. But I feel silenced, relegated to the too-hard-basket. So stop trying to fix me. Listen to me first and offer prayer afterwards; this affirms my worth and value.

When people treat me as a healing project or testimony-in-the-making, I wonder if they see me as 'pre-healed' and nothing else. Which raises questions about imago dei (image of God). If we are all made in the image of God, do people see me as less than imago dei because of illness, hence the knee-jerk offers of prayer? What does that say about the way they see God? If we are all truly imago dei, that means people with sickness, chronic pain, intellectual disabilities, mental distress, Down Syndrome and missing limbs are all imago dei. God may not heal us; he may not want to.

> If we are all truly imago dei, that means people with sickness, chronic pain, intellectual disabilities, mental distress, Down Syndrome and missing limbs are all imago dei.

So enough with prayer formulas, OK? Stop it. God is love, not a formula, and faith is relational, not transactional. The challenge is sitting with uncertainty: the possibility that God will not heal, that healing may come in the form of going home, or that things may get worse instead of better. It means embracing each other the way we are, not the way we could be.

This book will talk a lot about faith ambivalence, that in-between space, and how God is strong when our faith is not. It's one of the most uncomfortable places to be. And it's often where we live.

Asking for prayer

When I request prayer, I ask for things other than physical healing. Sure, pray for physical healing if you like. Knock yourself out. But assuming God won't heal me this time, not because he is incapable but because so far he hasn't healed me the previous thousand times I have asked, please pray:

- For my mental health as I endure.
- The medication will bring relief.
- I can sleep tonight, despite the pain.
- For wisdom for my doctors.
- For money for surgery.
- For courage to face whatever comes next.
- I will respond with grace, not irritability or self-pity.
- For my worries and worst-case scenarios.
- For God's sovereign peace to envelop me.
- I will be assured of God's love as everything else becomes uncertain and unpredictable.
- The joy of the Lord will truly be my strength. (Nehemiah 8:10 NIV)
- I will grow in the grace and knowledge of Jesus. (2 Peter 3:18)

- For the fruit of the Spirit in my life.
- I can rest in body and spirit.
- I will be patient and kind with myself, just as God is patient and kind with me.
- For healing in my relationships, especially my relationship with God.
- For God's nearness, his supernatural comfort, his matchless, unbroken companionship. (Isaiah 30:18 AMPC)
- God will build my spiritual maturity and fortitude.
- God will make me holy and more like Jesus.

That last one is pretty terrifying isn't it? A prayer like that, total surrender, is probably the scariest prayer I could pray. Yet that is what God wants. He wants us yielded to him, not to torture us or gloat, but to mould and shape us more like him.

If we belong to Jesus, there is no other destination for us, and no higher goal.

Surviving sermons

Sermons on healing can be powerful and inspiring. They often prompt a prayer-slash-healing bit at their end, which is wonderful. I love seeing people get healed. But they often miss a crucial elephant in the room: what about people who don't get healed?

> They often miss a crucial elephant in the room: what about people who don't get healed?

I suspect most preachers don't touch on that because it's incredibly difficult. I have no idea what I would say either, so I do not envy the job of preachers. However, when I am in the throes of illness and a preacher starts waxing lyrical about healing, I have to ask: what about me? Don't worry, I'm not embarking on a self-pity spiral. I'm simply posing the problem with healing, namely, that people do not always get healed.

A preacher once told me some healing is delayed or gradual. I think this means God might begin the healing work at the moment of prayer but you might not see or feel the effects until later. This is a legitimate form of healing. (My profound thanks to preachers who mention this.)

There is another form of healing too: the kind that comes from good doctors, medicines, treatment and forced rest. So God's answer is yes, but we don't see it until we get treatment.

Interestingly, God's answer is sometimes 'Yes—but not yet.' Some healing might be the chipping-away variety, whereby we invest much prayer over a prolonged period of time until God says, 'OK, I can't deny your healing any longer. There you go!' This is akin to the parable of the persistent woman who pestered the judge until he gave in and helped her because she refused to give up. (Luke 18:1-8)

Persistent prayers are worth considering. The bible exhorts us to 'Ask, and keep on asking' (Matthew 7:7 AMP), so when it comes to persistent medical problems, it's an apt response. Although sometimes we get sick of asking too. We feel like we are repeating ourselves. We are exhausted. Or we worry we are hassling God, turning into one of those dreaded naggers, imposing on his time. Or maybe he gets bored with the same old requests. (I know I do.) We forget he is our Father and 'He loves to help' (James 1:5 MSG).

Often he is waiting for us to stop leaning on ourselves and lean on him for a change. One way we can do that is 'pray in the Spirit on all occasions with all kinds of prayers and requests'. (Ephesians 6:18 NIV) Praying in tongues, for those who are able, or praying with sounds or sighs or silence, are good alternatives.

But we still have the issue of non-healing to tackle. And most preachers neatly side-step this one. 'Oh, that's a topic for another day,' they artfully deflect, breathing an internal sigh of relief. (Facetious alert.) I have no idea how to tackle it either. I mean, if God is capable of healing, and if God loves and cares about us, why doesn't he heal? Why does he heal the next person and not me? Why does he heal some ailments but not others? (If you ever hear a sermon that addresses this question, please let me know.)

I don't have an answer to this one (at least, not a pat answer), but here are my thoughts:

First, it is legitimate to pray for healing, and sometimes this might be a complaint about not being healed. 'Why, God?' is valid. In fact, when we protest our circumstances, our prayers become more like Job's. Job protested mightily about what happened to him, protested loud and long, asking if God could still hear him. Job was not embarrassed to raise his voice. Perhaps we can learn from him.

Second, healing is one of the big mysteries of the universe. Mystery is central to our faith. I don't like it either. But we already believe without seeing; this tells us we are capable of tolerating mystery. When we are not healed, we come smack-bang against this mystery.

Third, non-healing forces us to look to eternity. Many broken things in this life will not be made whole until the next. It would be great if God sorted them immediately, but for now, I hope one day he will make all things new.

I don't know what the answer is, and I'm not sure there is one. Until we get to heaven, I'm putting my hope in God. (Or trying to anyway.)

'Everything happens for a reason'

You've probably heard this form of spiritual bypassing. While many things do happen for sound reasons, I am not convinced everything happens for a good and meaningful reason.

I don't think war happens for a reason.

I doubt that child abuse and neglect happen for a reason.

I am unsure whether the suffering in third-world countries happens for a reason.

And I am not convinced chronic illness and pain happen for a reason.

When we entertain such platitudes, we are often trying to convince ourselves there is purpose or meaning in our suffering. The thing is—and I may get tarred and feathered for this—I am not sure there is inherent meaning in our suffering. Some suffering is just suffering for no good reason.

Isn't that a little defeatist, Steph?

Bear with me. If we believe God plans meaning within our suffering, we are in danger of believing God plans the suffering itself—and we'd better just grin and bear it. We can lose hope, joy and trust in God. We can resent him. At worst, suffering can drive us away from God. Because if he planned it, it's his fault.

Is suffering part of God's plan? I don't think so. I mean, it's possible (he is God, after all), but I don't think God is like this. I cannot believe our loving, kind, compassionate God goes around making people sick to see how long they can endure like some kind of spiritual experiment. Or divine schadenfreude (taking pleasure in others' pain).

Suffering is part of life, and some of us get bigger servings of 'life' than others. We get sick because we're in a fallen world and our bodies can break. We're going to have accidents, catch viruses, live in pandemics, succumb to diseases and grow old, God willing. I don't think God necessarily *plans* sickness. But he makes the most of sickness to refine us and make us more Christ-like.

> Suffering is part of life, and some of us get bigger servings of 'life' than others.

If I dropped a glass on the floor, it would smash to bits. I didn't deliberately drop the glass. But now that I have, I'll get the vacuum cleaner out and do the room. The floor was dirty anyway. In fact, while I'm here, I'll do the whole house. Or pay a cleaner to do it.

God is like that. He doesn't make us drop glasses and he doesn't intentionally shatter our lives. Neither does the shattering throw him into a panic; he knew it was coming. But if we do shatter, he'll take the opportunity to do a clean-up. He'll give us a good scrub. Maybe he'll polish us so we sparkle. Maybe we'll realise the floor was always supposed to be that colour.

There may not be a 'plan' for our suffering, but God can spontaneously bring good stuff out of it like a master improviser.

He'll work it into something that's good (Romans 8:28). I'm learning that following God is less about following a plan or map as it is improvising well with our Creator. Ivy Armstrong says it like this:

> This spiritual life—that Jesus absolutely calls us to live—is far beyond what could be mapped out. It requires us to go into spaces unknown, to take a journey, to open doorways that haven't been opened, to say things that haven't been put to air and imagine and explore new ways forward that have not yet been carved into the ground in front of us, to listen and pay attention to the fullness of the world around us (as it's ever-changing). This life, with God in the mix, requires us to improvise.[11]

Living with chronic illness involves constant improvisation with the Holy Spirit. I don't know if we can find meaning in sickness per se. But sickness affords us opportunities to search for and create meaning in our lives.

In her thought-provoking book, *God, Improv, and the Art of Living*, Maryann McKibben Dana tells the story of musician Keith Snyder who loves (and laments the loss of) analog synthesisers. Apparently, when these synthesisers break, they are capable of producing incredible and unique sounds that cannot be produced any other way. And once fixed, the unique sound is lost forever. Snyder turned this idea into a prayer:

> 'May I break in interesting ways.'

'May I break in interesting ways.'[12]

Whew. That is a revolutionary way to pray.

An older lady went into hospital. There, she chatted to other patients about Jesus. God didn't deliberately make her sick, but when she became sick, she and God together made the most of that opportunity.

A young girl became sick with an autoimmune condition. She found a great specialist and she referred friends and family to this specialist. She had an opportunity to help others.

I am writing a book about my own illness. Reaching out and comforting others injects meaning into my suffering. In fact, illness now fuels my writing fire. Does it compensate for my illness? Of course not. I still fantasise that one day I will wake up and be normal. Until then, I can find opportunistic meaning in this illness-ridden life.

Viktor Frankl, a prisoner of war and author of *Man's Search for Meaning*, wrote about finding meaning in a concentration camp:

> ...Everything can be taken from a man but one thing: the last of the human freedoms—to choose one's attitude in any given set of circumstances...The way in which a man accepts his fate and all the suffering it entails, the way in which he takes up his cross, gives him ample opportunity—even under the most difficult circumstances—to add a deeper meaning to his life...When a man finds that it is his destiny to suffer, he will have to accept his suffering as

his task; his single and unique task. He will have to acknowledge the fact that even in suffering he is unique and alone in the universe. No one can relieve him of his suffering or suffer in his place. His unique opportunity lies in the way in which he bears his burden.[13]

Frankl identifies mindset as the single thing we can control. He calls this 'attitudinal heroism'. One may not be able to stop being marched to a gas chamber, but one can march with one's head held high. We cannot control our bodies, but we can control how we respond to our particular 'concentration camp'.

Jerry Long, who became quadriplegic following a diving accident, went on to get a PhD in psychology. He wanted to help people. He famously said, 'I broke my neck. It didn't break me.'[14] That's attitudinal heroism.

When people tell me, 'Everything happens for a reason', I have a few options. I can tell them where to get off. I can politely disagree. Or I can say even though there may not be a reason for my suffering, I can still find meaning in it. And God is with me, even in the absence of reasons.

We can choose attitudinal heroism—even in a concentration camp. And God accompanies us there.

> One may not be able to stop being marched to a gas chamber, but one can march with one's head held high.

The prosperity gospel

The prosperity gospel or health and wealth movement says we can live victorious lives by 'claiming' it in faith. It states physical and monetary prosperity is God's plan for us, therefore our divine right. Sign me up. *Snorts*

According to this 'gospel' (sorry, lots of sarcasm in this section), God wants to bless us—money, a fabulous house, full health, a spouse and children, travel, food and luxuries of every kind—provided we have enough faith. Apart from being ludicrously unchristian (did Jesus walk around in luxury?), this teaching backfires when we do not receive 'guaranteed' blessings.

What if everyone else appears to be prospering except you?

What if you don't have money?

What if you lose your job—as many did during the COVID-19 lockdowns?

What if your house burns down?

What if you are single or childless?

What if you get sick and never get better?

Is there a place in the church for people like us: sick, and likely to remain so? Or is the church inaccessible to us?

According to prosperity teaching, I am to blame for my lack of apparent prosperity. I need to pray more, give more, find more faith (perhaps at the faith store), because it can't be God's fault. God wants to bless me.

I sincerely hope you have never been told this. It is deeply harmful. Plus it is shallow, ableist, untrue, spiritually bypassing and totally lacking in comfort. The so-called gospel of prosperity has no answer for those of us without it. We cannot claim healing 'by faith'. If we could have, we would have long ago. Plus, some of my chronically ill friends have the deepest and most durable faith I have ever seen.

We chronically ill folk are bad adverts for successful Christianity. We get blamed for illness, rather like the blind man in the bible accused of being a victim of someone's sin, either his own or his parents. In that example, Jesus insisted that sin did not cause his blindness, and told his disciples to stop looking for someone to blame. (John 9:1-5 MSG) Sometimes no one is at fault.

> I wonder when we will stop over-spiritualising sickness.

I wonder when we will stop over-spiritualising sickness.

Maybe we are not to blame for being sick. I mean, if you are neglecting your health or abusing substances, then sure. But most people I know with chronic illness are doing everything in their power to feel better. Other factors are at play: genes, injuries, viruses, medications, hormones, hidden vulnerabilities, doctors, the weather, seasons, the lunar cycle and a host of other factors affect our health. Maybe faith is not a cure-all.

True 'prosperity' does not mean material success, money, houses or the avoidance of pain and suffering. Eugene Peterson defines prosperity thusly:

> It has nothing to do with insurance policies or large bank accounts or stockpiles of weapons. The root meaning is leisure—the relaxed stance of one who knows that everything is all right

> because God is over us, with us and for us in Jesus Christ. It is the security of being at home in a history that has a cross at its center. It is the leisure of the person who knows that every moment of our existence is at the disposal of God, lived under the mercy of God.[15]

May we know that prosperity, that calm confidence in God, regardless of our health status. May we, the poor in spirit, know God in full and rich ways. May our souls rest in deep contentment, entrusting our bodies and futures to the care of Emmanuel.

And may no one accuse us of lacking faith, just because we remain sick.

Spiritual jealousy

It is hard watching other Christians get healed. It is hard hearing prophecies of healing. It's bittersweet rejoicing with them when I feel overlooked, let alone praying for their miracle when my non-miracle is staring me in the face. Cognitive dissonance, that disagreement between what I believe and what I actually do, is not a nice place to be. (I feel a similar mental wrestling when singing songs about our miracle-working God.)

For the record, I totally believe in 'rejoicing with those who rejoice.' (Romans 12:15) It is a beautiful thing to celebrate the healing of my brothers and sisters. I am genuinely glad for them. I praise God for it. It just smarts when I consider how badly I need healing too.

I realise the core issue here is unhelpful comparison. I want what they're having, please and thank you. It's possible to feel overlooked without it leading to jealousy, but if I am already feeling the void of unanswered prayer, I am more likely to envy my brother's or sister's answered prayer.

How do we deal with this? How do we get honest about our feelings without stealing God's limelight when he heals? And how in the world do I pray for others' healing when I wonder if God is listening to my own prayers?

Here's what I've done so far. I publicly rejoice with those who have been healed. I verbally give God praise. God deserves it, regardless of how I feel. I am not about to suggest we stop sharing their testimonies in church. That would be ridiculous. However, I need to confess my ugly jealousy to someone. I don't want to ignore that. So when it arises, I call one of my safe people and confess that I am a wretched sinner. I don't want to feel this bitterness, yet there it is. I ask for prayer.

I tell God about it. It's not a particularly pretty prayer, nor the most eloquent. It's normally fragments of sentences: 'Oh God…I feel…I don't want to, but there's jealousy there…I'm so happy for them…but I've prayed that prayer multiple times myself…sorry God…will you…look, I'm gonna need your help with this…' I ask God to heal my heart, if not my body, so I can genuinely rejoice with my friends. I don't want to do it grudgingly. Hence my need for God's help. I pray God will help me be supportive. I pray for them; I can put my own stuff on the shelf long enough to do that. And I ask for help with my cognitive dissonance and ongoing wrestling. The honesty in prayer is important, as we'll see throughout this book.

No, I am not perfect. There will be times when I have ugly, immature, selfish feelings about being sick. Despite my best efforts, I will fall into this trap. The least I can do is present those struggles to God, trusting his all-encompassing grace to cover me once again.

The pressure of 'usefulness'

There are implicit and explicit expectations in church circles that everyone should 'do' something. There is a legit idea that everyone in the body of Christ can contribute. I agree with this, and that anyone with the right calling, gifting and character can enter ministry.

But. How does it feel to be someone who cannot 'do' anything? What if you can't serve at your local church, or even attend in person? What if you can't meet the expectations or criteria set for you? What if your health deteriorates and you are no longer capable of doing the ministry you once loved? What then?

I have been in churches that explicitly ask members to participate in rostered ministry. They expect tangible, ongoing contributions. The rationale is to integrate new and fringe members into the church. It's a good rationale. In practice, however, it excludes those who cannot serve regularly or reliably. It's ableism.

Some ministries are flexible. In my current church, which sets up and packs up every Sunday, I play the keyboard—a really heavy instrument, too heavy for me to move. So my fellow band members help me move it. Flexibility. Some churches, however, are not so adaptable or accessible.

When we tell church members they need to serve in certain ways, we send the message, intentionally or otherwise, they are less useful—and therefore less valuable—if they can't. Some of us can't. If we give messages to ill or disabled people that they are less valuable, we cause harm to our brothers and sisters in Christ.

This bothers me. Churches should be more understanding and adaptable toward people like us. We should feel able to serve and participate in some way, including online options or outside formal services. We should not believe we are useless, less valued and less worthy than the rest of the church.

> We are already in ministry; just not in a church building.

We can minister through sharing our faith and testimonies, praying for others, helping fellow patients and role-modelling how to follow Jesus in illness. We are already in ministry; just not in a church building.

We are not less valuable.

We are not less worthy.

We are the Church.

Ways to serve

Serving looks different depending on our illness and level of disability. It also depends on spiritual giftings, personality traits, availability and general life circumstances. So feel free to take my learnings with a ladle of salt.

My main church-based ministry is serving on the worship team. I always ask for help with setting up. This is harder than it sounds. The voice of the Perfectionist yells in my ear: 'You should be able to carry that. Pull your weight!' Unhelpful, right? Reminds me of Luisa from the movie *Encanto*, the unwitting shoulderer of the family's burdens, unable to ask for help or show weakness. The best thing I can do is swallow my pride and ask for help. Every. Single. Time.

I sit during rehearsal to pace myself. If I jump around like an idiot during rehearsal, I won't have anything left in the tank for the service. Which is, you know, the important bit. Coz it's not about me. It's about others. So I take pains (forgive the pun) to conserve energy. I also bring sustenance as I experience a massive energy dive between rehearsal and service.

I don't serve out of some ridiculous compulsion to soldier on. I do it purely because God is worth it. Whether in pain or not, I give him everything. Then I go home and collapse.

Here are my top tips for surviving ministry:

- Let others know when you're ill. They can keep an eye on you and support you.
- Ask for prayer. Pray God will fill you with his own energy and be glorified.
- Have a contingency plan if you need to stop mid-service.
- Make concessions to your body. Sit rather than stand. Carry a bottle of water. Take painkillers.
- Plan recovery time. I never cook after serving.
- Give your immediate leader a heads-up if it is likely you won't be able to serve that week. See if someone else can go stand-by for you.
- Pace your week. When I am rostered on a Sunday, I clear the Saturday beforehand. Come Sunday, I have maximum possible energy, rather than feeling depleted.
- When you first join a ministry team, inform your leader

about chronic illness to the extent it might affect your serving—but don't divulge anything you're not comfortable sharing.
- Clarify upfront the consequences of not being able to serve on your rostered day.
- Try not to compare yourself to others. So what if they serve more? So what if they're younger or more physically capable? That way leads to madness.
- Discuss accessibility. Sometimes churches don't think about this stuff (because ableism) until someone shines a spotlight on it. Can people with mobility issues still participate? What about those who cannot serve—are they still valued? What about those who are neurodivergent or on the spectrum? How can the church be more accessible to them?
- Ask the Holy Spirit for help. Always.

I was once disabled by breathlessness. I couldn't play or sing for months. So I changed the way I served: I offered band members support behind the scenes, helped with rosters and songlists, and followed up with new members. I was still serving; it just looked different.

> *I was still serving; it just looked different.*

I once went to Africa on a short-term mission trip, leading worship in various churches. One Sunday I was supposed to sing but barely slept the night before. Chalk it up to strange neighbourhood sounds echoing through the night and mosquitoes from hell. I was sooo sleep deprived.

I had a desperate prayer moment with God: 'Holy Spirit, I feel absolutely putrid. I'm gonna lean on you today for everything. Is that...OK?' I heard a sigh of relief from the Holy Spirit: 'Of course it's OK, you daft chook. Now I can move through you.' I chuckled. The Holy Spirit had been waiting for my complete surrender all along. Nowadays, when I rock up to church feeling absolutely crap, I say to the Holy Spirit, 'I'm gonna lean on you a whole lot today!' And we giggle.

The Holy Spirit is always waiting, ready to help.

What about prophecies?

Have you received prophecies for healing? I have. No, I don't know what to do with them.

Prophecies do not always come true. I don't know why. The whole region of prophecy is fraught with weirdness and misinterpretation. Not to mention the symbolism of Revelation that totally defies understanding.

This doesn't mean we shouldn't give or receive prophecies. It means prophecies are not always literal, they can be symbolic, they can have more than one meaning, they can be for right now or for wayyyy down the track, they may be coloured by our biases and wishes, and they might not even be for us.

Some prophecies are not meant to be shared. They are for our own understanding, perhaps for prayer or intercession on the behalf of others. Other prophecies are straightforward (or they appear to be).

But not all prophecies come to pass. Prophecies for healing don't always result in healing. That's a rabbit hole! To be promised healing and not get it can be confusing, anxiety-provoking and depressing. It can shake our faith in God and ourselves, and our trust in prophecy. We might feel like we were fed false hope or outright deceived.

I'm still looking for that elusive balance in prophecy. In the meantime, here is what I'm learning:

1. It is healthy to test prophecy. That's in line with scripture. (1 Thessalonians 5:19-22) We can check it doesn't run contrary to God's commands.

2. We are encouraged not to suppress prophecy or quench the Holy Spirit, who often works beyond our understanding. Practise prophecy and apply wisdom to what is prophesied.

3. God normally confirms prophecy in three ways: through others; through circumstances aligning with the prophecy; and through peace in our spirits about it.

4. According to New Testament models, the purpose of prophecy is to edify (even if a word of rebuke), encourage and comfort. Test prophecy along those lines.

5. The ultimate test of prophecy is its fulfilment. If it comes true, praise God! If it does not, we might need to take that back to God and surrender it afresh. Perhaps he will give us clarity about it. If he does not and that prophecy remains a mystery, so be it. That takes real faith and courage: trusting God in the absence of answers.

I have seen prophecies come true. I have seen God heal. I have experienced God's healing firsthand in my life. So I am wary of discouraging prophecy, in the same way that I do not want to discourage prayer. Still, we must apply wisdom to prophecy, both in giving and receiving.

Otherwise, we cause pain to those already hurting and vulnerable.

Testimonies

The typical healing testimony goes like this:

First: I was sick, disabled, in mental distress.

Next: I prayed to God.

And: God healed me—hallelujah!

These are great testimonies. I love hearing them. I love praising God for them. But a little part of myself—forgive me, God—says, 'Lord, this isn't fair!' Have mercy on me, God. I do not begrudge anyone their healing. It would just be great if all of us got healed.

OK, tantrum over.

I rarely hear a testimony about not getting healed. I mean, imagine someone standing up in church and saying, 'Hey guys, I got really sick, and I prayed, and I'm still sick! Can I get an amen?' Never happened. Yet many of us are in this situation: we have not been healed, or healing has come gradually, or we got better but don't know if it was God or the medication.

> Just once I would like to hear a testimony of endurance, fortitude or perseverance.

Just once I would like to hear a testimony of endurance,

fortitude or perseverance. A story about God being faithful but not necessarily delivering us from horrible circumstances. A story about disability that was not a 'problem' per se and did not require 'healing'. A story of inner healing and reconciliation with God, a huge part of faith. (It gets its own chapter in this book.) Surely those kinds of testimonies are just as valid.

Dr Shane Clifton, scholar, quadriplegic and writer about disabilities in the church, says this about inclusivity:

> Embracing the ministry of Spirit-filled people with disabilities starts with providing space for their testimonies in congregational gatherings, in empowering and acknowledging the unique way in which the Spirit can work through all people, in all situations.[16]

Clifton says if believers with disabilities are part of the body of Christ, they have 'vital contributions to make to the life of the church at *every* level of leadership and ministry'. They are not an add-on to the church; they are the church. If nothing else, that should validate their testimony, irrespective of whether that includes 'healing'.

For many disabled people, healing is not wanted or necessary. They are embracing life, limited, different, but not bad. They don't need to be 'normal', whatever that is. God may also be quite happy with the way he made them. That's their testimony. (Acquired disability can be harder to tolerate. Those living with worsening or fluctuating disability often desire healing. I know I do.)

Professor John Swinton, theologian on disability, tells a story of a German man he met in a disability live-in community. The German entered the community as a self-described 'rampant atheist', and his job was to take another resident in a wheelchair, living with profound intellectual disability, to chapel every day for communion. Then he'd wheel him home again. Every day, for two years, he wheeled that man to chapel and home again.

One day, the man in the wheelchair died. Guess what? The German found he missed communion. That kickstarted his journey toward God. The man in the wheelchair was no evangelist. He just took communion and stayed alive. Sometimes our vocation is simply existing, simply being in the world.[17]

> Sometimes our vocation is simply existing, simply being in the world.

The danger of having only progressive-narrative testimonies is we set an expectation that God will always heal, which is fine until you are the exception. We need to know this so-called exception is far more common. By all means, let's tell those stories of God-miracles. Let's also include testimonies of I-got-sick-and-I'm-still-sick-and-I-trust-God, God-has-stayed-by-my-side-during-this-trial, and I-praise-God-for-all-he-has-done-even-though-he-has-not-healed-me.

Just because we're sick or diverse or disabled, it doesn't mean God is any less caring or present. Sometimes our testimony is God's nearness and comfort despite our illness.

And sometimes God works through our simple existence.

Startled by God

I completely believe in God's healing power. I have seen it

firsthand in my own life. God healed me of dislocated knees as a child. He healed me of acute whiplash. When lupus stole my voice, I asked everyone to pray and my voice spontaneously healed. Three times. So when I say I believe God can and does heal, it is not an intellectual exercise. It is experience.

Why does God heal certain problems and not others? I have prayed repeatedly to be healed of lupus and God has never healed it, although at times he has healed me of acute pain and manifestations of lupus such as the voice problem mentioned earlier. I have revisited this prayer a few times. Who knows? God is merciful; if I persist in prayer, he may grant my request. Not that God adheres to formulas or anything. But there are times when I feel prompted to pray specifically for this healing once more.

The last time I asked God about it, I was startled by his answer:

'Steph, you will not have the usual testimony of being sick and getting healed. Most testimonies are like that, but that is not your testimony. Instead, your testimony will be you got sick and *continued to worship me in the middle of that illness*.'

> Your testimony will be you got sick and continued to worship me in the middle of that illness.

I wasn't totally happy about it. I complained at the time. But it was a revolutionary concept, that one could remain sick and still have a testimony, that healing was not the only form of testimony. Since then, I have worshiped him while sick, and when I have asked God for help, he has whispered, 'Through you, I will show my wonders.'

Imagine that. Imagine a God so wonderful he will use imperfect, sick, complaining humans like me to show his glory. If you have asked for healing and have not been healed, take heart. God intends to work in and through you, putting his glory on display.

Lame feet at the table

I often feel like an outsider at church.

Mephibosheth was an outsider too. The son of Jonathan was lame in both feet. King David sought him out, gave him Saul's land and insisted he eat at the King's table. Forever. Mephibosheth's response? 'What is your servant, that you should notice a dead dog like me?' (2 Samuel 9:8) He felt his outsiderness rather keenly, like some of us do. But he was welcomed into the King's house, his dignity and inheritance restored. He lived in Jerusalem for the rest of his days.

God did the same for us. He sought us out with our lame feet and disfigurements, we who feel ashamed and outsiderly, showed us kindness and welcomed us at his table. He bestowed us with dignity and grace. That's the good news of the gospel: God has pulled out a seat at his table for each of us, regardless of health status, disability or disfigurement. If people with lame feet are welcome, there's a place for you and me.

> If people with lame feet are welcome, there's a place for you and me.

Jesus levelled the field. 'It was *our* pains he carried—*our* disfigurements, all the things wrong with *us*.' (Isaiah 53:3 MSG) In God's kingdom the last shall be first. I often wonder, when we get to heaven, if people with disabilities and mental distress and chronic pain will receive heaven's highest honours—not because they suffered, but because God equalises and sets right everything put wrong by our broken world.

I invite churches to value and prize those who are not the most well or 'normal', recognising them as imago dei. I would hate to get to heaven and suffer the culture shock of not knowing the disabled person sitting beside me on Sundays (or attending online) would get the seat at the head of God's table.

We are one in Christ, redeemed, welcome at the table. If anyone ever suggests otherwise, I hope you remember Mephibosheth.

Take a moment to notice how you are feeling after the chapter, and whether anything stood out for you or resonated with you. Time for some self-care.

I am walking around a theme park, hopelessly lost, trying to find the nearest massive park map on display.

I want to locate the big X telling me, 'You are here'. But I've been turned around by winding pathways and off-road trails, and I have no idea how to find my way back.

I wonder if there are any tour guides around. I wander aimlessly, hoping to be rescued. I am in limbo, stuck in between being lost and found, caught in the wood between the worlds[18].

5
SOCIETY
But You Don't Look Sick

An infamous disability meme did the rounds on social media in 2022. It featured a car's front windscreen with a note stuck in a wiper that said sarcastically, 'Did you forget your wheelchair?' The car was parked in a disabled spot.

The owner responded on social media, saying she was a legitimate holder of disability status, her disability was invisible, and she did not currently use a wheelchair. The meme went viral as disabled and chronically ill people rallied and railed against the widespread misconception of 'disabled = wheelchair'.

I resonate with this story. I don't qualify for disability status because I'm currently working part-time, able to shower and dress and feed myself, and do not require the services of an in-home carer. However, there are days when my illness flares and I am rendered paralysed or housebound.

But no one knows because my illness is invisible. And I don't look sick.

Invisibility

When I broke my shoulder and wore a sling for two weeks, I noticed a terrific advantage: people could see there was something wrong. They asked how I was feeling. They offered to help. I was touched by their thoughtfulness. At the same time, I noticed the disparity between a visible illness—like a fractured shoulder—and an invisible one—like lupus.

I have often been temporarily disabled by illness. But because I have not worn a sling or used crutches or a wheelchair, others have summarily dismissed me. Even doctors have treated my skyrocketing pain with levity, disinterest and dismissal. Imagine the indignity of not only living with chronic illness but having to prove it as well.

> *Imagine the indignity of not only living with chronic illness but having to prove it as well.*

I wish my illness appeared visibly on my skin. I wish pain showed up like fire or lightning bolts, like those painkiller ads. But I only have words to convey my pain and disability. As for tests, many symptoms don't show up on scans or bloodwork.

There is invisible mental and emotional pain as well. Mental distress such as anxiety is just as real as a medical condition, yet won't show up on an x-ray. Doctors can't tap you on the knee and watch the depression react. And invisibility invites disbelief from others.

Then there is the absurdity of pain scales. Don't get me started. OK then, I will.

Pain scales are ridiculous. There are many different kinds of pain, and most are invisible. Burning pain. Dull, aching pain. Constant pain versus throbbing pain. Searing hot pain. Pounding pain. Tight, squeezing pain. Pressure-pain. Gripping, twisting pain AKA gastro. Pain that reduces me to tears. Pain that goes beyond a ten like I'll pass out. Pain that freezes muscles. Pinching, stinging pain. Radiating pain. Referring pain from other parts of the body. Grinding pain. Have I missed anything?

When I broke my shoulder, the paramedics asked me to rate the pain out of ten. 'Eight,' I replied, 'But you're talking to someone who's had pericarditis.' I was genuinely surprised when the fracture showed up on x-ray. I live with eight-out-of-ten chronic pain all the time. Just shows how relative pain is.

Soon after my shoulder break, I developed blinding pain in one ear. I wound up in hospital, rocking back and forth, trying not to scream as the pain drilled into my skull. The triage nurse asked, 'How bad is the pain out of ten?' 'Eleven!' I cried from my doubled-over position. It turned out to be shingles. It shot the pain scale to pieces.

To add complexity to the mix, I am one of those 'Highly Sensitive People' (HSPs). HSPs are often more sensitive to pain than the general population. That doesn't mean we have a lower pain threshold. It means we're attuned to our bodies. Arguably, we have higher pain thresholds because we are forced to adapt to chronic pain. So my pain 'out of ten' is relative to the less sensitive population.

Because pain is so relative, I try to use metaphors:

A fracture feels like whiplash.

Shingles feels like a screwdriver grinding through my eardrum.

Pericarditis is a concrete slab laid across my chest.

Migraines are a sledgehammer on the side of my head.

Bursitis is my leg on fire.

I'm trying to make the invisible visible. I am relieved when symptoms take on visible forms such as sweating, tremors, rashes or flushing, sores, swelling or positive test results. It validates my illness and gives me credibility as a patient. It sounds silly to say that I care about what people think, but I do.

It matters that emergency staff believe me.

It matters that doctors take my concerns seriously.

It matters that specialists send me for the right tests.

It matters that my health team thinks outside of the box. Especially when my tests come back normal.

It matters that health professionals partner with me. Because when the chameleon is on the prowl, there's nothing worse than not being believed.

> When the chameleon is on the prowl, there's nothing worse than not being believed.

Ableism and the face of privilege

But what, you say, is ableism?

I am so glad you asked.

Let's start with privilege. Privilege is the subconscious position held by virtue of one's circumstances. Privilege cannot be learned like a skill; it's gained by fortune or favour. The privileged often do not realise they have it.

I hold white privilege. I have never been denied treatment at a hospital because of my skin colour. I have never had strangers cross to the other side of the road because they suspect me of aggressive tendencies due to my skin colour. I have never been accused of theft in a shop because of my skin colour. I never had to think about my white privilege until I saw the world through the eyes of my underprivileged Aboriginal brothers and sisters. Until then, I took it completely for granted.

I am, however, subjected to the effects of male privilege. I have been talked down to because I am female. I have been stood over, intimidated and touched uninvitedly because I am female. I have had men swindle and sweet-talk and mansplain to me because I am female. Which is something most men do not have to contend with. Male privilege makes men blind to what is happening to non-males, just like white privilege makes me blind to what is happening to people of colour around the world.

Ableism is another form of privilege. Those who are able-bodied do not consider the needs of less-abled people. It is not necessarily because they are self-absorbed or inconsiderate. The very nature of privilege renders people blind to it.

Asking neurodivergent kids to sit still in class is ableism.

Telling chronically ill people to 'Get more exercise' is ableism.

Expecting us to use what is left of our precious sick leave or spoons is ableism.

Working harder, increasing hours at work, working late and working back are products of ableism (and workaholism).

Saying, 'There's nothing more important than your health'—thanks for that—is ableism.

Advice can be fuelled by ableism. Chronically ill people have tried many treatments without effect (hence 'chronic'). They have tried exercise. They have tried yoga—or have baulked at forcing their bodies into unfeasible positions. We don't need advice. But most of us get lumped with it.

Accessibility is a major part of ableism (or inaccessibility, to be more accurate). Accessibility is more than ramps and elevators, which are immensely helpful, but there are other forms of inaccessibility. When I suffered severe breathlessness, I could not talk for long or walk far. I couldn't go shopping, clean the house, or do my counselling job. Accessibility became more than a disabled parking spot: I needed a scooter, shopping delivery, chauffeurs to medical appointments, in-home care, and an alternative role at work. Unrealistic, yes, but that would have made my previous life accessible to me.

> Illness and disability can cause less distress than being denied access by an ableist society.

Illness and disability can cause less distress than being denied access by an ableist society. That is a problem I cannot fix. It is bigger than me, bigger than a positive mindset. It is society's problem.

To their credit, the Australian government instituted the National Disability Insurance Scheme (NDIS) in 2013 for those who qualify. (Don't get me started on the deservedness of some disabilities over others.) It's not a perfect system—there are lots of hoops to jump through, not to mention accessibility issues—but it's a step in the right direction.

For those with mental distress or who are neurodivergent, accessibility may look like online or telehealth support rather than face-to-face contact. It might look like flexibility with schedules. It might look like support with reading or socialising or sensory sensitivities. It might look less like assumption and more like consultation.

I encounter ableism when friends discuss exercise or outdoorsy activities. 'How wonderful!' I enthuse, adding yet another item to my mental list of 'Things I will never be able to do again.' I am alone in an ableist crowd.

At worst, ableism shames and dismisses our lived experience:

'It's not that bad.'

'You don't look sick.'

'Surely you can do a little exercise.'

'But you've done this before, haven't you?'

'You were fine yesterday!'

'Can't you try?'

'I don't believe you.'

I am not immune to the effects of ableism. I have made suggestions to others: 'Why don't you try [insert seemingly innocuous activity here]?' only to be told that is ableism. It has opened my eyes. Some people are housebound, even bedbound, by chronic illness; as sick as I am, I have no idea what that is like.

The antidote to ableism is not pity or walking on eggshells around us. It is asking rather than telling, enquiring rather than advice-giving. It is a stance of curiosity: 'What is this like for you? What do you find helpful?' It says, 'You are the expert on your body and your illness.' It is willingness to address privilege around health, function and access.

It honours and centralises the lived experience of those with chronic illness. It de-centralises the gurus of medicine and government. It demands we be believed.

It's something society badly needs to do.

'How are you?'

This deceptively simple question can be quite loaded.

How honest should I be? I usually fake good, as you know. I feel shame associated with being *still* sick instead of better and embarrassment of losing all hope, not to mention my sense of humour.

Not only do I get sick of talking about it, but people get sick of hearing about chronic illness, even the ones who genuinely care. They don't have to live with it. They tune us out. They forget about our pain and limitations. As chronically-ill comrade Meghan O'Rourke writes:

> Healthy people, as you're painfully aware, have the luxury of forgetting that our existence depends on a cascade of precise cellular interactions. Not you.[19]

She goes on to quote the nineteenth-century French writer Alphonse Daudet, in his account of living with syphilis, *In the Land of Pain*:

> Pain is always new to the sufferer, but loses its originality for those around him...Everyone will get used to it except me.[20]

Others won't always get it. I try to remember this.

Sometimes I break my own disclosure rules. Today I got a scan on my foot which had inexplicably stopped working, and the technician asked how I was. I surprised myself with a straight answer: 'Not great—that's why I'm here!' They must get that all the time, right?

There are times I fake good because I feel acutely vulnerable. It's the If-I-start-talking-now-I'm-going-to-become-a-sobbing-mess vibe. So I say something vague like 'I'll get there' or 'I'm seeing the doc this afternoon' or the classic 'I'd love you to pray for me'.

Slightly trickier is the well-meaning query, 'Are you better?' It's really hard to give an honest 'Nope'. It's hard enough not feeling better and knowing I may never get better; it's soul-crushing to tell a friend and see their disappointment.

Then there's 'I hope it's nothing serious?' I appreciate their genuine concern, but I never know how to answer. What is 'serious'? A heart attack? Cancer? A death sentence? For me, 'serious' means I can't go to work, they can't find a reason for my symptoms, I am disabled, I need surgery or I feel suicidal. But others have a different definition of 'serious'. So I usually reply, 'Don't think so'. But we always have the back-up answer: 'Well, for me it is.'

If I do fess up, people often respond with suggestions: 'Have you tried...?' As though they hold the secret ingredient to the cure I've been missing all my life. Honey, thanks for trying to help, but I'm not looking for advice today. Can you just listen while I vent or scream or sob uncontrollably?

Workplace queries can be tricky. I want to protect my privacy, but sometimes I let them know what's going on because I might need time off. I don't give the names of diseases or anything, just enough so they can manage things. A little more detail can help them re-allocate work, especially if I have something potentially long-term or disabling.

Because this is complex and navigating innocent enquiries can be exhausting, I find it easier to over-function instead. I fly under the radar, raising health issues only when it becomes absolutely necessary. But that gets complex too because people think I'm fine. They don't realise I am struggling. Faking good can backfire.

> *Faking good can backfire.*

My judgement isn't perfect. Sometimes I share too much, especially when the pain reaches unbearable heights. Sometimes I under-share, and then it's harder to get help later. It's a bit experimental. But the sense of agency is something I sorely need. I may not be able to control what my body does from one day to the next but I can control who I give information to and how vulnerable I make myself.

Yes, control can be a double-edged sword. But retaining some sense of control can help us survive. I'm all about the survival things.

Stigma and the sick role

Society makes assumptions about sick people:

'They're lazy.'

'They're exaggerating.'

'They're faking for the welfare payments.'

'They're attention-seeking.'

'They're a hypochondriac.'

'They like the sick role.'

Twaddle.

Most people with chronic illness would give their right arm (or immune system) to be well again. Most wish they could return to work, care for their family or earn an income without relying on the government. Most are proud and value their independence. They hate asking for help and leaning on others. Not exactly the picture of the 'sick role'.

> Most people with chronic illness would give their right arm (or immune system) to be well again.

Yes, there are people who take advantage of government systems, who fake or exaggerate illness. Malingering, they call it. Like the unfortunate cliché, it ruins it for the rest of us. But most people with chronic illness are not exaggerating. If anything, people play down illness in order to work, maintain friendships and do important things. When people get sick, they don't like giving those up.

Some assume we're playing the victim. A person with this victim mentality may have, at some point, experienced a genuinely victimising situation. But the victim *mentality* is different; it's a mindset of 'Why me?' and 'Everyone else needs to fix this for me, coz I can't'. But most people with chronic illness do not like feeling helpless. They would rather take action to improve their health.

How about the lazy assumption? This assumes we are unmotivated moochers with little sense of self-responsibility who don't care about society. We who live with chronic illness are supposedly out to rip people off and have a good time of it. We are selfish, uncaring, self-seeking individuals.

More stigmatising twaddle. (I love that word, don't you?)

OK, there is some truth to feeling unmotivated. I am unmotivated when every movement triggers enormous pain and debilitating fatigue. Demotivation can be a direct result of living with chronic illness. However, that does not mean people living with chronic illness are trying to take advantage of the government or anyone else. Most people with chronic illness are in desperate need of assistance, and—once again—hate having to ask for it. They tend to feel guilty and ashamed, not lazy and selfish.

Having said this, it is possible to play into the sick role and victim mentality. If these resonate with you and you feel you have adopted one of these roles, there are things you can do. Start doing some of the little things you normally ask others to do. Maybe not all at once, but even one thing. It's a great way to challenge the 'I'm helpless' self-talk.

If you're a wallower in self-pity, challenge this by including gratitude in your day. Remind yourself of good things still present, despite chronic illness. Take a moment to laugh or enjoy the sunshine. Thank God for his goodness. Thank others and do something for them. It's a cliché, but honestly, helping others can shift our self-absorption. When I listen to others, fully present, it gives me mental respite from my own crap. It's also good for connection—no small thing.

Especially as friendships can suffer when we're constantly sick.

Surviving friendships

When I make plans, I cannot guarantee I can keep them.

In 2022 I booked a retreat with friends and warned the

organiser, 'I may have to pull out because I've been sick for a fortnight and may not be better.' I needed to cancel in the end. Gutting. The organiser was gracious about it. I have some forgiving friends, but many with chronic illness are not so lucky.

Another time I planned to meet a friend but came down with terrible pain and nausea. I swallowed painkillers but all I wanted to do was curl into a ball. I sent that awkward text: 'Sorry but I have to cancel, I'm sick'. She was really good about it, but I wasn't. I felt wretched for doing that. Even when my friends cut me a lot of slack, it is hard to do that for myself.

One of my friends lives with chronic illness that can hit as hard and fast as my own. We have an agreement for our meet-ups: if one of us wakes up feeling awful, we can cancel or amend plans at short notice. Instead of her coming to me, I can go to her. Instead of shopping, we can watch a movie. There's far less guilt when the agreement goes both ways.

> There's far less guilt when the agreement goes both ways.

Friendship takes effort. This is true of any worthwhile investment. The problem is I have to be selective with my energy. I am fine with calling or texting friends. (Here comes the 'but' bit.) But I can only follow up so many times before I become exhausted. This means if I text a friend who refuses to reply, I ultimately lose that friendship.

I can hear the accusations now:

'Steph, you have to be a friend to keep a friend.'

'Don't be lazy, give them a call.'

'What if they forgot or they're busy? Just send another text, how hard is it?!'

I have enjoyed many beautiful friendships over the years, some of which span decades. That's a beautiful thing. I do not take it for granted. But I cannot endlessly pursue friends who do not reply. I don't have spoons for that.

Chronic illness is isolating in other ways. People my age simply do not understand why a fortysomething cannot squat or kneel, let alone hike or do yoga. It is frankly distressing to be with a group of people my age—or twice my age—who are doing great physical exploits, while I wince every time I stand up. That's lonelifying.

A group at work once chatted about the activities they were doing—which I cannot do. I mentioned this out loud. One of them replied, 'You need to do strengthening exercises. Your muscles are too weak.' I don't always rise to the bait. But this time I latched on. 'No, it's not a muscle problem. It's a problem with my knees.' She carried on undeterred: 'You need to do more squats.' 'I can't,' I shot back. At that point she paused. 'Well,' she sighed, 'That's a problem.' And that's where our limping conversation finally expired.

Often people do offer genuinely helpful ideas. 'This mop/vacuum cleaner/time-saving device will change your life' might be legit good advice. So I do not complain when the advice is a poor fit. I try not to shoot people down. They're not being insensitive. They just don't comprehend the extent of my limitations. Usually because I haven't told them.

The most helpful approach is to own my illness. If I can't do something, I let people know. If I want advice, I say so. If I do not want answers, I specify this so people don't leap into knee-jerk fix-it mode. I ask for whatever I need: sympathy, prayer, a venting session.

Most people are understanding when I am clear. It keeps the friendship intact a little longer.

Surviving workplaces

I will never be able to work full-time again.

I worked this out at age thirty-five when my part-time job temporarily expanded to full-time. Extra money? Yes please. One month later, I was ready to drop dead on the spot. I was out of my mind with exhaustion. I was doing a terrible job, and I knew it. I came to an important realisation: I can't do this. Never mind that 99% of the population can cope with the rigours of full-time work. Never mind how I feel about it. My illness dictates I cannot work full-time.

> My illness dictates I cannot work full-time.
>
> This puts me at a disadvantage.

This puts me at a disadvantage. Most workplaces prefer full-time employees. Most struggle to accommodate part-timers, especially when it's not for the sake of kids (coz I'm childless too). I constantly remind people that I work part-time and request updates on information or express confusion about details discussed on my day off. Sometimes I stop the conversation to say, 'Wait, when did this happen?' It happened when I wasn't there, but no one remembered to tell me. And it's not hard. They could, oh I don't know, send me a one-line email. They could make a mental note to consult me before making a 'team' decision.

Even more complex than part-time work is the no-work

decision. At what point do I decide to throw in the towel? I have plenty of days when I wonder how much longer I can keep this up. But I also love my work. Do I quit work only when something dramatic happens? What if I gradually decline—how do I know when I have crossed that line into unable-to-work? There's no clear-cut answer to this, as it depends on our level of functionality, workplace support, financial situation and disability eligibility. It may take years of monitoring, reflection and research to determine the answer. If I do quit work, an even more important question must be answered: what now?

Many workplaces are inaccessible to those with limitations. They should be more accessible, and many workplaces make efforts to their credit. Most workplaces have lifts, for example; but what if the lift breaks down? Someone with mobility issues might be truly stuck.

Thanks to COVID-19, workplace accessibility has improved with the advent of working from home arrangements, online meetings and telehealth services. But working from home is a double-edged sword. People may be more tempted to work when sick on a working-from-home day; after all, I'm at home anyway, why not do a little work while I'm here? Initially, during COVID-19, people were good at not working when sick. The workaholic culture shifted toward healthy boundaries. But now it seems—this could be purely my experience—things are shifting back the other way again.

I have become increasingly intolerant of heat, especially the stuffy, office kind of heat. We're not just talking mild uncomfortability. We're talking full-blown heat stroke, about to vomit or pass out, severe brain fog rendering work impossible. Naturally, no one else has the same climatic preferences as me, so they constantly turn up the heat. They walk around wearing winter coats or blankets while I sit in a sleeveless top going, 'Finally, I'm comfortable.' They look at me like I'm crazy. That's OK. I look at them like they're crazy too.

It is embarrassing to have a flare in front of my team. I don't want to repeatedly say, 'Do you mind if I turn the temperature down?' The quips about hot flushes get old. (I have wondered about perimenopause, but that's tricky. Many lupus symptoms overlap with menopause symptoms. Thank you, chameleon.) I am forced to disclose my invisible symptoms. I mean, I know I won't die from mortification or anything. But people without chronic illness do not have to endure this.

I feel driven to over-compensate for my illness. I suffer from terminal presenteeism: working when I really should not. I'm guilty of that—because I feel guilty. Being part-time, I feel compelled to prove myself: that I can handle the workload and be a team player. I take more time off than others due to illness, so I feel obliged to show up when I am not deathly ill. (If the shoe was on the other foot, I would look my colleague in the eye and tell them to go home. Apparently I don't practise what I preach.)

> I feel driven to over-compensate for my illness.

There is something particularly demoralising about sitting at my desk, unable to work, watching everyone else get stuff done. On those days, there is little point in staying, except to satisfy my stubborn streak. Still, I find it hard to gauge how sick I really am. I'm sick all the time, so symptoms tend to blur. I lose perspective of what 'sick' is. When people ask if I should take the day off, my honest answer often is, 'I don't know'. I hover somewhere between sick and well: too sick to be well, and too well to be sick.

Presenteeism heroises or martyrises those who 'soldier on'. If I were in such a toxic work culture, I would feel obligated to show up even when physically unfit. But different illnesses affect us differently. We cannot compare ourselves: 'They pushed through their pain, so should I!' because our experience of illness is unique. Only we know how we are affected. I can push through (some) physical pain, but the flu completely disables me. But my colleague might be semi-functional on the flu. So it's not a one-size-fits-all thing.

We moan about having 'so much to do!' but in reality that's all of us. Been there, bought the t-shirt. The world will continue to turn without us, we are not indispensable, and we are not humankind's saviour.

I also suffer from a poverty of sick leave. I use annual leave to supplement sick leave, and then I run out of annual leave. I still need a holiday like anyone else. Sick leave is not a holiday.

I'm trying to get better at calling in sick—regardless of what the voice of Guilt might say.

Benefits of sharing

Sharing can be worrying. People might view or treat you differently once they know about your illness. You might experience discrimination, even though you shouldn't. People might tell you what to do, try their doctor, try their medicine, try sitting atop a mountain in a contortionist position until you achieve enlightenment.

Fear of pity is another reason we might be hesitant to speak up. We don't want anyone walking on eggshells around us, worrying about us, hovering like helicopter parents.

Fear of judgement is a barrier. A few years ago I was in a very dark place. I was flaring, feeling isolated, thinking no one knew what was going on and no one could help me. I decided to prove those thoughts wrong. I reached out to three closes friends. They got back to me straight away. One invited me to dinner. I was relieved to know they cared. And the dinner at my friend's house was lovely. We didn't talk about my depressing thoughts. We hung out, ate good food, listened to music; they basically spoiled me rotten.

> If you get into a dark place, I highly recommend asking someone to spoil you.

If you get into a dark place, I highly recommend asking someone to spoil you. I also encourage you to tell others if something stressful happens, like you go to hospital or get a new diagnosis. Sure, we have to endure this alone, but we don't have to be alone while we're doing it.

It can be hard to speak these things out loud, and you might experience what Brené Brown calls a 'vulnerability hangover'[21] afterwards. Look after yourself if that happens. It's normal to feel a bit raw and exposed after sharing. There's no shame in that.

If I'm not in the mood for talking, I ask people to pray for me. Often that is enough. I ask people for check-ins after medical appointments. I ask to have coffee. I ask for visits. I usually contact more than one person, so if one says they can't visit, another might say they can. I ask for support when I'm going to hospital. If people offer to visit me there, I usually say yes. I don't care how independent you are, it's nice to have a visitor when you're in hospital.

Accepting help is hard on the ego. So I talk myself through it. I say gentle things like, 'Steph, don't be an idiot. You obviously can't do it; ask for help!' I also ask myself this reflective question: 'If a friend were in my shoes, what would I say to them?' That normally gives me a clear answer.

Telling people at church can be hard. Some Christians blame sick people for being sick. It's another fancy variety of victim blaming (and spiritual bypassing). This blaming depends, in part, on their locus of control: they might believe we're the source of our illness (internal locus of control) and therefore can cure ourselves; or they might believe external forces are the cause (external locus of control) therefore control of our illness is limited. It also comes from a just-world bias: we want to believe the world is fair so we believe people get what they deserve, ergo, if you are sick, you somehow caused or deserved it. Hence victim blaming.

So I don't set myself up to be unnecessarily vulnerable. I am honest but selective. It's called 'wisdom gained from experience'. Occasionally, though, I share everything because I'm past caring. My filters evaporate and I become as blunt as a sledgehammer. If people want to shame or judge me, they can go right ahead.

If I sound feisty about all this, it's because I am. I hate seeing people I care about (that's you, by the way) being blamed for their horrible circumstances, especially when they already feel bad. I hate the injustice of it. So you can bet I'll speak up about it. I'll be wary with people I don't trust, but sometimes I'll be bolshie too. It's part of my survival toolkit.

It's OK to be selective about your personal information.

It's OK to save your tender stuff for trustworthy people.

It's OK to not give a hoot what anyone thinks of you.

And it's OK to ask for help.

Illness tribes

There is something special about friends with lived experience of chronic illness. They get it. There is an implicit understanding of the need to vent and break down walls of isolation that illness invariably brings. Prolonged illness is lonelifying by nature. We are limited, homebound or bedbound, when we do not want to be. It can be hard to maintain friendships. It is vital we have support from people who implicitly understand that. We don't have to do this alone.

> There is something special about friends with lived experience of chronic illness.

I find it easier to relate to people with multiple chronic illnesses, especially when they are autoimmune. Autoimmune disease seems to be a special kind of monster (or chameleon). So I love talking to people with complex issues. It throws my angst into sharp relief.

We can pray for each other. Honestly, if I'm going to get prayer I'd rather it be from someone who has walked through the manure of chronic illness, their mind on the cusp of madness, their faith shaken to the core. That is someone who knows about prayer.

There isn't much available by way of support groups for lupus here in Australia. But we can keep looking, keep searching for one another. It requires some effort from us, which is tricky when energy is one thing we do not have. But please keep going, keep persisting, until you find your tribe.

We won't tell you what to do. We won't get overwhelmed or frightened by your complexity. We won't shame you for being who you are. We are here for you.

We are your tribe.

Take a moment to notice how you are feeling after the chapter, and whether anything stood out for you or resonated with you. Time for some self-care.

SECTION THREE
BUSHFIRE!

I have been treading water for days without rest. I am growing weary, physically and mentally, with the constant movement and constant fear of sinking.

Fatigue is taking over. I fear my body will reach a point of simply giving out, unable to continue. I will lose the strength to fight and the will to live.

And then I will slowly drown.

6
GRIEF AND TRAUMA
I'm Not Crazy, I'm Just … Living with Chronic Illness

Content warning: *suicide and thoughts of dying are discussed in this chapter. Means or methods of dying are not discussed and there is no graphic content. Coping strategies are covered, including helplines.*

I awoke with searing pain in my shoulder. I turned over in bed, gasping as I did so. *What's going on? Did I sleep twisted?*

The chameleon had struck.

I made my way to the bathroom. The shoulder felt stiff; I could hardly move it. I tried to stretch it but it wouldn't budge. *Maybe I'll shower. The hot water might help.* But it didn't. I stood under the streaming water, the high-pressure jets pummelling my aching shoulder. *Please*, I prayed silently. *Please get better.* But it didn't. I started washing, but the pain stopped me in my tracks. I couldn't raise my arm, meaning I couldn't wash my hair.

I gritted my teeth. *OK, let's try something else.* I started scrubbing my legs but I couldn't reach my feet. My shoulder simply would not move. That's when I burst into tears. *I'm in my forties*, I thought bitterly. *I should be able to shower myself.* I stood there under the pouring water, sobbing freely, crippled by pain. Thoughts came flooding thick and fast.

I can't do this anymore.
I don't want to live like this.
I'm geriatric.
This will never get better.
I want out.

I staggered out of the shower and burst into tears again at the thought of trying to dress myself, let alone go to work. My mind started brainstorming ways of getting out of this situation. Permanently. That's when I knew I needed help.

This is not the only time I have been suicidal. Illness has a way of crippling you physically, emotionally and psychologically. It breaks down your mind and any resilience you might have accrued in your coping bank. My triggers can be as simple as losing sleep or flaring pain. My wellbeing falls off a cliff. If you know what I'm talking about, you are not alone.

This is secondary mental distress resulting from chronic illness, different from mental distress independent of illness (or primary mental distress); secondary mental distress will be the focus of this chapter.

Depression

Christians can get depressed! Some believe we shouldn't, that Jesus should be all we need. But faith does not inoculate against depression, just as it does not inoculate against physical sickness.

Illness can be depressing. It's a reasonable reaction, isn't it? I mean, talk to anyone who has their normal rights and privileges taken away, and they have a reaction. (Look at how people reacted to COVID-19 lockdowns.) Anyone who feels constrained or limited will be impacted by that. Tell someone they can't do something and they'll feel the impulse to do it. That is a natural, human response. But when your body fights your own instincts—when willpower isn't enough—when your own positivity and optimism runs out? Depressing.

> Faith does not inoculate against depression, just as it does not inoculate against physical sickness.

Everyone feels depressed at some point. Depressed mood is a normal emotion. But a clinical level of depression is different: it's persistently depressed mood or loss of enjoyment in things that once brought you joy for at least two weeks. It's more than crying or a mood swing. It's accompanied by other changes: not eating (or binge-eating comfort foods), not sleeping (or oversleeping), trouble concentrating or making decisions, having no energy, feeling empty or worthless inside, feeling persistently guilty, and thinking about ending one's life.

People with chronic illness, especially chronic pain, are more likely to experience depression and thoughts of suicide.[22]

Depression also has a physiological link: our mood is connected to our energy levels. If we are not eating or sleeping properly, that can bring our mood down and interfere with our thinking. Then we feel down, which feeds back into problems with eating and sleeping. It becomes a self-perpetuating cycle.

So if illness affects our energy—and when does it not?—it increases the chances of depression. In fact, if you are *not* experiencing depression, you are doing supremely well, and I would like to sit at your feet and learn how you do it!

Depression is isolating. You cannot see the point in doing anything. You stop reaching out or answering calls or texts. You withdraw from the world. You feel like it's just you: 'I'm the only person in the world who feels this way. No one can possibly understand.' Not true.

> Depression sounds convincing. But depression lies.

That's the voice of depression speaking. Depression sounds convincing. But depression lies. It tells us no one cares (not true). It tells us things are hopeless (not true). It tells us we're worthless (also not true). It tells us to keep quiet about it.

My depression speaks in Shoulds: 'You shouldn't need antidepressants,' it hisses. 'After all, you're a psychologist, and a Christian, and a very resilient person! You've got this!' Not true.

Mental distress, especially suicidal thoughts, thrives on silence and secrecy. 'Keep quiet,' it whispers, 'Or people will think you're crazy. They'll reject you. They'll throw you into a psychiatric ward. You can't tell anyone.' Not true.

When I want to turn the volume down on the lies of

Depression, I watch TV shows that make me laugh. I go back to nature. I eat chocolate and cuddle my furbaby. I pull out all the stops of self-care. I also find music helpful when I feel depressed. Songs like *Intact* by Falcon, *It's a Wonderful Life* by John Lucas and *Closer than a Brother* by Josh Garrels have saved my life. Literally.

I once spoke to a specialist about the depression resulting from lupus. I wanted to get off the anti-depressants; at the same time, my depression symptoms were real. He gave me a sideways look. 'Well then,' he commented, 'Let's fix the problems causing the depression!' We giggled about it but often this is missed. Doctors can be quick to medicate mental distress arising from genuine medical conditions. While I appreciate the value of anti-depressants, especially during times of acute suicidal thoughts, there is a danger we'll forget to address the problem that triggered the depression in the first place.

When we are in utter despair, we need doctors who are determined to get to the root of the problem. They need to fight for us. We need support people—friends, loved ones, professionals—who refuse to quit when we badly want to.

Also, sometimes having a laugh at depression—the ridiculousness and absurdity and even the agony of our situation—can be the best medicine of all.

Suicidal thoughts

Suicidal thoughts are an understandable response to a prison sentence.

Being permanently limited, or in pain, or at the mercy of an invisible disease, can feel like a life sentence. Sure, it won't kill you, but so what? You can't do anything you want to do. You can't be the person you want to be. Your work, social and daily living plans are constrained by your own body. It feels like living in lockdown. Pretty soon, those four walls close in on you. Many people living in housebound or bedbound situations can relate.

> *Suicidal thoughts are an understandable response to a prison sentence.*

Thinking of a way out is our brain's natural response to being cornered. We feel trapped, so we look for an exit. We feel like everything is out of our control, including our own bodies, so we look for something we can control. Sometimes ending our lives feels like the only solution.

The biggest trigger for my suicidal thoughts is extreme pain. My second biggest is lack of sleep. There's a reason sleep deprivation is used as a method of torture. There is something about not sleeping and getting up in the morning feeling like roadkill that saps the will to live. Plus, when I'm sick, sleep is literally the only escape in the whole wide world. If I can't even do that, how can I go on? Sometimes the desire to die is about extending the relief promised by sleep. It's not necessarily about wanting life to end; it's that I don't know how to keep on living.

Now, let's get some stigmatising stuff out of the way. We should talk about suicide more. It's more common than we think, even in Christian circles. How I wish the church would discuss suicide openly. Same goes for all kinds of mental distress.

Thinking about dying and suicide does not make you a bad Christian. Let me say that again: thinking about suicide does not make you a bad Christian. It does not make you weak or cowardly. Don't let anyone accuse you of that. It does not mean you are inherently flawed. It does not mean you lack faith. It does not make you selfish. It does not mean you haven't thought about how it would impact everyone else. It means you're in a horrible situation. It means you need support. It means God still loves you—with extravagant, unconditional love.

Some believe their suicidal thoughts mean they're turning away from God. Maybe someone told them that. That's a double-whammy of feeling like they want to die and believing they're hurting or disobeying God in the process. Not true. You can want to die and love God at the same time.

When people with chronic illness think about suicide, it's usually not about attention-seeking. It's about escaping unbearable pain. It's a way of saying, 'I'm not putting up with this anymore.' It's an attempt to put a stop to the madness. It could even be viewed as an act of defiance. It's not so much 'I'm sick of living' as 'I'm sick of living with *this*.'

There is nothing wrong with those thoughts per se. The important bit is choosing whether we act on those thoughts. That's been one of my saving graces: thoughts are just thoughts, and we do not have to act on them. Just like you might hate someone and feel the urge to punch their lights out—what matters is whether you act on it!

> *Do something that helps you feel safe right now.*

A good action to take when feeling suicidal is to do something that helps you feel safe right now. It might be self-care, grounding techniques, talking to someone, taking medication (as prescribed), getting rid of things you might be tempted to use to hurt yourself, going to a safe place, having someone stay with you and reminding yourself of your reasons for living. The goal is not necessarily to get rid of the thoughts—sometimes they stick around like a bad smell—but to keep safe for now.

For those living with chronic illness, suicidal thoughts can become chronic too. You may not want to take your life every day, but the thoughts may be there in the background, always on, always waiting. When pain or illness flares, thoughts of suicide can flare too. It's like living with yet another unwelcome roommate: we've got to learn how to coexist with distressing thoughts that might never go away, while using our safe-for-now strategies.

Defiance can be a good thing. It lets us know we're still alive. It shows we haven't completely given up yet. Let's harness that fighting spirit, that energy of resistance. I channel my inner defiance into reaching out. I call people. I ask for prayer. I post on my private online forum, telling them I'm having a bad time and I need support. That is often enough. I have been flooded with support. People get it. They understand. They say they are here for me. That makes a big difference. It's not a cure, but it creates breathing space in my world, a chance to catch my breath again. A little breathing space can save my life.

> Defiance can be a good thing. It lets us know we're still alive.

I once checked in with a GP who didn't cringe at the mention of suicide. They asked questions like, 'Would you consider seeing someone about those thoughts?' and 'How have those thoughts been in the last three days since I saw you?' I need doctors who won't dance around the issue. It helps normalise it.

Lots of people experience depression and suicidal thoughts or know someone who has. One in six Australians aged 16-85 have thought seriously about suicide at some point in their lives.[23] People are surprisingly understanding when they find out how bad we are really feeling. So one of the most helpful things we can do is tell someone. I don't care who it is. Tell a trusted friend. Tell a partner or spouse. Tell a doctor. Tell a counsellor. Tell a helpline confidante. That's why they exist.

Telling someone breaks the silence and shame around depression. It throws our helplessness and embarrassment into sharp relief. It reminds us we're not alone, or not as alone as we thought. Sure, we still have to wade through the swamps of chronic illness. But we can wade together.

Depression does not know what the future holds. Depression does not get to dictate my life. So when depression starts lying, I can notice those thoughts as they pass by like clouds drifting across the sky, without having to act on them. And I can take safe-for-now actions instead.

Helplines. Use them. I'm not just saying that because I'm a counsellor. I'm saying it as a human being, living with the realities of chronic illness including mental health complications. I'm saying it as a consumer of mental health services. I have used helplines and online chat services when thinking about harming myself. The counsellors have been great. They praised my courage in reaching out. They highlighted my capacity to make good self-care decisions (including chocolate). They even booked follow-up phone calls so I didn't have to chase them or remember to call back. They made it easy to get help. They're a good option for the middle of the night or when others aren't available. I recommend helplines without hesitation (see list below and at the end of the book).

Here are some beliefs that get in the way of using helplines:

- This isn't a big deal.
- I should be able to sort this out myself.
- I don't want to be a bother.
- I don't want to take up their valuable time.
- They can't help me anyway, so what's the point?
- They're busy.
- And my trump card: I'm a counsellor; I shouldn't need another counsellor!

Notice what we're doing? We're coming up with excuses. We're justifying to ourselves why we shouldn't make that call. We're talking ourselves out of it. Why are we doing that? When we try to talk ourselves out of something helpful, it is often because we know, deep down, we really need it.

So here are my counter-justifications:

- This is important enough that I am thinking about it. Clearly, this matters.
- If I call them, it might give me a little breathing space.
- If I call them, they might say something helpful.
- If I call them, they know their service is needed.
- If I call them, it will increase their stats, thereby justifying

their ongoing existence to their funding bodies.
- If I call them, it's not a sign of weakness; it's proof of my inner courage to reach out.
- People make themselves a 'bother' to me. It's my turn!
- Maybe I can sort this out myself; but there's nothing wrong with getting a leg-up.
- Being a 'counsellor' does not inoculate me against problems. Even counsellors need counsellors!

In Australia, there are several helplines including Lifeline (13 1114), Beyond Blue (1300 22 46 36), Suicide Call Back Service (1300 659 467) and the Mental Health Line (1800 011 511). All are 24/7 helplines and they are free. They are staffed by trained counsellors who do this for a living. They are not shocked by thoughts of suicide. They will not judge you. They can help.

Beyond Blue has a website with online chat too. This is handy when there are people nearby and you don't want to be overheard. Their website is www.beyondblue.org.au. Plus there's a safety planning app called Beyond Now (download from the Apple store or Google Play, or fill it out on the Beyond Blue website). You can write down your support people to call when feeling suicidal, practical things you can do to distract yourself, ideas for self-care, and ways to talk yourself through. This is useful when suicidal thoughts are overwhelming. Who wants to try and come up with a safety plan when one's headspace is shot? Not me! Far better to come up with a plan beforehand. If you need it, it is on your phone, ready to go.

Personally, comedy shows have saved my life. They helped me laugh when I seriously believed I would never laugh again. They have given me brief mental respite from the horrific thoughts swirling in my mind. They weren't a cure, but they took the edge off. They reminded me life is not over. Not yet.

I need that when I want to die. I need to smile, laugh, catch glimpses of joy. I need to hang on to threads of hope. Sometimes I feel like a ninja in a video game, swinging from rope to rope, clinging to each one like it might be the last. I cling to moments of fleeting joy until the next one arrives. I can get through entire days that way. I encourage you to do those things that give you ninja ropes of joy, even if it's only one thing, one little thing.

> I cling to moments of fleeting joy until the next one arrives.

Grief

I'm standing on a cliff-edge, looking down over a dark, swirling abyss. The wind whips around me, tearing at my hair and clothes, threatening to toss me over the edge. My feet slip and pebbles scatter into the void below. I gasp for breath. I peer over the edge, wondering what lies at the bottom. Rocks? Hard earth? Air?

I falter. I fling out my arms, grasping for a railing, a wall, anything to steady myself. My hands grip air. There is nothing. The darkness seems to call me. It is terrifying, yet I feel the pull of the wind, dragging me closer to the edge. I don't have breath to cry out. My heart beats wildly in silent prayer. I hope no matter what happens, God's strong hands will catch me should I fall.

I don't want to fall into the abyss. But some days it seems to swallow up my whole world. This whirling darkness comes and goes like the night. There are times when I'm OK and I face the future with confidence, looking on the bright side, counting my blessings. Then grief knocks me off my feet like a tsunami.

It is like a pendulum swing. I am constantly retreating from and returning to the cliff-edge of despair. Sometimes the swing hovers mid-arc and I am numb; numbness often precedes the fall back into utter despair. If illness was a one-time thing, I could grieve that loss once and for all. But the losses are ongoing. No sooner do you come to terms with one loss then another knocks you sideways. Grief is part of chronic illness. I don't care how optimistic or resilient you are, if you live with chronic and complex illness, you have lost something. Grief is a reasonable response to that loss. In that way, grief can be lifelong.

Depression and grief are sometimes used interchangeably, but they are different entities. Both often feel the same: no energy, no motivation, a persistent feeling of emptiness, no appetite, sleep and concentration problems, spells of crying. Whereas depression can strike without rhyme or reason, there is always a reason for grief. If you feel down, you might say you are depressed. But if you feel down after losing something, I would say you are grieving.

Some losses are obvious, like losing hair or a leg. I am facing the grief of losing my original joints when I have corrective surgery soon. But many losses are intangible. I have lost the capacity to work full-time. I have accepted that, and now see the benefits of working part-time. It does wonders for your mental health! But the loss of opportunity in the work sphere is real. My world has shrunk.

I have lost the carefree enjoyment of holidays and travel. There

> My world has shrunk.

is always the shadow of illness looming. I have lost an incalculable amount of holiday leave and holidays. Once I lost three days of my precious Christmas week off due to medical tests. Three. Days. Then I got sick for the remainder of the week. I am forever losing my plans, breaks and relaxation to illness.

I live with chronic, unabating dizziness. There's grief around that: I will never walk clear-headed again.

There are intangible losses of identity. I want to be a fun-loving, playful, energetic middle-aged person. Perhaps I still carry aspects of that. But most of the time, I feel the acute absence of energy. I feel run-down, like I am perpetually coming down with the flu. (Perhaps that's why the real flu knocks me sideways; it's a double flu.) I make careful choices about how much shopping I do. I selectively choose how many appointments I attend in one day. If something big is coming up, I spend several days conserving energy beforehand.

This is not the kind of person I wanted to be.

This is not how I wanted to live my life.

I have lost my old self.

People are quick to dismiss intangible losses. 'What are you complaining about? At least you still get to travel!' 'At least you have a job!' 'At least you aren't bed-ridden!' This kind of dismissal effectively disenfranchises our grief, denying us the opportunity to publicly grieve what we have lost.[24]

Sentences that start with 'At least' are devoid of empathy and understanding. (See Brené Brown's excellent work on this subject.[25]) I am mighty fortunate to be working. I am profoundly grateful to get out of bed every day. I am totally blessed to be able to travel to some degree. But gratitude and grief are not mutually exclusive. It is possible to be grateful for what you have while feeling the absence of what you once had. I experience gratitude every day. I also experience constant grief.

Grief is an act of protest. I object to this lifestyle. I object to feeling like an eighty-year-old in my forties, having aged prematurely my whole life, and the ensuing loneliness as I identify less and less with my peers. I object to the loss of the simple life. I have become fussy, picky, high-maintenance.

I am currently in the phase of hating my body. Not hating myself—I love my quirky, observant, passionate, anally-retentive self—but hating this gravity suit. You could say my relationship with my body is ruptured at present. I feel let down by my body, disappointed, betrayed. My body has broken my trust in the simplest activities: going out to dinner, travelling, eating an apple, showering. I do not know how to repair this, or even if I should.

Even as I type this, I can hear Christians gasping in horror. 'How can you hate your body? It's a gift from God!' Do we really want to go down the rabbit hole of why God gifted me with such a dysfunctional body? Never-ending illness has the capacity to affect our faith. For now, I accept that hating my body is part of grief. This is the body I have, not the body I want. I cannot take it to the Body Store and get an exchange. (But it's a nice fantasy, isn't it?)

Illness has taken my resonance with my peers. I relate more to people in their seventies and eighties than I do my own age group. When I read medical articles, it is the geriatric ones that speak to me. This is overwhelmingly sad.

It has taken my peace. I am surprised how much anxiety lives in chronic illness. C.S. Lewis rightly said, 'No one ever told me that grief felt so like fear.'[26] Losing something inevitably brings worries about what else I will lose. Everything is at stake, and I may lose it all. And it might not be in my seventies—it might be next week.

There are new losses with chronic illness. Grief is a constant process of coming to terms with yet another limit as we experience further world shrinkage. It's always swinging between hope—'Maybe tomorrow will be better'—and loss—'Oh great, another thing I can't do anymore.' Every time I see a doctor, I hold my breath. I am anticipating more bad news.

> Grief is a constant process of coming to terms with yet another limit as we experience further world shrinkage.

When I turned forty, I found out I had osteoporosis. I lost my healthy adulthood. My body was eating away my bones from the inside out. Can you blame me for being angry at my body?

Grieving is real and necessary. We might need to grieve for the rest of our lives.

There are times when I feel like writing my own obituary:

> Here lies Steph's health and wellbeing. It lived for fourteen years before illness took over. It has now been absent so long it has been deemed missing, presumed dead. Ordinarily we would bury the body at this point, but it seems Steph still needs it for...something. Steph's health and wellbeing brought great joy when it was

> around. It gave Steph the satisfaction of being able to work, see friends and go on adventures. Farewell, old friend. It was good while it lasted.

It is appropriate to memorialise what we have lost.

I move in and out of grief, like a kid running through a sprinkler. There are times when I shelve it. There are moments when I give way to the tears. I let it surface, like a kick-board held underwater and finally released, rushing to the surface. I feel all of it.

I take this mess to God. I give him the full force of it. Sometimes I even use words. I let him know the good, the bad and the ugly, especially the ugly. Prayer is not a job interview, and I am not on my best behaviour. I give God the lot. I ask for what I need: peace, answers, healing of the heart as well as the body, a good nights' sleep, an infilling of his love. He meets me there. He waits for me with acres of grace. Sometimes he even uses words too.

Give grief quality time. Don't ignore it; it won't go away on its own. Not too much in one sitting either, lest the abyss swallow you whole. I visit the abyss regularly, like an old friend, but I wouldn't want to live there. Sometimes I process just a sliver of it.

And grace, fathomless grace, awaits us in the abyss.

Rage

When I can't face grief, I get angry instead. There is a theory that depression is rage turned inward. I wholeheartedly agree.

I rage against the loss and limitations of my body. I get sick and tired of feeling sick and tired. Chronic illness has ceased

> *When I can't face grief, I get angry instead.*

to be a novelty. I watch others being active and think, *Why can't I do that anymore?* It doesn't seem fair that others have so much capacity when I have nearly none by comparison. Rightly or wrongly, I experience normalcy-jealousy. I have lost my normal. Everything, down to my split nails, is a reminder there is something fundamentally wrong with me. I know comparison is unhelpful; it only makes me more angry and upset. Yet the reminders are all around me, people in their sixties, seventies and eighties being busy and outdoorsy, while here I sit, conserving energy at every turn. That's not OK.

It's not OK we live with unrelenting pain and fatigue.

It's not OK we are losing our movement, energy and lifestyles.

It's not OK we feel double our age.

It's not OK to lose work and ministry opportunities.

It's not OK illness affects our friendships and relationships.

Anger is not necessarily bad. It's a normal and understandable reaction to something that is not OK. Usually we feel angry for two reasons: we have been wronged or violated in some way, or our needs are going unmet.

Experiencing the emotion of anger is not a sin. God got angry plenty of times in the bible (the idolatrous Israelites in Exodus 32:7-10, the whingeing Israelites in Numbers 11, the Pharisees in Matthew 23:13-36). Aggressive behaviour, on the other hand, is not OK. It's not OK to hurt ourselves or someone else, yell at people or 'kick the dog'. There's a difference between feeling angry and acting aggressively. I have no problem with the former.

Anger can even be a good thing. It can be an act of defiance.

It says, 'I don't accept this.' It is a decision to resist, to stand against something, to seek out another way. Healthy anger can also motivate us to take action, like a parent leaping between their child and a bully. Anger can be an incentive to look for another treatment, another doctor, another cure. It can prompt us to ask questions. It can compel us to persevere.

There is a time for acceptance too. Prolonged anger that goes nowhere can be unhealthy, like a car spinning its wheels. Anger eventually needs a resolution, or we burn through our reserves and collapse. That's not good for our health. If you experience the health-related rage that I do, you can harness your anger to push for better treatment or answers. Or channel your anger into something productive or grounding, or an outlet.

I have been incandescent with rage at the indignity and relentlessness of illness. I need to rant and rave. So I channel my anger into writing and music, a form of expression that harms no one and might even resonate with others. That's healthy. It doesn't take away my illness or make me better, but it gets it off my chest. I anticipate ongoing anger alongside ongoing illness like parallel train tracks, because illness stinks. It's not pretty. It's hateful, mind-bending and life-altering. May as well get honest about that. When my rage surfaces, I can't sweep it under the carpet. The silent treatment doesn't work. I've got to face it and find a way of expressing it.

> I anticipate ongoing anger alongside ongoing illness like parallel train tracks, because illness stinks.

Eugene Peterson, in an interview with U2 singer Bono, talks

about how to 'cuss without cussing'[27]. Peterson suggests the brutal honesty of the Psalms can help us do that by giving vent to our feelings. When chronic illness gets under my skin and on my nerves, I want to swear. (Sometimes a swear word might be the most appropriate descriptor!) But regardless of whether you swear or not, the important thing is to express that emotion. You have permission to cry, rage, journal, pray, sing, feel irritable, get snarky, punch the pillow, scream into the wind, whatever it takes. Then do something nice for yourself. Anger has a way of dropping us like a sugar crash, so self-care helps restore equilibrium.

God gets angry when we get angry; not necessarily angry *with* us but angry *about* the things that anger us. He cares deeply about those things that deeply concern us. He hates it when things are not right. He gets just as angry about unfairness, inequity and injustice as we do—possibly more so. So talk to God about the rage, secure in the knowledge he really does understand. He is a safe person. He won't punish or reject you for having those feelings. If anything, he is the one person you can tell without fear of reprisal. He doesn't get defensive or offended. That's good news!

Honesty with God is more important than 'nice' or 'polite' prayer. He wants your life—all of it.

Anxiety

Anxiety is correlated with chronic illness[28] and depression.[29] Oh joy!

If you have lost control of your body and world, it is understandable to have worries. Worry is normal. Anxiety is a human emotion. However, anxiety sits on a spectrum, and if it gets carried away, it can carry us away with it. It can lead to phobias (irrational or exaggerated fears) or panic attacks (intense, rapidly increasing anxiety that becomes overwhelming or paralysing).

Illness affords us many opportunities for worry. Everything from the stress of organising medical appointments to making future plans promotes anxiety. It is an environment ripe for worries like weeds in a garden. Even when we feel physically good, we might worry about the next flare or relapse. It is the proverbial ticking time bomb. Except the bomb is real.

After my pericarditis, I did a little research. (Yes, I know the pitfalls of Dr Googling. Don't judge me.) I found that statistically speaking, one is more prone to getting pericarditis a second time after having it the first time. Awesome. How am I supposed to live with that? Pericarditis is not something I want to relive. I worried about it. For years. That stifling fear followed me wherever I went, haunting my waking hours and sometimes my sleeping ones too. It got to the point where I spent the better part of a holiday in a near-panic state about it.

What if it happens again?

What if I get chest pain on top of a mountain?

How on earth do I get to the nearest hospital?

I felt like I was in a perpetual fight-or-flight state, batting away the hands of anxiety creeping around my throat, threatening to choke me. It was horrible. And no amount of 'Well, that's very unlikely' was going to help. Because I had already had it. It was not unlikely. It was, in fact, more likely to happen.

Rarity also increases my anxiety. When I get concerning

symptoms or test results, doctors are quick to tell me, 'Oh don't worry, it's probably not [insert worst-case medical scenario here], that's very rare.' I stare back at them. 'Honey, I was born rare. I eat rare for breakfast.' I'm living with a rare disease, the very first symptom of which was the incredibly rare bamboo nodules. I embody rarity.

I've received some terrible news in doctor's surgeries. This has triggered a kind of appointment-anxiety in me. I worry about what bad news I'll receive at my next appointment. That's why I take a support person whenever an appointment threatens to deliver bad news. (Blood tests, I'm fine on my own. Brain MRI? Support person, please.)

Anxiety pops its head up in unexpected places. I spent two years getting tested for heart-related symptoms that have no apparent cause. I have worn heart monitors, been scanned within an inch of my life, undertaken every blood test known to humankind, attended hospital eight times and seen countless doctors, all for heart problems of unknown origin. Doctors have done their best to reassure me, and rightly so. 'You do not have a problem with your heart,' they insisted. 'Your heart is just...working too hard.' What kind of diagnosis is that? I can't fix that!

Getting good news about your heart is always good. But I worry about the next 'heart episode'. I worry about going to hospital for the ninth time, knowing they will find nothing wrong. I worry about becoming incapacitated next time it hits at work, which has happened several times.

This is a time when negative or normal test results are more worrying than positive ones. Being told there is nothing wrong when you have chest pain and trouble breathing, or when you are so dizzy you cannot stand, is the opposite of reassuring. I need to know what the problem is so I can do something. I am an action type of girl. I need a plan. If the test results come back normal, I have no plan, no direction, no control. I am living on the whim of my disease. For people living with chronic illness, anxiety is an understandable reaction to a situation beyond their control.

> This is a time when negative or normal test results are more worrying than positive ones.

Those who live with chronic illness are frequently accused of being a 'hypochondriac'. Hypochondriasis means you imagine or exaggerate your health issues. People with chronic illness rarely exaggerate or imagine things; if anything, they play them down. Still, the fear of being labelled a 'hypochondriac' causes me considerable stress. If my doctors think I am a hypochondriac they will dismiss me. It is vitally important I present as calm and non-alarmist, while describing my illness with sufficient drama to convince them there really is a problem. It is a tightrope walk: I want them to believe I am ill without thinking me hysterical. This calm-yet-defensive position does my head in. After all, I reject my own illness at times. I do not want to accept how sick I am. But I want the medical profession to accept it. Mind-bending.

Anxiety is acute vulnerability. My anxiety is about being vulnerable to physical harm, future disease, pain, job loss, gaslighting (being blamed for illness which is not my fault), dismissal and lifelong disability. Worry says something about our vulnerable spots. It thrives on worst-case scenarios and 'what if's, turning every problem into a catastrophe. As far as worst-cases go,

I've come up with some beauties:

'I'll never get better.'

'They're never going to find out what's wrong.'

'This isn't just a skin spot. It's a blood clot.'

'I'm going to lose my job.'

'My career is over.'

'This is the end of the line.'

You can add 'What if' to the start of all those worries.

People with chronic illness have good reason to catastrophise: they have experienced catastrophes. They have had near misses and brushes with death. Telling them not to worry is like saying to Superman, 'Surely kryptonite isn't that bad?'

> People with chronic illness have good reason to catastrophise: they have experienced catastrophes.

My worst-cases do not involve dying. That's because, for me, death is not the worst-case scenario. But you might be different. Personally, death would be a welcome relief from the pain and madness I experience. No, my worst-case is living a long and increasingly disabled life, lupus gradually usurping my body like one country invading another. My worst-case is losing my mind, slowly, agonisingly, till I die. My worst-case is uncontrollable pain from which there is no escape. My worst-case is acquiring a disability that takes my mind and my job—maybe my entire career—from me.

I actually love my work. I worked hard to get where I am today. I would hate to lose that. Even though my identity sits firmly in Christ, my profession holds part of my identity too. It's no wonder anxiety and depression go hand in hand. And my illness-related anxiety does not go away. It is always there, sitting quietly in the background or screaming in my face, or somewhere in between.

I wish there was a cure for these fears. But most of us have to co-exist with anxiety just as we co-exist with illness. For now, I can only tell you what helps me. I selectively share my anxieties. When I need grounding or talking down from the ledge, I tell my support people. They remind me what is true. When everything is uncertain, it helps to remember the few things that are certain.

I know I have lupus.

I know people love me.

I know my doctors believe me.

I know I belong to God.

Sometimes that's enough. But there are times when helpful reminders do not cut it. On those days, when fear is asphyxiating, I hang on to Jesus for dear life. There seems to be a pervasive belief among Christians that trusting God will eradicate all fear and mental distress from your life. Not true. I can experience rapidly escalating anxiety while trusting in God whole-heartedly—at the same time. The two can co-exist. I can hold two opposing things in my mind, similar to George Orwell's 'doublethink' in *1984*.

It doesn't make me crazy. (Even if it feels crazy.)

It doesn't make be a bad Christian. (Even if I feel distant from God.)

It doesn't make me weak or a failure. (Even if I feel that way.)

It is an understandable reaction to a crazy situation.

Some Christians, whom I love, drive me crazy with their 'Jesus will fix your mental distress' talk. It is possible to love Jesus and have anxiety. Don't let anyone add guilt or shame to your already burdened plate. If Jesus, in his distress, produced sweat like blood and yet was the Messiah, we too can experience bouts of anxiety and still be Christians.

> It is possible to love Jesus and have anxiety.

It's hard to imagine life with chronic illness that does not include anxiety. But even if we can't completely eradicate it, there might be ways to limit it, like turning down the volume on a radio station. We can drown it out with helpful noise. And I'm not talking about alcohol. In case you were wondering. I'm talking about self-care. I'm talking things like chocolate and being in nature. I'm talking about warm baths with epsom salts, good for the body and the mind. I'm talking reading, music and debriefing with supportive friends. I'm talking whatever healthy coping strategies work for you. Sometimes it's helpful to channel anxiety into rage instead and scream it out.

Contingency plans can help. When I go out, I notice the exits. When travelling, I make a mental note of the nearest hospital, just in case. 'Hope for the best, plan for the worst' is a helpful adage, especially when living with such a wild and uncontrollable disease. I make a plan, then get on with what I want to do.

Songs that help me when I'm anxious include *You'll Always Be* by Kim Walker-Smith, *P E A C E* by Hillsong Young & Free, and *Sweet River* by Paul Coleman. They remind me every fear ultimately bows to Jesus Christ. It doesn't delete anxiety, but it does tell it where to go. I have playlists for certain moods. It's a system that works for me, not just because I'm a musician, but because music is a big part of my life. It grounds me and helps me experience God's presence even if it's not 'Christian'.

I once started singing *In Christ Alone* aloud in hospital while awaiting test results. It anchored me in a moment of intense pain and distress. I sang it over myself, reminding me my life is in God's hands and no one can pluck me from them. He was there, smiling. 'Do you trust me?' he enquired. 'Always,' I answered.

One more thought about fear:

> For the Spirit that God has given you does not make you slaves and cause you to be afraid; instead, the Spirit makes you God's children, and by the Spirit's power we cry out to God, 'Father! My Father!' (Romans 8:15 GNT)

We are no longer slaves to fear. We are his children. We can cry out to the Father. We belong to him.

Trauma

Can one be traumatised by one's own body? I'm starting to think so.

We have long understood the traumatic effects of extensive medical treatment on children. The evidence suggests these children and their immediate families are profoundly impacted by both illness and treatment.[30] So how about adults?

The more I live with illness, the more I believe we can be traumatised by it. Think about how many survival situations we have experienced, how often we have called an ambulance or gone to hospital, how frequently we have been confused and bamboozled by inarticulable symptoms. Plus, how do you live with a body that has betrayed you?

There have been many frightening times in the course of my illness. At times I have received multiple diagnoses in rapid succession; even one diagnosis can be life changing. There have been moments when I was not sure I would make it or questioned whether I would survive the night.

Such legit traumas, however, do not fit the widely understood trauma definitions. When you say 'trauma', most people think of one-off events like a car accident or bushfire. These are known as single-incident traumas, common and totally valid. There are, however, other kinds of trauma caused by repeated and cumulative exposure to dangerous or horrific situations. Things like living with a violent person in the home, being bullied at work over a prolonged period, or working as an emergency responder. The traumatic impact of cumulative stress is well documented.[31]

Chronic illness is another form of cumulative stress, punctuated by painful, horrifying, frightening and even life-threatening situations—coupled with the knowledge that this thing may never go away. And at any time, the frightening thing may happen again.

> *Chronic illness can trigger its own unique and legitimate form of post-traumatic stress, specifically, the kind of Enduring Somatic Threat (EST) that occurs when the threat exists inside your own body.*

Research is now indicating what we have long known anecdotally: chronic illness can trigger its own unique and legitimate form of post-traumatic stress, specifically, the kind of

Enduring Somatic Threat (EST) that occurs when the threat exists inside your own body.[32]

When you think about the major criteria for Post-Traumatic Stress Disorder (PTSD) through the lens of enduring illness, it makes sense:

- Exposure to frightening or horrifying incidents with harm or threat of harm, causing feelings of powerlessness and helplessness.
- Re-experiencing those incidents in flashbacks, intrusive thoughts or nightmares.
- Avoidance of reminders: places, people, conversations and thoughts about illness.
- Changes in thoughts, beliefs or mood: amnesia, believing the world is bad or we are bad, self-blame, ongoing fear or horror, inability to feel happiness or connect with others.
- Hypervigilance: trouble concentrating, difficulty sleeping, loss of appetite, irritability, anger outbursts, reckless behaviour, increased startle response (someone taps you on the shoulder and you jump through the roof).[33]

We cannot escape our traumatising situation. Normally, if we find ourselves in a dangerous place like a fire, our first priority is safety: we either leave or maximise our safety like firefighters wearing protective gear. But what do we do when our own bodies make us unsafe? How do we escape that ever-present threat? This is why it is so traumatising. If we could ensure our safety, it wouldn't impact us the same way. We would not experience the heights of powerlessness and helplessness. It is precisely this lack of control in the face of physical and mental threat that causes the traumatic stress response.

I am just realising how illness might have traumatically affected me. I am still piecing this together, but here are some thoughts that help me process this.

First, I remind myself that illness, and traumatic stress responses, are not my fault. I am doing everything in my power to mitigate the effects of illness. The rest is outside my control. Trauma is an understandable and even expected result. How can anyone live with crazy-making illness and NOT be affected by it?

Second, I tell myself I am safe. I may not have been safe yesterday, or an hour ago, but right now, I am safe. I don't know what the future holds, but it is not within my responsibility (or ability) to know the future. All I have is this present moment. Right here and now, I am safe.

Third, I remember that trauma is anxiety on steroids, and anxiety thrives on future-oriented worries. What's going to happen tomorrow, or an hours' time? I tell myself the future is outside my control and bring my focus back to things I can control: the present moment, my choices and decisions, my responses.

Fourth, I ground myself physically, using the five senses: things I can see, hear, taste, touch and smell, like music, the scent of orange, or the warm sunshine or cool wind on my skin. It's a form of mindfulness, but it's also about small moments of pleasure. If I am doomed to endure chronic illness for the rest of my life, I'm going to find any enjoyment I can!

Fifth, I tell God everything. I tell him how bad I feel. I describe my fears about the future. I ask for his help. Some of my simplest and most heartfelt prayers are 'God—help!' He hears our prayers. I pray with this in mind, knowing he is listening intently, not bored or annoyed but hanging on every word. He really does love us.

Finally, words are sometimes unnecessary. I love words—I am a writer, after all—but they can reach saturation point. I have unpacked my issues until there is nothing left to unpack. At those times, I go to other forms of expression. I speak in tears. I speak in tongues. I sit at the piano and play out my feelings.

The Holy Spirit speaks through us with sighs and groans that words cannot express (Romans 8:26). There is something holy in silence and the absence of words, something special about reaching the end of our vocabulary. The silences I've shared with God have been some of the most meaningful 'conversations'. We are both taking a breath, sharing that space. He holds me, and I let him. I rest my head on his love like a pillow and feel the relief of not needing to do anything, just be.

> There is something holy in silence and the absence of words.

I want to embrace those holy moments more often.

Emotional whiplash

I acquired whiplash after a car accident. I did not feel the full force of it until a week later when I tried to pull down the garage door. My neck went into spasms and I was paralysed for a week. It certainly made driving a new adventure in faith.

What no one tells us about chronic illness is the mental and emotional whiplash that comes with it. Shock, disbelief, sadness, rage, trauma, anxiety about the future—this is the whiplash of living with chronic illness. Sometimes whiplash is delayed. We can cope with our illness until one little thing goes wrong and we are completely discombobulated. All the stuff we have been suppressing, the stress and frustration and not-coping, suddenly rush to the surface. We go into emotional 'spasm', paralysed with pain and fear.

> Shock, disbelief, sadness, rage, trauma, anxiety about the future—this is the whiplash of living with chronic illness.

I think I have chronic whiplash.

After my car accident, my whiplash was retriggered years later after another one. It then became chronic, an ongoing point of vulnerability in my body, a weak spot triggered by small accidents like falling over or being startled suddenly. Emotionally, we may find ourselves in a similar state of greater vulnerability. It might take one little thing for anxiety or depression or trauma to come rushing back. It is not our fault. It is a consequence of illness. Just like whiplash from a car accident is a consequence of physics, emotional whiplash is a consequence of the violence and insanity in our bodies.

If we have ongoing emotional whiplash, we might need ongoing emotional expression and outlets. Just like rain falls repeatedly to keep the earth nourished, so we cry and rage and grieve repeatedly to give our emotions the nourishment they need. My physical whiplash required a very gentle approach at first. It still requires special attention: I stretch it daily. Give your emotions some special attention. They will not always need intensive care; they might only need a little time to stretch. Give them that space.

Grant them the kindness you would give actual whiplash.

What I need most when I'm angry is self-compassion. 'Steph, I understand. I know why you are angry. Your situation is unfair and unjust. It is only right to feel angry.' That's the voice of a compassionate parent. That's an opportunity to see and care for ourselves like we would for a child. We are nurturing our inner child. That's kindness.

I have felt tenderness for my overworked heart that carries so much pain. I have held my heart and cried for the suffering—mine, and others—it has borne. In those moments, I have experienced self-kindness. It's the voice that says, 'You are doing the best you can.' Sometimes I stand in the rain and let it seep into my skin, and knowing the earth is drinking it in, breathing and sighing as I breathe and sigh, seems comforting. It might sound strange, but I find connecting with the earth helps me in times of emotional turmoil.

As Petrea King, cancer survivor, says, 'You are not your body; you have a body. It is your responsibility to nourish it, rest it, exercise it and "fluff it up".'[34] Our bodies and illnesses are not the sum total of who we are, but they need our care. Make sure you have some quality 'fluffing' time.

> Make sure you have some quality 'fluffing' time.

Can Jesus fix my mental health?

Ah, this old chestnut. Here we go. *Cracks knuckles*

Yes and no.

In the church where I grew up, I often heard about God being our healer. 'Why would you go to a doctor,' the preacher would shout, 'When you can go to the Great Physician?' 'Yes!' I would cheer with the rest of the congregation. 'Who needs doctors? All we need is God!'

The spiritual bypassing runs deep.

Then I went to university to study psychology and become a counsellor. I valued my chosen profession. But my pastor saw things differently. 'Why,' he preached from the pulpit, 'would anyone go to a counsellor when you have Jesus? He is the Wonderful Counsellor!' 'Yes!' cried the congregation, while I silently cringed.

Is my chosen vocation less valuable because Jesus is already our Counsellor? No.

Should Christians avoid counsellors? No.

Do other Christians question my choice of vocation? Maybe.

The belief that Jesus is all we need for mental distress is both true and misleading. It is true Jesus can, and sometimes does, bring wonderful relief and healing to mental distress. But it is also true God can and does bring healing through medication, trusted friends and the counsel of professionals.

Over the course of my life, I have consulted plumbers (even though God is the water of life). I have consulted electricians for lighting solutions (even though Jesus is the light of the world). I have hired cleaners (even though the Holy Spirit is our helper). I have consulted dozens of doctors and specialists (even though God is our healer). I pray about my health; I also do back stretches, take medications and get regular bloods done. When I broke my shoulder I prayed about it; I also went to hospital, got x-rays, took painkillers and did physio. Imagine if I had avoided hospital because God 'could have' healed my shoulder.

It is wise to ask God for help. It is also wise to go to those with wisdom in those areas. God placed us in community with one another for wise reasons. We need each other. I hope you can see the parallel with mental distress. Mental health is a specialist area and it is wise to seek counsel from the experts. Yes, pray about it. I hope you do. I also hope you get help from those with extensive wisdom to offer. Picking a good counsellor is a bit like finding a good doctor: you want someone who knows what they're talking about, who listens to you, who is a good personality fit, and who will offer you real options without taking over. A good counsellor can make all the difference.

There is a great need for a trauma-informed approach in church. We need to support people in seeking specialist help. Being trauma-informed does not mean we become trauma therapists; it means we are aware of potential triggers, recognise signs of trauma when we see them, and know what to do about it, such as referring people to appropriate services. It's vital pastoral care.

Pastors, want to help your congregation? Be vulnerable. Talk about your own struggles. That gives others permission to struggle. And make sure they're current struggles, not struggles you had ten years ago. Let people know you're still human. A great resource is suicide first aid training through LivingWorks (see resource page at the end).

Mental distress is not a moral failing. It is not weakness. It is certainly not an indicator of spiritual maturity or sin. So let's stop treating it like one. Mental health issues are not necessarily spiritual ones. Mental distress can be triggered by stressful events (such as death in the family), chronic illness, chemical imbalances in the brain, genetic factors, gut issues, hormone cycles and the onset of puberty. So it is erroneous to assume one's mental distress is spiritual in origin and therefore requires a spiritual solution.

> Mental distress is not a moral failing. It is not weakness. It is certainly not an indicator of spiritual maturity or sin. So let's stop treating it like one.

Can Jesus help with non-spiritual problems? Of course. And it would be wonderful if Jesus fixed our problems with a snap of his fingers like a holy Mary Poppins. But my experience tells me he does not always intervene. Some things we learn for ourselves—the hard way.

If you are like me and your mental distress is secondary to chronic illness, then you are not in sin. Mental distress happens when the pressure is too much for the brain. Like pressure on a leg will eventually break the strongest femur, mental stress will eventually break the most resilient mind. Mental distress says something about the daily stress with which we live.

So what's the answer? Do we look to God, or others, or ourselves for help?

Yes. Seriously, why not a combination of all three? Tell God what is going on with your mental health and ask for his help and healing. Reach out to others and think about treatment options, including medication. Come up with a plan for yourself, things you can do when your mental distress gets triggered; plan it when you are feeling good, so next time you are feeling bad, you won't have to.

I moved house a few years ago, and let me tell you, there's a whole bunch of stuff I can't lift: heavy furniture, awkwardly shaped pieces, boxed filled with books (why are books so heavy?). Some things are just too big for me. Same with our minds and emotions. Some problems are too big; we need a hand with the mental and emotional heavy lifting.

It's like a friend giving us a leg-up to climb over a wall. Sure, we probably could do it ourselves (give me all day for that one), but it's so much easier with a leg-up.

Wonderful counsellor

The older I get, the more I realise how vulnerable Jesus was.

His parents fled from Herod to stave off Jesus being murdered. (Talk about childhood trauma.)

He endured threats and ridicule during his ministry years.

He grieved the loss of John the Baptist and wept at the tomb of Lazarus.

He faced the brutal reality of impending crucifixion in Gethsemane. His sweat became like drops of blood (Luke 22:44). Apparently, the threat of crucifixion affected Jesus' mental health. He took his disciples with him. They couldn't stay awake, but he reached out to them in his time of need. Even Jesus asked for help.

So when I say Jesus is our wonderful counsellor, I am saying he understands the pain of human existence first-hand. He got stressed. He got upset. He got hurt by others. Jesus knew what it was like to need support. Even Jesus did not face Gethsemane alone.

Our wonderful counsellor can truly empathise with us. As Hebrews 4:15 says,

> For we do not have a high priest who is unable

to empathize with our weaknesses, but we have one who has been tempted in every way, just as we are—yet he did not sin.

This empathy is much more than pity; he is right in the middle of our pain with us. He made himself vulnerable on earth, and he continues to make himself vulnerable to us. He feels what we feel. He weeps with us. He feels our anger, fear of the future, the grief of all we have lost.

> This empathy is much more than pity; he is right in the middle of our pain with us.

He gets it. He is God with us.

When nothing else helps, I hold on to the truth of Emmanuel. No, Jesus will not always heal me. He will not always deliver me from ghastly situations. Sometimes he will let me walk through those dark places. But I don't have to do it alone. He will walk through those graveyards with me.

Even in the valley of the shadow of death, he is right here with me.

Take a moment to notice how you are feeling after the chapter, and whether anything stood out for you or resonated with you. Time for some self-care.

*This lifeboat keeps springing leaks.
Every time I turn around, there's another one.
I keep plugging the leaks as best I can.*

*The smaller ones are manageable, but I just copped
a big one and water keeps getting in, no matter how
I stuff the hole or how fast I bail.*

*This leak has a feeling of inevitability about it,
like a puncture in a gravity suit. It might mean
the end of the lifeboat—and me.*

7

RELATIONSHIPS

Sex, Singledom and Childlessness

When I got a new job, my husband and I relocated so I would be closer to work. It meant I could physically handle the drive. One problem: it made his daily commute far longer. What a hero!

Chronic illness does not just affect the person with illness. It affects the people we love and who love us. It affects our friendships, collegial relationships and social lives.

Illness can affect every relationship we have.

Relationships

I was diagnosed with lupus two years into my marriage. Perhaps things might have been different had we known about lupus beforehand. (Sounds like a premise for *The Twilight Zone*.)

It can be hard not to feel guilty for what our loved ones go through. It is not just me who lives with lupus. Everyone in my household lives with it too, the uncertainty, worry and madness. I eat differently because of my illness. I travel differently because of it. I even moved houses because of it. This can put a very real strain on relationships, and even bring some to an end.

While illness can be stressful for our loved ones, it also means they are with us through it all. There is undeniable benefit in having companions for the journey. Personally, it is great to have a witness and ally at my medical appointments. Instead of travelling this road alone, trying to work out my illness like a medical Sherlock, I have a Watson to assist. Our Watsons can bring fresh eyes to the problems, brainstorm with us, and bring us back to the pertinent facts when our brains go walkabout. Watsons are life savers.

> Watsons are life savers.

We can find Watsons online too. It can be hard to find support in our existing social circles, so online avenues are an option (though we can also be susceptible to trolling there too, so please take care of yourself). It's hard to find online groups for rare diseases, but you might be able to find something broader that fits for you, such as groups for pain, arthritis, fatigue or simply chronic illness. You might also find online support that centres on common interests or hobbies such as sci-fi, pets or online gaming. Those kinds of connections can bring meaning and relief into our lives just when we need them.

When illness feels like an unceasing volley of bullets flying overhead, it is good to have comrades in the trenches.

Sex

Illness and disability can affect one's sex life. So I've heard.

Just imagine it. You start fooling around, and your knee seizes up. Or your hip. Or your jaw locks up from...kissing. Your muscles go into spasm as other things do. It can be hard to get excited over the noise of pain.

Many things can get in the way of enjoyable sex. Tension in the relationship, exhaustion and depression can affect your libido. A partner who is a carer may need time alone to recharge. Maybe you've lost interest in sex...and everything. If that's you, you're not alone.

Sexual satisfaction is, or should be, about mutual enjoyment rather than 'performing'. If sex is about serving one another—and I think it is—it's important to work out how best to do that. Within our means. So, not that I'm an expert or anything, but here are my top tips for satisfying sex while living with chronic illness:

- Talk. Get honest with your partner or spouse about sex. Tell them what works for you, when something hurts, or when you can't do something. It sounds simple, but a lot of things go unsaid in the bedroom (or wherever). Especially when you're trying to serve the other person. So speak up if something no longer works and try something different.
- Experiment. It's worth trying another approach when things get uncomfortable. Experiment with another position. Another room. Focus on pleasure, rather than sprinting to the supposed finish line of orgasm. (Sure, orgasms are great, but have you tried chocolate? In fact, chocolate might help things along.)

- Laugh. Funny things can happen during sex. Apparently. It's OK to laugh at yourself and each other, say, if your leg gets stuck in a weird position, or things seize up, or you have to stop because you're laughing so hard. Turn it into a funny story. You can relive it for years to come. It could make a great icebreaker at your next party.

There are some great sex resources online, including fact sheets for those with intellectual disabilities,[35] myths and misconceptions about disability and sex,[36] [37] and legal and public health rights of those with disabilities.[38]

Sex can still be enjoyable. While it can be difficult to enjoy sex when our bodies feel bad, sex may also be the only enjoyment our bodies get!

Singledom

Dating is hard when you're sick.

I didn't meet my husband till I was twenty-nine. Before that, I was reluctant to date. This wasn't just because of the normal dating perils; I worried about broaching the subject of illness.

When is a good time to break the news of chronic illness to your date?

How do you explain you can't do anything outdoorsy?

> *How do you approach a date as a date, not as an interview for a prospective carer?*

And how do you approach a date as a date, not as an interview for a prospective carer? (More on the challenges of marrying a carer later.)

During my singledom, I was exhausted. All. The. Time. I had no spoons for anything, including dating. It wasn't just romantic relationships that suffered. Having visitors was a major endeavour. Driving to see friends was taxing. Don't get me wrong; they were worthwhile things. I would not have done them if they weren't. But they came with hefty price tags.

Beyond dating, it just sucked to be sick and single. I struggled to do the shopping. Shopping trolleys were the bane of my existence. (Why don't they move in a straight line? Why?) So I started ordering online. Wonder of wonders, I turned back into a sane person.

When you are deathly ill, there is nothing worse than dragging your sick carcass down to the shops because you need painkillers NOW. There's nothing worse than taking two hours to dress because you simply have to see the doctor. Thankfully, my church family came to the rescue. They went shopping for me. They visited and squeezed money into my hands—they knew I was struggling. They weren't always readily available as they had their own families, but they did what they could.

One night, I was acutely unwell and the toilet was rapidly becoming my new best friend. A church friend dropped round. She had gone shopping for me unasked. She brought lemonade and soup. That's friendship. Single people need that. Church, friends and family, if you know single people with chronic illness, please take the initiative. Check on them, even if it's only a text. Ask how they're *really* doing. We get good at faking it. Even if they do not accept your help, they will appreciate it. They will know they are loved. That's what matters.

For more helpful tips on navigating singleness, check out my other book *Surviving Singledom*[39] (subtle, eh?) which is more entertaining than it sounds.

Childlessness

I am childless because of lupus. (That's why there's no parenting section in this book. We need a parent for that. If you know a parent living with chronic illness, feel free to mention to them the appalling lack of literature in this area.)

Lupus never made me miscarry or anything. It merely carries a terrifying risk of miscarriage and other pregnancy problems (google 'antiphospholipid syndrome' FYI). Because of this and other factors like endometriosis, I made the difficult decision not to try for children. It might sound like a choice, but it was a forced choice. Not everyone with lupus or chronic illness will make this decision. Having children is a very personal decision, and there is no right or wrong.

I feel ongoing grief about childlessness. I had dreams for my children. I had names for them. I had things I wanted to hand down to them. Chronic illness smashed those dreams to pieces. Sometimes this grief sits quietly in the corner, minding its own business. But other times, like at Christmas, that childless grief plants itself front and centre. That's when the temptation to rail against lupus hits. That's when I feel like my body has let me down.

It affects my self-identity. A woman's body is supposed to be a safe haven for life. But a body riddled with autoimmune disease is primed to kill 'intruders'. Lupus has programmed my body to search for and destroy babies. I

> *I am still processing what it means for my body to be a baby-killer.*

am still processing what it means for my body to be a baby-killer.

Grief is rarely a case of 'Move through the stages of grief in a linear fashion'. Grief comes and goes, sometimes in ripples, sometimes tidal waves. The trick is to surf the waves, in whatever fashion works for you. The waves aren't good or bad; they just are. The only way to heal grief is to grieve.

If you're interested in my full childlessness story, check out my other book *Surviving Childlessness*[40] which includes stories of other childless people too—some with their own chronic illness tales.

Abuse

People living with illness and disability are statistically more likely to experience domestic violence (DV) and sexual assault.[41]

DV is more than hitting; it's manipulation, denial, blame, fear and other forms of abuse underpinned by a drive for power and control. For a great list of DV warning signs, see the *DVConnect* site.[42]

It's easy to exert power over someone who is physically, cognitively or otherwise disadvantaged. In the context of both illness and Christianity, a person using DV tactics may blame the chronically sick person for their illness, accuse them of being in sin, prevent them from seeking medical treatment, insist on spiritual solutions for their illness, and otherwise take advantage of their fatigue and incapacity to take independent action.

Escape from DV is particularly problematic for those with chronic illness. How can you leave when you're in severe pain? What if your mobility is limited? Who can you live with, knowing they will have to care for you? What if you have no savings because illness has taken your ability to work? What if you have trouble asking for help because of neurodivergence or mental distress or deafness?

The obstacles are plentiful. But there is help. In Australia, you can call 1800 RESPECT (1800 737 732), the DV Line (1800 63 64 65), or DVConnect (1800 811 811—based in QLD). These are all 24/7 helplines. If you feel unsafe, call 000. Every police station or LAC (Local Area Command) has DVLOs (Domestic Violence Liaison Officers), special police officers trained in understanding DV patterns and behaviours. They can answer your questions and give you information about your rights and options. If you aren't sure if the abuse you've experienced is a crime, they can help.

I hope you can ask your church family for help. Church is supposed to protect and care for the disadvantaged, including us. But sometimes we can't ask the church for help. Sometimes we're not in a church, or don't trust the church enough to reach out. Sometimes the church is the source of hurt and abuse.

What do we do in these scenarios? First, there's absolutely no pressure to reach out to someone you don't trust. I wouldn't do that, nor would I recommend it. Find someone who is trustworthy—a friend, colleague, carer, neighbour, helpline counsellor or doctor. Even if you only tell them a little bit. That's OK. Just don't bear this burden alone.

Being physically or sexually hurt by anyone, including members of the church, is a crime. You have the right to report church abuse to the police (you don't have to, I just want you to know you have that right. You may choose not to.) You might report it to someone within the church. You might prefer to keep your distance or leave the church altogether or stay to protect others. There are no right or wrong choices here. The decision is entirely up to you, and you are free to choose.

There are online places that can help such as *Wilderness to WILD*[43], a website by Sarah McDugal and Bren Wise-Mays, for mothers leaving faith-based abusive situations.

It can be hard to tell whether a relationship has become abusive or is just under strain. A healthy relationship is marked by mutual respect, boundaries, openness and honesty, effective communication, trust, equality and, above all, safety. The *National Domestic Violence Hotline*[44] website has a more complete checklist of healthy, unhealthy and abusive relationship traits.

No one has the right to abuse, control or manipulate you. Regardless of what illness has done to you, regardless of what disability has taken away from you, no one has the right to punish or take advantage of you for that. Being sick or disabled is not a crime. It is a circumstance.

> Being sick or disabled is not a crime.

If you cannot leave an unsafe situation, stay as safe as possible within it. Put some support people on standby. Set up a safety plan in case things get dicey. Hopefully you will never need it—but if you do, it's ready to go. Just as with illness, contingencies for DV are always helpful.

Keeping it real

It's a struggle to keep relationships healthy when chronic illness is third-wheeling.

Communication is vital. Others don't live in our skin, so how can they know what's going on? We need to tell them what we need, physically and emotionally. Unfortunately, communication can sometimes be misinterpreted as complaining. Especially when we're communicating about *that* issue again. Instead of rehashing my old complaint, I try to communicate what is fresh today, like 'I'm a bit irritable this morning' or 'I'm starting to feel isolated'. This is better than reruns of the same old symptoms. It's also better than taking things out on others. It's not their fault I'm irritable or frustrated. Those emotions belong to me, no one else. Sure, I can ask for support with those feelings, but it's not up to others to solve them.

I used to be passive-aggressive. (Hard to imagine, I know.) I would drop hints, deep sighing and wincing when I walked. Others had no idea, of course, because they're not psychic, and because I didn't tell them I was playing mind games with them. They carried on with their day while I got increasingly frustrated and upset at their apparent neglect. Until I finally exploded. Not healthy.

It's much simpler to come out and say, 'I'm feeling overwhelmed.' Or 'I don't need you to say anything, just let me cry'. It tells the other person exactly what's going on and what to do. No mind-reading required.

> *Keeping things fun is not always easy, but it's necessary.*

Doing enjoyable things together keeps things healthy, even if it's as simple as going out for breakfast. If I know there are horrible health-related things on the horizon like surgery, I plan for a big holiday beforehand, like having one last fling. Life does not (always) have to revolve around illness. Keeping things fun is not always easy, but it's necessary.

Pray with and for one another. Sometimes simple is best: 'God, please heal them, and help me.' It reminds us we are loved. It puts God front and centre, displacing chronic illness at the core of our lives.

That's keeping it real.

Take a moment to notice how you are feeling after the chapter, and whether anything stood out for you or resonated with you. Time for some self-care.

I am walking on a tightrope.
I am terrified with every step that it will be my last.

My heart is in my mouth and I hold my breath, willing myself to keep my balance and not look down. I don't know if I will fall to my death; this may be the last thing I do. With immense relief I finally reach the end and step off, shaky and out of breath. I am happy just to be alive.

I look back along the tightrope, realisation dawning that I was attached to a safety harness the whole time.

8

GOD

Through Many Dangers, Toils and Snares

I have wrestled with God throughout this illness.

I wish it weren't so. I wish I could be one of those Christians who says, 'I have been to hell and back, and my faith in God has never wavered.' If you're looking for that kind of inspiration, better put this book down right now.

At times, yes, my faith has been strong and secure. I have sung songs of praise in the desert, sought God in the sleepless nights, been thankful at every turn. I have been the very model of a modern major Christian.

Then there's the rest of the time. I feel despair. I want out. I look for someone to blame, and God is a convenient choice. After all, he could just heal me, couldn't he? I feel torn about God: on the one hand, I love him more dearly than anything; on the other, I am tormented by questions.

Why won't you heal me?

You've healed me before; why not now?

It's not fair that you heal others and not me! (Not a question, but valid.)

How come you listen but don't say anything?

God, are you avoiding me? (Psalm 10:1 MSG)

Is there something you're trying to teach me through this illness?

Why do I have to rely on you over and over again? I've already learned that lesson!

Am I missing something?

Have I done something wrong?

Do you still care? I mean, I know you do…but do you?

God, I'm so angry with you; does this make me a bad Christian?

Sometimes I feel like a push-me-pull-you animal from *Doctor Dolittle*, constantly reaching out to God while recoiling at the thought of seeming like an ungrateful child. I need him, yet I worry about my relationship with him too. It's possible I'm overthinking things. Sometimes my brain likes to pretend it's running a spiritual marathon. Mile after mile, it keeps rehashing these things.

This is my ongoing wrestle with God. It's not a nice place to be. I would rather be in a state of constant peace with God, trusting him with childlike simplicity. Some days it is that simple. But other days are fraught with stress and head miles and despair. On those days, it can be difficult to pray—or be sure I am still a Christian.

I mean, I think I am. For today, at least.

Safety and other illusions

I grew up believing God would protect me from harm. I was taught God will keep you safe, if you simply trust him. So I did. I trusted him, straightforwardly and naïvely believing in his protection, AKA Psalm 91:9-12:

Safety is an illusion.

> If you say, 'The Lord is my refuge,'
> And you make the Most High your dwelling,
> No harm will overtake you,
> No disaster will come near your tent.
> For he will command his angels concerning you
> To guard you in all your ways;
> They will lift you up in their hands,
> So that you will not strike your foot against a stone.

Then, in my early twenties, I went through a horrendous experience (a story for another book). God eventually brought complete healing to my life. But I learned some important lessons, the primary one being that safety is an illusion. We are currently safe insofar as nothing has gone wrong. Feeling safe and well and healthy are temporary states. It only takes a moment for disaster to strike.

Ask anyone who has been assaulted.

Ask any Australian who has lost their home to a bushfire.

Ask those who have survived a cyclone or tornado.

Ask someone in the middle of an illness flare.

Our subjective sense of safety is subject to change without notice. Being Christian does not inoculate us against harm. Does God care when we are hurt? I believe he does—even if he seems strangely silent or absent at the time. He sees us. He hears our cries. He knows what is going on. Unfortunately he does not always intervene.

God won't always 'take the bullet' for us. God does not necessarily protect us from harm or the traumatic consequences of same. Sometimes Christians experience terrible things. So why follow God at all? Why follow him if he is not going to keep us safe?

That is the question every one of us must answer. I cannot tell you to follow God, or why you should. I can only give you my answer: because the centre of God's hands is still the safest place to be. With all the dangers of this world, with everything that can go wrong around me and within me, with pandemics and disasters and upheaval, the best place to live is in God's steadfast grip.

Eugene Peterson addresses this in the example of Psalm 121:

> He won't let you stumble,
> Your Guardian God won't fall asleep.
> Not on your life!
> Israel's Guardian will never doze or sleep.
> God's your Guardian,
> Right at your side to protect you—
> Shielding you from sunstroke,
> Sheltering you from moonstroke.
> God guards you from every evil,
> He guards your very life. (Psalm 121:3-7 MSG)

What the psalm is saying, according to Peterson, is '...not that we shall never stub our toes but that no injury, no illness, no accident, no distress will have evil power over us, that is, will be able to separate us from God's purposes in us.'[45] We will certainly stub our toes. (I know I will.) We will be affected by things going wrong. God does not promise us a spiritual 'Get out of jail free' card. Instead, he promises to be our Guardian, protect us in the face of evil, and not fall asleep on the job. God has been near in my troubles. He has preserved me and continues to preserve me. Nothing can separate me from him—and nothing has.

(By the way, Peterson explains the 'moonstroke' bit is a reference to insanity—where we get the word 'lunacy' from. It is reassuring to know God intends to preserve us in the face of both physical and mental distress.)

Adrian Plass once said:

> The safety we find in Jesus is only discovered at a price, which may be suffering or the witnessing of suffering. Jesus himself was able to battle through the agony of Gethsemane because at the deepest level he was safe in the love of his Father.[46]

'Safe' does not necessarily mean we are well, uninjured or even alive. It means we are held in the Father's hands. It is eternal safety, in the same way as we will one day be eternally healed.

Despite my fallings-out with God, despite my misgivings and unresolved questions, he is still the rock that is higher than me (Psalm

61:2). I will run to him when the world collapses around my ears. He is the one thing that stands firm. As much as I want my faith to be immovable, it is possible to shake my faith down to its foundation. But God can never be shaken. He is all I've got. God loves it when we turn to him. He looks for it. He rejoices in it. Even now, I can sense him anticipating the next moment when I will turn in his direction.

> 'Safe' does not necessarily mean we are well, uninjured or even alive. It means we are held in the Father's hands.

Safety doesn't always look like sitting pretty. It doesn't look like champion-level faith. It doesn't look like Psalm 91. For me, safety is crying into my pillow at night, hearing nothing but silence from God and turning to him anyway. Safety is the sigh of surrender when I have run out of words. Safety is the tremulous whisper: 'Maybe tomorrow will be better. Let's try again tomorrow, God.'

And safety is knowing when I turn to him, he is completely wild with joy.

Attachment

In his book, *Attached to God*,[47] Krispin Mayfield explores how our styles of attachment—ways we seek connection—can impact our faith. It explains why some Christians are anxious around God, work hard to avoid him, or have a push-me-pull-you relationship with him. These behaviours relate to specific attachment styles, stemming from our childhoods and how our caregivers met our needs—or not.

But what, you may ask, are attachment styles?

There are four broad attachment styles split into secure and insecure styles. Secure attachment is feeling confident in another person to support us if we need help, but also confident enough in ourselves to try new things. It is the picture of child in the playground who is happy to explore, knowing their parent is nearby if they run into any problems.

Then we have three insecure styles: anxious (sometimes called ambivalent), avoidant and disorganised. The anxious style is typified by clingy and dependent behaviour. It is the child with separation anxiety, always looking to their parent for answers and afraid to try anything new without their close supervision. The avoidant style is the opposite: complete independence from others, driven by a belief that others will only let you down so it is best not to depend on them. It is the child whose parent never answers when they call, so they grow up fast and learn to fend for themselves. The disorganised style is the push-me-pull-you style, the person who can never decide whether others are safe or not. The child with a disorganised style may simultaneously draw near to their parent while trying to run away, because they have experienced their parent as being frightened or frightening.

The notion of attachments shaping our relationship with God is not a new one (see, for example, Kirkpatrick and Shaver's revolutionary 1990 paper on attachment theory and religion[48]). Attachments also relate to childhood trauma (check out Dr Nadine Burke Harris' TED talk on her groundbreaking ACE [Adverse Childhood Experiences] study[49]).

We develop patterns when it comes to relationships. Yes, we behave in a myriad of ways, but we have a default setting for how to deal with other humans, especially when under stress. As highlighted by Mayfield, we also develop patterns of relating to God. So what might be your pattern with God? Do you tend to run toward him, away from him, a little bit of both? Do you trust him, avoid him until absolutely necessary, cling to him for fear of trying new things?

Trauma, like chronic illness, has an impact on our relationships and attachment styles. If your attachment to God has been blind-sided by illness and you want to experience a more secure attachment with him, it is possible to do so. They are a pattern, or habit, of behaviour, and habits can be changed.

> If your attachment to God has been blind-sided by illness and you want to experience a more secure attachment with him, it is possible to do so.

People with insecure attachments in childhood can be healed through secure attachments in adulthood. People with secure attachments with God can be rocked by illness and other trauma. Attachments are elastic, and there are things we can do to repair our attachment to God.

Here are a couple of things that can help:

Talk to people with healthy, secure attachments. Observe what that looks like in human terms: how they accept others, how they handle rejection or differences of opinion without becoming anxious or detached, how they remain confident and loving during a disagreement. That will give you a comparison for God. Go through the scriptures and see what they say about God's attributes. I like to read about God's fatherly and motherly traits. It paints a picture of how God cares for us as a parent. Remind yourself God is different from imperfect people. Whereas people can abandon us, God is near. Remember God's promises: not that he will prevent illness, but he will be with us through it, and he will guard our eternal safety. Go back to the scriptures you believe about God, the ones you really believe, not the ones you are supposed to believe. The Holy Spirit will help you.

When trust has been broken by the trauma of illness, take heart. It is possible to repair that trust. Go slowly with God; there's no deadline. Pace yourself. Even if you only let him in a sliver at a time, and only for a fleeting moment, that tiny bit might help.

One day you might be able to turn toward him again.

The problem of omnipotence

OK, let's talk about the elephant in the room.

If God is all-powerful, why the donut doesn't he heal?

Sorry. Got donuts on the brain. (Hey, I don't judge your self-care.)

We know God is all-powerful. We know he can heal. We've heard stories of healing. (Especially if you, like me, grew up in Pentecostal circles.) Maybe we've witnessed healing or experienced it firsthand. And the bible is filled with testimonies of healing. Some methods were unusual, such as the washing-seven-times approach or the spitting-in-the-eyes style (just imagine going to church and the minister invites you to receive the spitting ministry...) The point is God can heal—if he chooses. So...

Why doesn't God heal all the time?

Why does God heal others and not me?

Why does God heal some conditions and not others?

Why does God heal non-Christians and not me?

There's no simple answer. (Yay!) Because if it was simple,

there'd be no need to write a book about this. It's enough to drive us mad. And for many of us, hope deferred quite literally makes the heart sick. (Proverbs 13:12)

Even looking for answers can be problematic. When we ask Why, we are typically looking for someone to blame. Whose fault is it that I am not healed? And we only have two contenders: me and God. So either God is at fault, or I am. This is where we can get really angry at God.

Cue the hard questions

God, why won't you heal me? Have you forgotten about me? Are you not as all-powerful as I've been led to believe? Are you asleep? Have you heard my prayers? Don't you care? What's going on? Hello? Anybody there?

Of course, if God doesn't answer, or the thought of questioning God makes us squirm (because he's perfect—isn't he?), we might start second-guessing ourselves. Have I done something wrong without knowing it? Have I displeased God? Is there secret sin in my life for which I need to repent? Have I changed God's plan somehow? Did I get in God's way? Did I really hear from God? Am I really a Christian? Should I pray differently, find a 'magic' word that will unlock God's healing power? Should I 'claim my victory'? Do I need more faith? Should I give more money? Should I get anointed with oil? Should I dance naked in the middle of a forest glade under a full moon?

You get the idea.

Blame is complicated for me because I don't have a solid cause for my illness, so I don't know if I caused it. If I fall and injure myself, that's easy: I am to blame for that one. But what do you do with a mysterious illness? I want to toss my anger at someone, but don't know who to target.

There's another side to the healing coin. Sometimes healing complicates things when an illness later returns. If God heals us and we have a relapse, what does that mean? Did God actually heal us the first time? If so, why wasn't the healing permanent? This can loop back to the 'Is this God's fault or mine?' question. Will God heal me again, or is this as good as it gets? And this is not hypothetical. This happens.

The heart of this problem is essentially relational. We feel let down by God, abandoned, betrayed. Our trust is broken. If our all-loving, all-powerful God doesn't heal us, can we really trust him? Is he still trustworthy when we are bent double with pain, crippled by disability?

> *If our all-loving, all-powerful God doesn't heal us, can we really trust him?*

As C.S. Lewis puts it in his gut-wrenchingly honest memoir, *A Grief Observed*:

> But go to Him when your need is desperate, when all other help is vain, and what do you find? A door slammed in your face, and a sound of bolting and double-bolting on the inside. After that, silence. You may as well turn away.[50]

There are times when cold indifference is the worst response of all.

It's reassuring to learn spiritual giants went through crap too. If C.S. Lewis struggled with his relationship with God, I feel slightly less of a fraud. Slightly.

Speaking of spiritual giants, Mother Teresa also went through a spiritual wilderness. As this article[51] details, Mother Teresa experienced a prolonged period of God's absence. She came to doubt the existence of heaven and God. She continued to serve others her whole life while enduring a sort of spiritual agony, as this excerpt from her private letters reveals:

> Lord, my God, who am I that You should forsake me? The Child of your Love—and now become as the most hated one—the one—You have thrown away as unwanted—unloved. I call, I cling, I want—and there is no One to answer—no One on Whom I can cling—no, No One.—Alone… Where is my Faith—even deep down right in there is nothing, but emptiness & darkness—My God—how painful is this unknown pain—I have no Faith—I dare not utter the words & thoughts that crowd in my heart—& make me suffer untold agony. So many unanswered questions live within me afraid to uncover them—because of the blasphemy—If there be God—please forgive me—When I try to raise my thoughts to Heaven—there is such convicting emptiness that those very thoughts return like sharp knives & hurt my very soul.—I am told God loves me—and yet the reality of darkness & coldness & emptiness is so great that nothing touches my soul.

Mother Teresa was not delivered from darkness. Rather, she discovered a strange light within the darkness:

> I can't express in words—the gratitude I owe you for your kindness to me—for the first time in…years—I have come to love the darkness—for I believe now that it is part of a very, very small part of Jesus' darkness & pain on earth. You have taught me to accept it [as] a 'spiritual side of your work' as you wrote—Today really I felt a deep joy—that Jesus can't go anymore through the agony—but that He wants to go through it in me.

Mother Teresa ultimately prayed she might be willing to suffer 'for all eternity'. God grant me such grace to surrender under his sovereign hand. I am not glad Mother Teresa went through such difficulty, but I am relieved to not be the only one. Perhaps the experience of spiritual drought, doubting, questioning our faith and despair is more human than we realise. I am not the only one to experience fractures in my relationship with God. And neither are you.

> Perhaps the experience of spiritual drought, doubting, questioning our faith and despair is more human than we realise.

If our core problem is relational, you can bet your bobcat the solution is relational too. If we have a problem with God, there's only one person with whom we can resolve it. That's God, folks.

We've got to get honest with God. We've got to ask the hard questions. We've got to tell him how hurt and disappointed we feel. We've got to let him know this has affected our faith and trust in him. Essentially, we've got to complain.

Complaining gets a bad rap. We think good Christians should never complain. But the bible is full of it. I'm thinking of the book of Job right now. He was straight up with God and his friends. He did not mince words or hide his true feelings. He was authentic and frank and open—without disrespecting God. I sometimes think my prayers are pretty honest. Then I reread Job's words and realise I have a lot to learn about real prayer:

'Why didn't I die at birth?' (Job 3:11 MSG)

'Don't you [God] have better things to do than pick on me?' (Job 7:20)

'I hate my life!' (Job 9:21)

God didn't answer Job's complaints. He didn't defend or justify himself. He didn't map out his plan for Job's life along a clear timeline. He didn't, in fact, give Job anything he asked for. Maddening. Instead, God described his creation and the care and power involved in creating it. He turned Job's complaints on their heads and challenged Job to defend and justify *his* actions. He defied Job to equal God's omnipotence. Job had nothing to say to that.

Sometimes I forget God does not just use his omnipotence for healing. He uses his power all the time, healing souls, creating new things, weaving his glorious story in and through our lives, knitting his family together. He creates new weather and clouds and sunrises and sunsets every single day.

I was once reminded of this while walking in a garden, chatting to God about a decision I needed to make. It was a yes or no decision, so I was hoping God might—well, you know—give me a yes or no. When will I learn?

God completely avoided my question. He pointed out a cool-looking tree in the garden. He urged me to notice the unusual shape of the leaves. 'Yeah, that's awesome, God,' I replied, 'Now, back to my question...' He cut me off, pointing out the other unique trees around me. That's when I realised he wasn't going to answer my question.

God was making a point. He wasn't just showing me the beauty of the garden, although I am certain he wanted me to notice and appreciate it. (And I did, once I was no longer distracted by my All-Important Question.) He was reminding me this world belongs to him and he's in charge; he notices all the fine details of my life, just like he notices the shapes of leaves; and he will attend to my question in due course, just not straight away. 'Don't get caught up in the Answer,' he seemed to be saying. 'I've got it all in hand. Just rest in that for now.' I had a feeling he was leaving it up to my judgement; sometimes he does that.

> *Sometimes the journey of the question is just as important.*

It reminded me of a quote from Rainer Maria Rilke about sitting with questions, because sometimes the journey of the question is just as important:

> Be patient towards all that is unresolved in your heart...try to love *the questions themselves* like locked rooms, like books written in a foreign tongue. Do not now strive to uncover answers:

> they cannot be given you because you have not been able to live them. And what matters is to live everything. *Live* the questions for now. Perhaps then you will gradually, without noticing it, live your way into the answer, one distant day in the future.[52]

There is nothing wrong with questions themselves. As poet and priest John Donne prayed:

> There is more boldness in the question than in the coming; I may do it though I fear thee; I cannot do it except I fear thee.[53]

Presenting our questions to God shows our respect for and trust in God in ways nothing else can. It demonstrates our healthy 'fear' for God, not anxiety but reverence for him. Sometimes questions are all we have. Trusting him, especially when we feel let down, is scary. Following him can feel like driving blind through the worst fog ever. He won't always dispel the fog. He won't always show us where we are going. He won't always heal us. But he can be everywhere at once—and he will never leave us. If you can't trust him right now, trust in his ever-presence. He is near. He is Emmanuel.

We may feel alone in illness. But we are never truly alone.

If only you had been here...

Jesus' friend, Lazarus, got sick and later died. Instead of going to him straight away, Jesus faffed about (actually, the bible says he waited a couple of days) before going to Lazarus. He found everyone in mourning, including Lazarus' two sisters, Mary and Martha.

Then a very interesting thing happens. Martha goes out to meet Jesus. (That's not the interesting thing. This is the interesting thing.) She says, 'Master, if you'd been here, my brother wouldn't have died.' Then Mary, the other sister, comes out. Guess what Mary says? 'Master, if only you had been here, my brother would not have died.' (John 11:1-32 MSG)

Isn't it interesting that both sisters, independently of each other, say exactly the same thing to Jesus? 'If only you had been here...'

Sometimes we feel like that with God. 'If only you had been here, God. My illness would not have got worse. I would not have gone to hospital. I wouldn't need surgery. I wouldn't live in pain. I needed you, and you weren't here.'

We who are familiar with the story know what happens. (Spoiler: Jesus raises Lazarus from the dead.) But Mary and Martha didn't know that. When they went out to meet Jesus, they only knew their brother had died. They were upset. They were hurting. They wished Jesus had shown up earlier.

We do not have the benefit of hindsight. We do not know if God might resurrect something in our lives. Nor can we know what God will do ahead of time. But perhaps the most honest prayer we can pray when God does appear is lament. 'God, I'm hurting, I'm upset, and I'm angry with you. If only you had been here...'

Jesus wept with Mary and Martha. Even though he knew Lazarus was about to be resurrected, he wept. Perhaps Jesus weeps with us too. And there's a promise in Revelation 21:4 that one day, Jesus will wipe every last tear from our eyes.

> *Perhaps Jesus weeps with us too.*

The God who allows pain

'God is good' is a well-worn cliché in church circles. I believe God is truly good. At the same time, God allows atrocities to occur: war, rape, child abuse and politicians. God allows his people, his children, to be hurt. In some parts of the world, his children are persecuted and even martyred. Is this a good God?

These are hard questions. I ask them not because I hold the answers (who does?) but because I already ask them in silence. I'm guessing I'm not the only one. Sometimes we do not give voice to our fears because they frighten us. Being angry with God, raging at God, blaming God can be scary. Facing the reality of a God who lets us down can be terrifying.

What do we do with a God who is supposedly good but allows the torture of chronic illness? How do we reconcile his apparent goodness with an absence of healing? How can we trust God knows what is best for us? How do we believe God cares when our midnight cries are met with stony silence? At times, our ever-present Emmanuel seems absent.

Even as I write this, I wonder if I am blinded and deluded by grief. Is it only when I am sick, facing mortality and despair, that I get really honest with myself? Or am I more of a wretch than I thought? I seem to have more questions than answers in this book.

Do you ask these kinds of questions too? Good. Then we are not alone. Remember, God does not mind questions. I truly believe that.

God lets all kinds of adventures befall us—good things, hard things, ecstatic things, heartbreaking things. Some adventures teach us; some offer friendship; some force our faith to dig deep. But this is not to say there is always a reason for our suffering. Sometimes there isn't. I am also not saying we should welcome suffering, be grateful for it, or seek it out. We want to stay sane, after all. But some forms of suffering can be helpful—and God can bring good things out of them, like a rose growing out of a great big pile of manure. Some adventures are good for us, but some are filled disproportionately with sorrow. And so my faith swings out of balance again.

One individual who can relate to see-saw faith is Jesus. Judging from his almost-last words on the cross, Jesus felt abandoned by God: 'My God, my God, why have you forsaken me?' (Matthew 27:46) Not exactly words of faith. I can only imagine how alone and betrayed he felt, not to mention the physical pain of crucifixion, the loneliness and utter lostness. And God allowed it. God allowed his only son to be crucified.

That's what I like about Jesus. He knows about being let down by God, forsaken, forgotten, hung out to dry. He questioned God. What if our Saviour knows exactly how it feels to doubt God? To feel that agony of separation, the tension between love and despair? What if Jesus really gets our situation? God might still be good, but he wasn't past putting his son through crucifixion. He's a God who allows pain. We won't always understand why. Sometimes it will hurt; Jesus' example shows us that.

But this God who allows pain is the same God who endures great pain with and for us. Jesus is the God-with-us part. He's the one who stepped into our humanity, who truly understands suffering, who experienced

> This God who allows pain is the same God who endures great pain with and for us.

the pain of abandonment. He's the one who continues to intercede for us. He understands.

When Jesus prayed for his disciples in John 17, he didn't pray for health, wellbeing or happiness. He didn't pray for protection. He didn't even pray they would stay alive:

> Holy Father, guard them as they pursue this life that you conferred as a gift through me, so they can be one heart and mind as we are one heart and mind. As long as I was with them, I guarded them in the pursuit of the life you gave through me; I even posted a night watch. And not one of them got away, except for the rebel bent on destruction…Now I'm returning to you. I'm saying these things in the world's hearing so my people can experience my joy completed in them. I gave them your word; the godless world hated them because of it, because they didn't join the world's ways, just as I didn't join the world's ways. I'm not asking that you take them out of the world but that you guard them from the Evil One. They are no more defined by the world than I am defined by the world. Make them holy—consecrated—with the truth; your word is consecrating truth. (John 17:11b-17 MSG)

Jesus prayed we would be guarded, not so we could live free from suffering, but so we could be 'one heart and mind'. Jesus wants us united with each other and him, just as he and his Father are united. Jesus prayed his joy would be completed in us. Joy, of course, is not dependent on mood or spiritual temperature and is not the same as happiness; it is a consequence of knowing Jesus and being secure in him, a fruit of the Holy Spirit dwelling within us. Jesus prayed not that the Father would remove us from the godless world but that he would guard us against the Evil One. He intends for us to stay here; our suffering may not ease, but he will guard us while we remain. Finally, Jesus prayed we would be made holy.

> Our suffering may not ease, but he will guard us while we remain.

Some of these prayers are pretty intimidating: unity, joy, protection from evil, holiness. Personally, I am gratified to learn Jesus prayed for us so earnestly, knowing our temptations would be plentiful and our sufferings immense. He prayed, and continues to pray, that God will keep us—and no one can pluck us from his hand. (Romans 8:34-39)

There is one more thing Jesus prayed:

Father, I want those you gave me to be with me, right where I am, so they can see my glory...(John 17:24a MSG)

Jesus won't leave us here forever. He wants us in heaven to see and share in his glory. He wants to be united with us. Can you imagine? The Saviour of the world wants us to live at his place! He wants it so badly he prayed about it right before he was crucified. He was going to his death—he knew it—and his prayer was for us, our oneness with him and each other.

That's our Saviour. That's our Emmanuel.

God with us

One of my most treasured encounters with the Narnian Aslan (symbolic of Jesus) is in *The Horse and his Boy*.[54] Shasta, our hero, is riding a horse alone having lost his riding companions. A fog descends and he finds himself blinded and frightened. He is completely lost and hopeless.

He slowly becomes aware of the sound of something—someone—walking beside him. He can hear the sound of breathing. He is terrified. Finally, he speaks, and Aslan answers him. Aslan keeps him company on the long walk. Only when they come out the other side and the fog lifts does Shasta see Aslan in all his lionly glory. And Aslan leaves.

Shasta reunites with the other riders and they head back the way they came. This time, there is no fog. They follow the trail up a narrow mountain pass where the road drops away on one side like a sheer cliff face. Aslan had been walking between Shasta and the cliff the whole time.

God does not always deliver us from difficulty. Sometimes he lets us walk through those terrifying places—and keeps us company there. We catch the sound of his footfalls, hear his breath, talk to him. He walks between us and the worst things imaginable.

As bad as my life has been, I occasionally wonder if I might look back with the benefit of hindsight and see that God protected me from the worst of it. Will I see how he kept me company through the loneliest nights, like the cat that

> *I occasionally wonder if I might look back with the benefit of hindsight and see that God protected me from the worst of it.*

kept Shasta company in the dark tombs? Will I see how those times I asked to be carried—and he refused—were times he shaped my faith and fortitude and character?

When I read stories like *The Horse and his Boy*, a little flash of hope lights up my heart, and I think, *It's possible. Maybe God is more present than I realise. Maybe he is here even when I can't hear or see him.* And maybe, when the fog hides him and all I can feel is the distance between us, maybe his grace will cover even that. Maybe he will hold me there, even when I hold him at a distance. Maybe that will be enough.

I have felt like a prisoner chained up in a dungeon. I have wondered if God is here—I mean, I believe he is, but it can get pretty cold and lonely in a prison cell. One day I realised he was sitting right beside me in the cell, chained up like me, suffering like me. The image disturbed me. 'That can't be right,' I chastised myself. 'God is our redeemer. He breaks chains, he doesn't wear them!' But the image persisted, God with chains around his wrists, enduring what I was enduring. That's when it hit me.

He's right beside me. He's in this with me.

Sometimes when we say, 'God is with us,' it feels distant, like he's watching our prison cell on security camera while sitting all nice and cushy in an office somewhere. But that's not God-with-us. God-with-us sits in our cells. He doesn't cash in his get-out-of-jail-free card. He stays with us by choice. Such is the force of his love.

That keeps me hanging on.

Stories and glory

'God's writing your story.'

'Let God write your next chapter.'

'Isn't it great how God keeps appearing in your story?'

Before I rip these statements to shreds, let me say I 100% agree with them. I agree God is the author of our stories. After all, he's the author of our faith. God shapes the narratives of our lives. God has ways of popping into our stories and interrupting the trajectories of our plot lines.

> *Maybe our tiny, short stories are mere threads in God's epic tapestry.*

But. Do you ever wonder if we have this backwards? If the point of our lives is not our stories, but God's majestic narrative that sweeps our plotlines into his eternal story? Maybe our tiny, short stories are mere threads in God's epic tapestry.

This difference matters. When we view our lives through the lens of 'My story' and try to make sense of illness in that light, it can be hard to see any point to the pain. We can spend our entire lives searching for meaning. However, if we view illness through the perspective of 'God's story', it changes the shape of illness entirely. We see our lives from an eternal point of view. We see how illness affects not just us but many people in God's family, over many centuries. We see how far-reaching these issues are. And we see God ever redeeming us.

That's a different story. That's not just about suffering. It's about grace showing up in unexpected and glorious ways. It's about God the redeemer stepping into the middle of our mess and bringing forth something. It's about God and his glory.

My church worship team once recorded a bunch of worship

songs to put online during one of the horrible COVID-19 lockdowns. It was a long day. I came prepared with plenty of sustenance. But the day pushed my body right over the edge. My energy fell off a cliff. I went from 'I'm a little tired' to 'I'm gonna faint' in a matter of minutes. Nothing helped. I ended up flat on my back on the floor.

As people prayed for me and I tried to breathe, I remembered God's words: 'Your testimony will be that you got sick, and I didn't heal you, and you continued to worship me anyway.' I knew this would be a testimony of worshiping God in the face of disabling illness. I knew I would stand again and record the next song with the band. It was all for God's glory. And it would indeed glorify God. Because anything I did from that point would be purely by the grace of God. I had nothing left to give. As if in response, I felt the Holy Spirit whisper: 'Just watch, Steph. Today I am going to show my wonders through you.'

He did just that. After a few minutes, I was fit to stand. We recorded the song. I played and sang my heart out. The presence of God grew in the room. In fact, the more we tired, the richer God's presence seemed to grow. But that's not all. We still had one more song to go, and seconds away from recording I was hit with severe pain. I couldn't breathe. I bent double and yelled to halt the recording. My muscles were so fatigued from the whole day they had pretty much quit on the spot. They were done. It was over. Except it wasn't.

I said to the guys, 'Let's go'. The only thing to do now was go ahead with the final song. I could collapse afterwards! So we recorded the last song and I gave everything I had, knowing this was it. I watched the recording afterwards and went, 'Wow'. You would never have known how much pain I was in. I danced and played like a caffeine fanatic. God showed his wonders.

The presence of God after that last song was palpable. I think we even burst into spontaneous applause. We were exhausted, pain-ridden and hardly able to move, but our hearts were glad. I took painkillers straight away and collapsed in a chair, regretting nothing. I had surrendered to God until nothing was left. I had trusted him with even the ability to stand. And he came through.

One friend present at the recording recently retold the story to a group. (Not at all embarrassing.) When he told them how sick I was right before the recordings and how God came through, those people made noises of wonderment. They weren't in awe of me or my stamina (coz I had none) or commitment (which was overshadowed by illness) or bravery (which is sometimes closer to stupidity). They were in awe of God.

When God empowers you to do something you cannot do in your own strength, that's God's story taking over yours. John Newton, the poet who penned *Amazing Grace*, once said:

> Some Christians are called to endure a disproportionate amount of suffering. Such Christians are a spectacle of grace to the church, like flaming bushes unconsumed, and cause us to ask, like Moses: "Why is this bush not burned up?"[55] (Thanks Alia Joy for the quote.)

Our 'disproportionate suffering' gives way to spectacles of grace.

It's about God, not us; God, showing his wonders in and through us; God, using every facet of our lives—even illness—to show his glory.

> God wants to tell his story and show his glory through you.

Speaking of Moses, God decided to show his glory through him and asked him to speak to Pharoah, even though he stuttered. When Moses pointed out the vital flaw in God's plan, God didn't heal him of his stutter. He sent him anyway and gave resources to help him. (Exodus 3:1-4:17) Sometimes God uses limited, diverse, disabled people at crucial moments.

God wants to tell his story and show his glory through you.

Praying and complaining

When I say praying, I also mean complaining, crying, venting, praying in tongues, writing, singing, pleading and collapsing. Every breath, every sigh, every groan is a form of prayer. Silence is prayer.

Having said that, I'd like to share some psalms that have helped me in the throes of sickness. They're especially helpful when my word-prayers have reached saturation point. Here's Psalm 22:

> Doubled up with pain, I call to God
> All the day long. No answer. Nothing.
> I keep at it all night, tossing and turning...
> I'm a bucket kicked over and spilled,
> Every joint in my body has been pulled apart.
> My heart is a blob
> Of melted wax in my gut.
> I'm dry as a bone,
> My tongue black and swollen.

> They have laid me out for burial
> In the dirt. (Psalm 22:2, 14-15 MSG)

We should set these words to music and sing them at church. Imagine rocking up to church and the worship team leads with, 'My heart is a blob…'

> [God] has never let you down,
> Never looked the other way
> When you were being kicked around.
> He has never wandered off to do his own thing;
> He has been right there, listening. (Psalm 22:23-24 MSG)

What a wonderful shift. God does not leave us alone in our misery; he is right alongside us, and he hears our cries.

Psalm 31:

> Be kind to me, God—
> I'm in deep, deep trouble again.
> I've cried my eyes out;
> I feel hollow inside.
> My life leaks away, groan by groan;
> My years fade out in sighs.
> My troubles have worn me out,
> Turned my bones to powder. (Psalm 31:9-10 MSG)

Psalm 41:

> Whenever we're sick and in bed,

> God becomes our nurse,
> Nurses us back to health…
> You know me inside and out, you hold me together;
> You never fail to stand me tall in your presence
> So I can look you in the eye. (Psalm 41:3, 12 MSG)

When our bodies tear themselves apart, God holds us together. When we collapse, God sets us on our feet again.

I'm absolutely nutty about the psalms. They are so relatable. No matter what mood I am in, I can find a psalm that resonates. When I pray the psalms, I feel like God really understands what I'm going through. Many of the psalms, even the most melancholy, shift toward God. They start off depressing, but then remember God's goodness and unrelenting love. Some even finish praising God.

> *When our bodies tear themselves apart, God holds us together.*

May we turn to God for help in times of need.

May he hold us together.

May he lift your spirits through the psalms.

Haven

I wrote a song called *Haven*[56] (shameless self-promo alert), inspired by a prolonged illness. You may not think illness can be inspirational, but here we are. You will find the YouTube link in the back of this book. It was also inspired by Psalm 62:2:

> He's solid rock under my feet,

> Breathing room for my soul,
> An impregnable castle:
> I'm set for life. (MSG)

We need that breathing room. We need moments of respite from illness, glimpses of wellness, breathers from constant pain. God can be that breathing room for us, like a much-needed retreat or holiday getaway.

He is our haven.

 Take a moment to notice how you are feeling after the chapter, and whether anything stood out for you or resonated with you. Time for some self-care.

SECTION FOUR
REGROWTH

*The sun shines down on all of us, weak and small,
great and strong, sick and well alike.
The sun has no favourites.*

*God makes his sunshine to bless us all. What a wonder.
As I marvel at his goodness and fairness, his wild generosity,
somewhere inside me a tiny seed stirs, as though perhaps,
one day, it might want to burst open.*

9

PHENOMENA
Alternative Stories to Illness

In her book *Phosphorescence*, Julia Baird writes about the soft luminescent light given off by human bodies. This light, Baird says, too subtle to be seen by the naked eye, can be viewed through a highly sensitive imaging system utilised by Japanese scientists Masaki Kobayashi, Daisuke Kikuchi and Hitoshi Okamura in 2009.[57] [58] Humans literally glimmer.

'Maybe it's just that we're all made of stardust,' says Baird.

There's more to our bodies than 'sick' or 'healthy', more to existence than pain or the medications rattling around inside us. We are accustomed to the illness dominant story, the story that springs to

> Apparently, God made us to sparkle.

our lips when others ask how we are. It is the verbal report we give to the doctor. It dominates our existence.

I'm tired today, like always. That is a dominant story.

I had to go to hospital again. Dominant story.

I'm still in pain. Dominant story.

Dominant stories roll readily off the tongue. But there is an alternative. To borrow a concept from Narrative Therapy, we're going to explore alternative stories: times when the dominant story of illness does not rule our lives. Let's deep dive into the phenomena of our bodies, the beauty and wonder not just the problems. Let's rediscover the awe of God's designs that means we are beautifully and wonderfully made, not just flawed and dysfunctional.

Because, apparently, God made us to sparkle.

Green and blue spaces

Baird's book describes the growing phenomena of 'forest bathing', the practice of immersing oneself in nature's 'green spaces'. Spending time in green spaces, even five minutes, is good for us. There is something nature does for us that nothing else can. It is not just healthy. It is magical.

One famous hospital study found people recover more quickly from illness and surgery if they have something green to look at.[59] Apparently, our bodies yearn for something in God's creation. Could this be God's design? And blue spaces, according to Baird, can be even more potent.[60] Blue spaces are water; being near or immersed in water can be healing for us.

Aboriginal Australians speak of being connected to country in ways I cannot fathom. When they go walkabout, they are seeking reconnection with their country. They listen to nature, remaining silent long enough to hear the whisper of the land. When they are unwell, they view it as loss of connection to country.

Why should our bodies be impacted by our environments? I cannot say, but it seems we are. Why else am I tempted to linger in the park? Why do I stop and stare at the lake? Why do I breathe differently in the forest? Why does the sight of a flowering Jacaranda move me to tears? What is it about the smell of cut grass that is so intoxicating—especially after the rain? Why do I talk to eucalyptus gums like confidantes? Maybe I'm just weird. (I'm OK with that.) Or maybe nature is part of our wellbeing. Maybe being connected to the earth is more important than we realise.

Maybe God designed us this way.

Luminescence

Humans are not the only beings giving off bioluminescence. Bacteria, earthworms, fireflies, fish, crustaceans, jellyfish and fungi also display this stunning phenomenon. Fireflies flash their lights in certain sequences as mating signals. But other luminescence does not appear to serve any purpose, such as certain underground mushrooms that glow.[61] I can understand above-ground mushrooms glowing to attract insects to spread the fungal spores, but underground mushrooms glowing where nobody can see them? What could be the function of their hidden light? Perhaps there is a reason, and we are yet to discover it. Perhaps we don't understand the purpose of bioluminescence. Or perhaps God just likes creating beautiful things.

What about our own bioluminescence? Has God created us

this way for a purpose? Or did he just want to make us beautiful? And does this change how we view ourselves? Perhaps this is an alternative to the dominant stories of 'broken', 'damaged', 'dysfunctional' and 'sick'. Perhaps there is beauty co-existing in us alongside imperfection.

The Japanese art of Kintsugi exemplifies this. Kintsugi, literally 'golden joinery', takes broken pottery and mends it using engoldened lacquer. It shows us broken stuff is never wasted; each of us is unique; and sometimes imperfections, like illness, can display the most stunning golden artwork.

> *Sometimes imperfections, like illness, can display the most stunning golden artwork.*

Ernest Hemingway is famously quoted saying, 'The world breaks everyone, and afterward many are strong at the broken places.'[62] That's our testimony. That's luminescence.

Heart- and gut-brains

Our brains are not the only brains we have. Our hearts and guts have the capacity to think, feel and make decisions completely independently of our head-brains.[63]

'My heart is broken.'

'I have a gut instinct about that.'

'The heart wants what the heart wants.'

'That was a gutsy thing to do.'

Our heads, hearts and guts are connected via the vagus nerve which runs up and down our spines. These organs communicate bidirectionally along this remarkable nerve. Which goes a long way toward understanding why certain foods, or butterflies in the stomach, or a broken heart, can interfere with our cognitive thinking and why good food and love can restore it.

> When I learn about phenomena such as these, I am inspired to stop asking God questions and simply say, 'Wow'.

The phenomena of heart- and gut-brains tells us there is more to these bodies than medicine tells us. And there's more to being human than illness.

When I learn about phenomena such as these, I am inspired to stop asking God questions and simply say, 'Wow'.

Coexistence

How can good things coexist with bad?

The metaphors are all around us. Roses have thorns. Gardens have bees. Chocolate has calories (not that it matters). Many things have imperfections or 'dark sides', to use a *Star Wars* analogy. They provide us with balance and at times bittersweetness. It's part of the package.

Our world holds opposites in its hands. There is both great poverty and great wealth, war-torn countries and nations of peace, sickness and people who are unbelievably fit and healthy. The sun can burn and warm us; rainwater can nourish and drown us. This world has both day and night, providing us with light and darkness. Both occur simultaneously, two sides of the same coin.

There is beauty throughout this world in plants and animals, sunrises and sunsets, birth and death. This planet resounds with God's glory, shouting his praises all day long. The grass hums with it. The morning lights thrills with it. The clouds resonate with it. His music abides in nature. God, the artist, gifts his art to us. His currency is not cash; it is the dewdrops glistening on leaves, beams of light breaking through rainclouds, songs bursting from the mouths of birds, roots stretching deep into the comfortable soil, flowers reaching for the sun. It is our skin receiving the warm daylight and the coolness of night, our lungs gratefully receiving oxygen and exhaling in contentment.

All creation boasts of him. Including our bodies. When my lungs—his creation—offer him praise, I join with creation's great chorus. When I speak, this mouth—his creation—gives him glory. When I work, serve and rest, this body—his creation—points to him.

How can the two coexist? How can such a broken piece of machinery be so beautiful in God's sight? Because just like he created roses with thorns, he created us with dark sides. He gave us bodies capable of breaking down—sometimes in devastating ways.

Does this make his work any less beautiful? For answer, I must turn to creation. I love the beauty God has created. I love the mountains, streams, birds and animals (although I still hold reservations about cockroaches). God's creation constantly inspires me to worship him. But creation isn't perfect. It is subject to floods, droughts, tornadoes, earthquakes, avalanches, volcanic eruptions, lightning strikes, hailstorms and bushfires. These things cause great loss and heartache. Not to mention insurance headaches.

This planet is broken too. Does that make it any less beautiful? Of course not. For all its flaws, creation shouts God's praises morning and night. If I go looking for beauty in this world, I will find it in bucketloads. Even though it misbehaves, its inherent wonder cannot be denied.

Now comes the tricky part. My body is part of God's creation. Is my body any less beautiful because it is flawed? I reluctantly admit it is not. I have hated my body for a long time, resenting it for its inadequacies. But if my body is part of the creation song, and if creation retains its beauty despite the mess that coexists with it...then my body must retain its inherent, God-breathed beauty. Somehow.

> My body is part of God's creation.

There are parts of this planet that don't appeal to me, like deserts and swamplands. But many parts of the world hold my affection: alpine mountains, fluorescent green hillsides, the coastal beauty of Australia, the stark wonder of snowfall and the stillness of the nighttime sky spread with stars.

What about my own body? It's easy to list things I hate about my body. (A wacky immune system, for starters.) But what do I genuinely like and appreciate about it?

I like that my skin tans nicely. (We've got to start somewhere. Baby steps.)

I like the colour of my eyes.

I like that I can bend my joints further than most people. (It's called hypermobility, and it's a cool party trick.)

I like that my fingers are crooked. They match my quirky personality.

I like that my taste buds love chocolate.

I like that I have a heart- and gut-brain. That's pretty neat.

I like that my vocal chords can sing.

There, that wasn't so bad. The coexistence mindset helps.

We live with illness; at the same time, we acknowledge where the beauty God created still shines through. Both can be true. We are sick *and* we are fearfully and wonderfully made.

> We are sick and we are fearfully and wonderfully made.

That's an alternative story.

God likes us

I am a (recovering) perfectionist. When I clean something, I want it spotless. If spots remain, the thing isn't clean. When I scrub my white kitchen bench top, I can easily tell if I have missed a spot. I cast a critical eye over it and mutter to myself, 'Missed a spot'.

I do that with myself too. It's hard for me to love myself when I am critically examining my body, declaring over and over, 'Missed a spot'.

God doesn't do that. He doesn't view me the same way I view myself. When God created the world, light and darkness, land and sea, plants and animals and humans, he cast his eye over it and declared, 'It is good'. He didn't grind his teeth and mutter about the spots he missed (if God does 'miss' anything). He might not have made things perfect—only he is perfect—but he did make them beautiful. He was pleased with what he saw. He thought it was good.

> He might not have made things perfect—only he is perfect—but he did make them beautiful.

The same applies to me. He didn't make my body and then say, 'Drat. Look at all those spots I missed.' He didn't forget to give me an immune system. No, he created me and said, 'It is good'. He actually liked what he saw. I am fearfully and wonderfully made. I may not like this body, this dilapidated house that is constantly falling apart, but he sure does. He made it and gifted it to me.

He made you too. When he sees you, he's not critiquing your body or himself as Creator. He's saying, 'It is good'. He really does like us the way we are.

May God help us rediscover the enjoyment and wonder of ourselves, his creation—just as we enjoy and wonder at the richness of a mountain or flower. May these broken vessels, these jars of clay, join with creation in singing his praises.

Take a moment to notice how you are feeling after the chapter, and whether anything stood out for you or resonated with you. Time for some self-care.

*I am walking through a forest in winter.
I trudge through the thick snow, longing for a rest.
Finally, I stumble upon a log cabin tucked away in the trees.*

*As I enter, I feel the warmth of a fire in the far corner
of the room. Others are there, huddled around it, and I
join them, shaking from the cold. Gratefully I rub my
hands together and hold them near the flames.*

*As embers dance and smoke fills my eyes, I feel my
body slowly beginning to thaw. The uncontrollable shivering
settles. This tiny fire will certainly not be enough to defrost
me, any more than it can thaw the winter outside,
but it will keep me from freezing.*

For now, that is enough.

10

CARERS

Whom I Love

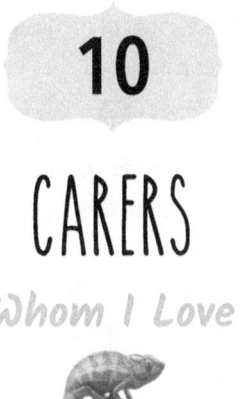

In Luke 5:17-26, a paralysed man wants to hear Jesus preach, but the house where Jesus is speaking is chock-full of people and he cannot get in. His friends climb on to the roof of the house and *pull the roof off*. They lower the paralysed man into the building, mat and all, so he can hear Jesus.

Jesus is astounded at their faith. I am too.

When I think of carers and all they do, I think of the friends of the paralysed man. They carried him, physically and spiritually, to be where Jesus was. I sometimes need assistance with showering, dressing, housecleaning and shopping. I also need intangible help. I need emotional help when feeling depressed or overwhelmed. I need mental help when I can't think through the brain fog. I need social help when I can't muster the energy to reach out. I definitely need spiritual help when my faith is flagging.

In this chapter I will be speaking mainly to carers, mostly of the unpaid variety, but some things will no doubt apply to paid carers as well. If you are a carer of a chronically ill family member or loved one, this chapter is for you.

Kinds of caring

I used to think being a carer meant showering and toileting. But there is more to caring than wiping someone's butt. I want to acknowledge the different things you might do as a carer.

Some carers pay the bills (financial caring).

Some worry about their loved one all day (mental caring).

Some become confidantes and sounding boards (emotional caring).

Some drive their loved one to hospitals and medical appointments (medical caring).

Some pray for their loved one (spiritual caring).

There's picking up medication, giving hugs to the chronically ill person, holding their hand during tests, hearing their bad news, planning for the future, advocacy, helping with paperwork, Dr Googling, shopping for walkers and other aids, arranging home visits and other services, and being a general dogsbody. Caring can be a full-time job.

Minor things like assisting your chronically ill loved one to remember and report their illness information to a doctor is a kind of medical and mental caring and can be a huge help. The constant emotional support carers provide makes a massive difference too. Not to mention those carers who cook, give massages, bring people out of panic attacks, talk, distract and pray for them. Carers are freaking amazing.

> Carers are freaking amazing.

Carers, take this moment to be seen and acknowledge all your caring. No one else knows exactly how much you do—in spite of your own stress, sickness and tiredness too!

Those of us who are cared for appreciate you.

Limits to caring

Even the strongest carers can't do everything. And you don't have to. You have limits. You have stuff you cannot do. You have other responsibilities, interests, hobbies and ministries. You will get sick, grow old and need caring yourself. This is your official permission to take time off.

People who are chronically ill do not always want carers around. Sometimes they want space. Sometimes they want to feel independent, if only for a little while. Sometimes they want to try things, even if they struggle. Sometimes the best thing you can do is balance your caring with healthy time away. Especially if you are an introvert.

It is OK to set limits with your chronically ill loved one. It is OK to say no when they ask for help. It is perfectly acceptable to have your own life. You will get sick of caring, just like chronically ill people get sick of being—well, sick. The important thing is to recognise your need for time out.

It can be hard to say no without feeling guilty or worrying

about letting them down. Sometimes carers expect a lot of themselves. Especially if you've made 'in sickness and in health' types of promises. But you're allowed to have boundaries. Here are a few ways of respectfully saying no to a chronically ill person:

'Sorry, I can't do that today, maybe another time?'

'How urgent is it? Can it wait?'

'Is there anyone else you can call?'

'Can I get back to you later today?'

'I know you're in pain; unfortunately, I can't make it.'

'I feel privileged you reached out to me; I just can't swing it today.'

'Here is the number of a service that can help.'

'I can't manage that, but I can pray for you?'

A no may be a not-yet, rather than a hard no. Having said that, there is a place for hard nos too, like if your loved one takes advantage of you. If they are calling day and night saying it's urgent when it's not, borrowing money endlessly without paying it back, abusing you or complaining endlessly (or countless other examples), it's OK to set a firm boundary.

'No, I won't lend you money.'

'No, I won't answer the phone in the middle of the night. Because I'm sleeping.'

'No, I'll turn my phone off when I need a break.'

'No, that can wait.'

'No, I'm not the right person to help with that. Call [insert name of willing volunteer] instead.'

'No, you can do that yourself.'

'No.'

While the needs of your loved one may be genuine, your needs are too. It might help to remind them of that. Maybe let them know when you need a break and have a Plan B for them: a friend, a service, a helpline. You might be able to negotiate and find a compromise.

> While the needs of your loved one may be genuine, your needs are too.

Remember, the person with chronic illness might be in a lot of pain. Maybe they haven't slept and they're feeling cranky. You might find yourself having arguments with them. Apologies and forgiveness can go a long way for both of you. Cut them some slack if things get a bit tense. Cut yourself some slack too—you're only human!

(And if you're reading this as a person living with chronic illness, try to respect your carers' limits and have a Plan B so you don't burn them out.)

Compassion fatigue, vicarious trauma and burnout

Who cares for the carer?

Caring can take a toll. You may become disinterested in your chronically ill loved one. You may find yourself switching off, distancing yourself or becoming emotionally detached.

That's compassion fatigue. It's a normal effect of caring. Compassion fatigue says, 'I've been giving for too long.' It doesn't mean you no longer care. It doesn't mean you've stopped loving them. It doesn't necessarily mean you should stop being their carer. It might mean you need some TLC, a break, a holiday.

Of course, it can also mean that you are caring for a loved one in a strained relationship, or caring for someone you no longer love. Perhaps you come from a culture that keeps illness and caring within the family, rather than asking friends or the government for assistance. You might be caring for them out of a sense of obligation or duty, or financial or practical necessity. That is a difficult, draining situation. You might need to consider your limits or minimise your contact with that person.

Compassion fatigue is different from burnout, the deep-seeded cynicism born of overwork and under-resourcedness over a prolonged period of time. It is exhaustion of the body, mind and spirit, a desire to escape or even give up. Burnout means you definitely need a break, possibly for good. At worst, burnout can change your personality and sense of who you are.

Some believe compassion fatigue and burnout are on the same spectrum with burnout at the extreme end and compassion fatigue an early warning sign. Before hitting compassion fatigue, you might feel weary, stressed, tired, strung out, anxious, overloaded, depressed, paralysed, held hostage, frustrated and resentful. You may have other warning signs.

These can also be signs of grief. Caring comes with its own unique version of loss. Perhaps, as a carer, you have lost the life you once had. Perhaps you have lost your freedom and independence because of caring responsibilities. Perhaps you lost your relationship with your chronically ill loved one, or the nature of your relationship has changed for the worse. Perhaps their personality has altered, or you feel like you don't know who they are anymore. Perhaps you find yourself wishing for a different life and feeling guilty about that. Please don't

> *You have the right to feel those feelings and grieve that loss.*

be too hard on yourself. These are legitimate impacts of caring and you have the right to feel those feelings and grieve that loss.

Vicarious trauma is different again. This is the traumatising effect of working with a traumatised person. Your chronically ill loved one may have been traumatised by illness or medical treatment. Witnessing your loved one being traumatised can be traumatising for you too.

This term was first coined for emergency responders (police, firefighters, ambulance workers) when they started displaying the same trauma signs as those they rescued. Anyone exposed to the trauma of others can potentially develop signs of vicarious trauma. For example, if your loved one suffers panic attacks and you begin experiencing the same panic, you might be developing vicarious trauma.

So what do you do? Taking a break can help you separate mentally and emotionally. It can remind you that you are safe and you do not have to absorb their trauma. Self-care is also helpful, so do something to unwind. Find those glimmers, the things that counteract the triggers in your life. Self-care should outweigh how badly you are feeling; if you have a particularly bad week, the self-care should be top shelf!

Ask your church for prayer—for *both* of you. When your family member or loved one is sick, it's easy for them to get the prayerful attention. Make sure people know you need prayer too!

If you think you might be experiencing compassion fatigue, burnout or vicarious trauma, or you are simply looking for support, talk to someone who gets it like *Carers NSW* (www.carersnsw.org.au),

Carer Gateway (www.carergateway.gov.au) or the *NDIS* (www.ndis.gov.au). They can help with counselling, peer support, information, in-home care, equipment, home and vehicle modifications, respite, transport, finances (such as the Carers Allowance), finding employment, linking to social or hobby groups and a host of other services. This support can make a big difference, especially if you are starting to feel traumatised and don't know where to turn. And also if you don't have family or children you can call on for help.

The other side of vicarious trauma is vicarious resilience (originally coined to describe how trauma therapists can be positively impacted by their work[64], but I think it applies nicely to carers too). Just as you can be negatively impacted by the sickness of your loved one, you can be inspired by their strength, resilience and bravery.

> Just as you can be negatively impacted by the sickness of your loved one, you can be inspired by their strength, resilience and bravery.

Is there anything you admire about your loved one? Have they displayed courage in the face of medical danger? How are they still capable and strong in the midst of illness? Have any silver linings surfaced out of your time together? Surprisingly good things can happen, even in the face of disaster. When beauty shines out of difficult and devastating situations, that's vicarious resilience. Reflecting on the resilience of your loved one and your own vicarious resilience can be an antidote for fatigue, burnout and trauma.

(Also, if you are reading this as a person with chronic illness, consider giving your carer the day off every now and again if you can manage. Tell them to clear off—respectfully. Call on other friends once in a while. Share the love around so you don't rely too heavily on one person.)

Standing together

It's tempting to see sick people as problems.

Don't get me wrong. Some sick people seem to have an endless string of problems. Some can become a pain in the proverbial about it (even without meaning to). There is nothing easy about caring. But sometimes the problem becomes the dominant story. It's all we can think about, all we can see, when we look at that person. As in, 'Steph is a lupie.'

An alternative approach is to externalise the problem (common practice in Narrative Therapy[65]), where sickness is viewed as a separate entity rather than dwelling inside a person. As in, 'There's Steph in that chair, and she lives with lupus, which sits in that other chair.' We have just externalised lupus.

What difference does that make, I hear you ask? It means I am not the problem. I live with the problem, but I am not to blame for lupus. If the problem lives inside me, I might believe I caused it. But if it lives outside me, I'm not the problem. The problem is the problem. Lupus is the problem. With lupus living outside of me, separate and distant, I can take a stand against it. Others can stand with me against lupus too.

My family and I stand against lupus.
My doctors stand with me against lupus.
My church stands with me against lupus.
God stands with me against lupus.

Carers, take a stand with your loved one against the problem. They are not the problem; the illness is the problem. Let them know that. Let them know you stand beside them against the sickness. Pray for your loved one; it's another way of standing against the illness. Chronically ill people need to know they are not alone and you are standing with them. It reassures them they are not to blame for the illness, and that you don't blame them.

No greater love

No greater love
Has a carer
Than to shower me
When I can't move,
Let me lean on them
When my legs are weak,
Dress me
When pain forbids.

No greater love
Has a carer
Than to hold me at midnight
While I cry into the darkness,
To stroke my hair,
To listen,
Until the tears are spent
And I can breathe again.

No greater love
Has a carer

CARERS

Than to stay
When they could so easily
Leave
When their shoulder is drenched in my tears,
Their back aching from standing up for me,
Their throat sore from reassurances,
Their hand numb from holding mine,
Yet they stay—
No small miracle.

No greater love
Has a carer
Than to pray for me
Day after day
Year after year
And in every magical moment,
In every finite gesture,
To show me
God's infinite love.

There is
No greater love
Than the love
Of a carer.

 Take a moment to notice how you are feeling after the chapter, and whether anything stood out for you or resonated with you. Time for some self-care.

*Sitting on a beach, wind blowing,
I feel able to breathe again.*

In this oasis, I have permission to sit, be still, settle into the sand, simply be. I feel the calm and space of a steadfast heart. I feel the gentleness of the breeze. I watch the water wash the sand, cleansing it.

I breathe slow, deep, full breaths, unhurried by the marching of time or disease. I sink into this peacefulness, letting it wash over me.

11

SANITY

Silliness and Other Survival Strategies

A priest, a rabbi and a lupus patient walk into a bar…

Just kidding. No lupie has the energy to go to a bar.

Life with chronic illness gets way too serious. Not to mention insane. So we're going to counteract that with laughter, play and self-care. Be warned: silliness and sarcasm awaits (along with some more mature sanity-saving suggestions). I figure if lupus can take over my life any time, I'm going to make the most of opportunities to mock and parody it—and laugh at myself too!

Humour

I have a couple of quippy (all right, sarcastic) retorts that help me. When I develop a new problem, my favourite responses is, 'Put it on my tab'. I have accrued so many symptoms and diagnoses over the years, what's a few more? I'll pay the bill at some point. Don't ask when.

I acquired several new diagnoses in 2021, and two of them happened in the same fortnight. To offset the shock and rage, I responded to the doctors with, 'Put it on my tab!' While a new diagnosis is not great news, I can handle it. Although this can backfire. I used this comeback once and my doctor said, 'You're so strong.' I laughed: 'Perhaps I should visit you on a bad day!' As nice as it is to be seen as 'strong', doctors need to know when I am struggling.

Another comeback is, 'I always knew I was special.' This is handy for the rare ones. When doctors look at my constellation of symptoms, I remind them how special I am. 'Aren't you glad you have such a rare and unique patient?' This normally produces a laugh.

I have a special kind of loathing for the negative-test-results letdown. This is when the symptoms are severe but every test comes back normal. Sure, it's great to be told one does not have, for example, heart disease or a lung clot. But why the fart am I so sick? And what the helium do I do about it? So even before they share the results, I say, 'Let me guess: I'm normal?' The doctors laugh. They understand the frustration of having problems with elusive answers. We giggle about how boring and normal I am. Of course, that opens me up to ridicule about being 'abnormal, but in a normal way'. The sky's the limit.

Sometimes my doctors simply shake their heads. They're not giving up; they are just baffled. Some are amazed I am still standing. They say, 'Gee, you weren't kidding about being complex.' I always rise to the bait. 'C'mon,' I egg them on, 'You wouldn't want to be bored in your work, would you? At least I present a challenge!' Even doctors need a little sanity.

On bad days, I get super sarcastic. It's not the doctor's fault. I'm just blowing off steam. (I do tell them that, by the way. Just in case you were worried.) When they ask, 'Why are you here?', I shoot back, 'Because I was bored', or 'Because it's been soooo long between visits', or 'Because I'm giving my new shoes a spin'. They can usually tell I'm kidding. If they can't, I hurriedly and red-facedly apologise.

Sometimes I go full-force:

> Long time, no see.

> [When they call me] I won! ('Bingo' is a fine alternative.)

> I just **love** the colour of your ceiling.

> You guys will be able to retire on me.

> Shall I set up my bed in your waiting room?

> This bed is so comfy!

> Wanna give me a tattoo while you're there?

> That medicine could use a little salt.

> Drugs? For me? You shouldn't have!

> [To pathologists] So you're my friendly neighbourhood vampire today?

Me: *Screaming in pain on examination*

Doctor: Does that hurt?

Me: No, why do you ask?

Doctor: How bad is the pain?

Me: Shall I show you?

I'm soooo glad I came today.

Let's do this again—not!

After this, I'm getting cake!

I hope I never see you again, in a good way!

The pleasure was all mine.

Pity my doctors. Please.

If a health professional accidentally hurts me, I take humorous advantage of that. If they rip my skin off, I say I have plenty to spare. If they hurt a limb, or an ear, or anything of which I have two, I tell them I have a spare part. If they hurt my head, I dramatically exclaim, 'And I didn't bring my spare!' My talent is wasted on them.

A recent addition to my humour repertoire is the plot twist. When something goes wrong or I get a new problem, I yell, 'Plot twist!' It appeals to the quirky writer in me. It acknowledges, just like a plot twist, medical curve balls can come out of nowhere and slap us sideways.

Makes me feel a little less helpless. Which is a good thing.

Distraction

One of my all-time favourite TV shows is *The Big Bang Theory*. That show has literally saved my life. When my body is riddled with pain, the fatigue so bad I can hardly lift my head, my mind in the darkest headspaces—watching that show has helped me smile again, if only briefly. It's made me laugh when I wondered if I could go on or if I should end it all. It's talked me down from the ledge. That is a worthy distraction.

Anything that makes us laugh is good medicine. Even black humour can give us a break. I highly recommend funny movies, TV shows, online videos, cat photos, humorous podcasts, comedic books and plays, anything that throws your melancholy into sharp relief.

Speaking of cats, my new furbaby Boba has been a quality distraction. He seems to know when I am unwell. Animals are great like that. Many times I have been in tears and Boba has jumped up and talked to me. Or jumped down and started playing with a piece of fluff, making me roar with laughter. It eases the pain.

> Anything that makes us laugh is good medicine.

Chocolate gives me momentary distraction. When I am in pain, chocolate reminds me my body is still capable of feeling good. It seems like a simple fix, and it is. It's an instant dopamine hit. I tend toward dark chocolate which is healthier and therefore easier to justify. If I am thinking of ending things, chocolate is a much better alternative. Cake is good too, and when life looks less like a neat slice of cake and more like an Eton mess slopped into a bowl, it's a good reminder life can still be good, even though it looks like a big ol' mess.

There's a Narrative Therapy practice known as 'exoticising the domestic'.[66] This means taking everyday things we take for granted—chocolate, sunshine, flowers, a text from a loved one—and making a big deal out of them. When I do this, I get a dopamine hit. I notice how good it feels to stand in the sun. I notice the colours of flowers, their generous tapestry of beauty. I notice how my mouth curves into a smile when a friend texts me. I loiter with that moment, extending it, deepening it. I take that taken-for-granted moment and exoticise it.

I have a repertoire of healthy distractions from which to choose. If one isn't working, like social media, I can choose something else from my menu. I can go for a walk instead. But if it's raining, I can choose an indoor menu item, like calling a friend. Or irritating the cat. Or grabbing a book. Or eating chocolate. Hey, it works no matter the weather.

Pick something that gives you even the briefest of distractions. Shop online or just browse. Paint your nails (guys, I'm looking at you too). Make a cup of tea. Pluck your eyebrows. Give yourself a five-minute break from the endless production line of worries.

Distractions aren't necessarily bad. Yes, they distract from the real problem. Sometimes we need a break from the real problem. Distractions are healthy, reasonable coping mechanisms for overwhelming things. If things weren't overwhelming, we wouldn't need coping strategies. We would just fix it.

Distractions can provide welcome relief from illness.

Escapism

In his book, *Whole Notes*, Ed Ayers says music is his superpower.

Music is his place of escape, a safe haven, that gives him abilities beyond himself.[67] I can relate to that.

Music has long been a source of escapism for me. Music does not judge. It simply is. It takes me away from this world while grounding me. It doesn't matter what I play or whether I produce anything. The process is just as important as the outcome. Music is about expression and playfulness. Improvisation gives me permission to have fun, be adventurous and experiment without knowing the result. This is the essence of play: there is no pressure to arrive at a specific destination. The point is to play. That is escapism.

When I sing and play, I enter a flow state, that spontaneous concentration where your entire being is caught up in the moment. It is not about forced concentration but being captivated, swept away, losing track of time. I can lose hours swept away by music. Same goes for writing. I look at the clock and gasp. 'Wow, I've been writing for three hours!' That's flow.

This is healthy escapism. Our brains need time to recharge. Fantasising about a holiday or becoming a hermit who lives in a cabin in the woods and eats berries is totally normal. Respite is good for us so long as it's healthy. There are unhealthy forms too: drug use, alcohol abuse, gambling, workaholism, porn, oversleeping, binge-eating and self-harm.

> Escapism is not bad. It's the way we go about it.

Escapism is not bad. It's the way we go about it.

The 'mindful colouring' movement is becoming increasingly popular. There's drawing, reading, gardening, being in nature, painting, doing diamond art or other fine artwork, building LEGO, bike riding, driving, playing games (video, board and role-player), walking, martial arts, going on holiday, self-pampering, cuddling pets, playing with kids, knitting, scrapbooking, writing poetry, coin collecting and painting *Lord of the Rings* figurines. Even standing in the sunshine can be escapism.

Your escapism might be slightly unusual. I have some less common hobbies including fossicking for semi-precious gemstones. I'm never going to polish or sell any of it—it's too small for that—but the joy of finding these gems is priceless.

Some of these choices may not be options for you if you are housebound or bedbound. Things you were previously able to do may be off the table now. For you, escapism might look different or experimental until you find something that fits. When I am unable to move, I find myself indulging more in cat videos, orchestral music, social media and scented candles. Do what works for you.

Struggling to pinpoint your kind of escapism? These questions might help:

What brings you joy?

When did you last lose track of time? What were you doing?

What did you enjoy doing as a child?

What brings a smile to your face?

What makes you inordinately happy?

When do you feel most free and most yourself?

Follow that path. Whatever brings delight and lightness of spirit is likely to be a good escape for you.

Leaning on others

God once kicked my butt about my ego.

I was setting up for church band, wrestling with the weighty and awkward keyboard. 'No, I'm right,' I said to passing band members, faking good. 'I got it.' Until my leader swept past. He knows I shouldn't lift heavy things, and he immediately ticked me off. 'Leave it, Steph. Lift within your means.' Before I could protest, he'd grabbed the keyboard and hauled it away. I grabbed the cables and followed him, muttering to God under my breath. 'God, it's not fair,' I complained. 'I hate feeling useless. Why can't I carry a keyboard like everyone else?'

Why don't I ever learn? God took me by the scruff of the neck. 'Oh, poor Steph,' he said, 'Having to lean on your church family like that. Poor you!' I went scarlet. 'OK God, point made.' I told the band what God had just said, and we all had a good-natured laugh at my expense. Sometimes I can be so childish.

Ego can get in the way of accepting help. We like to feel independent and capable, especially when we have been robbed of so much. But we need others. God has placed us in community for good reasons. All of us are dependent to some degree and all of us have limitations. We need each other.

I used to feel bad about reaching out for help. 'I should always be giving to others,' my naïve brain used to admonish me. 'To receive is selfish.' Until I realised 'never receiving' means others never experience the joy of giving to me. Giving has to be two-way. If I freely give to others, I must also freely receive. It's only fair. To reject their generosity is like handing back a Christmas present. 'No thanks, I don't want anything from

> Some of us can get better at graciously receiving.

you.' They have offered a gift. Regardless of what the gift is, I hurt them when I reject it. Some of us can get better at graciously receiving. It takes courage and vulnerability to ask for help. I pray we get better at it.

C.S. Lewis said:

> Suffering is not good in itself. What is good in any painful experience is, for the sufferer, his submission to the will of God, and, for the spectators, the compassion aroused and the acts of mercy to which it leads.[68]

Acts of mercy are always a good thing. No, they do not make up for the suffering we have endured. But they are moments of kindness, glimpses of grace, silver linings. Let's accept those acts of mercy from others, just as we accept God's grace. Totally unmerited. Totally undeserved. Gratefully received.

Voices in my head

Thought that would get your attention.

On a bad day, I am visited by supportive voices of friends, family, pastors and professionals. Their encouragements return to mind, seemingly just when I need them. They are my invisible support team. They come with me wherever I go.

My husband says, 'You'll be OK'. My pastor says, 'The joy of the Lord is your strength'. Several friends say, 'I love you'. Members of my family crowd around, giving me compelling reasons for living. People from work chip in, telling me my health comes first. My cat climbs into my lap, kissing me on the nose. I know furbabies can't talk, but they can be part of our support team. People who don't know me show up. Lines from movies, books and songs come prancing to mind. (My thoughts prance, OK?) They sing of stillness, rest, and God's peace that surpasses understanding. They remind me of beauty. They encourage me to keep going, or fall apart, depending on what I need.

I think this is the Holy Spirit at work. He often uses people, music, books, movies and a host of resources to comfort me. He helps me remember something God spoke to me. He uses wonderful and creative things to do it. I am sure the Holy Spirit is one of the voices in my head.

> I am sure the Holy Spirit is one of the voices in my head.

You might hear voices in your head too. Perhaps you can call upon your voices when you're having a rough time. Even deceased voices can help. Perhaps you can take the lyrics from a favourite song to nourish your soul. Perhaps you have a favourite mantra or life motto. You can recruit characters from stories. I don't mean in an 'I believe Superman is real' kind of way. I mean in an 'If Black Widow was here, what would she do?' fashion that can inspire and motivate you. Pick a strong, tough character you admire. Add them to your repertoire.

A similar concept in Narrative Therapy is the 'Team of Life'. Originally conceived to help young people address trauma, the Team of Life invites us to identify members of our support 'team'. We can do the same with illness. One member in the Team of Life is the Coach. If I were to ask you about your illness Coach, I would ask who you have learned the most from and what they have taught you. I would also ask about the rest of your Team of Life:[69]

- Who makes up your team? These people can be alive, no longer living, or people you have known in the past. Who are the people who have been most influential, in a positive way, in your life?
- Who is your goal keeper, the person who looks out for you, guards your goals, and is the most reliable?
- Who are the other team-mates in your life, those you play with, those whose company you enjoy?
- Where is your home ground, the place you feel most at home? You may have more than one. Your home ground might be somewhere you go regularly, or somewhere you visit in your memories or dreams.

If sporting metaphors aren't your thing, an alternative could be the Band of Life. This appeals to me as a musician. If you are the lead singer of your band, who is your drummer who keeps you in time, the one who sets the rhythm and groove for your life? Who is your bass player, the one who provides a solid musical foundation? Who is your keyboardist, the glue who keeps you together? Who are your guitarists, the ones providing drive and harmonics for your life? Do you have backing vocalists who help you sound better? Who is your sound person, the one who mixes the band? Do you have a band manager, someone who knows where the next gig will be?

The Team of Life, Band of Life and voices in our heads are possibilities for hope. They are lifelines on bad days.

Next time you have to do a hard thing, take your team with you.

Pacing

No, I don't mean pacing like a caged animal. Although that may apply. I mean listening to our bodies.

Why do we find the concept of 'pacing' so distasteful? Perhaps it's just me. I hate the idea of not being able to do everything I want. If I have plans, I want to follow through with them. I don't want to wake up in the morning and go, 'I feel like rubbish. There go my plans for the day.'

Pacing is countercultural. Our society values busyness, over-scheduling and over-productivity. Everything about pacing goes against that grain. The culture of busyness says, 'Do as much as possible.' Pacing says, 'Work within your means.'

We have given way to busyness before—and paid for it. If we push ourselves today, we will pay, maybe for days or even weeks afterwards. Pushing comes with a hefty price tag. Pacing is not just about getting through today. Pacing is about after today. It is the long haul of chronic illness. It is the inner wisdom of lived experience.

I know when I move outside my body's pace. I feel it when I'm stressed. If there's a work crisis and I stay back to deal with it, I feel the fatigue burrowing into my brain and bones. My mind slides sideways, my body slipping away from me. I know instinctively it will take me about a week to recover from this fatigue.

Now, that is not a reason to avoid work crises. I will stay and deal with it. That is my work ethic. However, I know the impact it will have on my health. That's why I pace when I can. If I do not pace myself today, I might need a week off sick. I cannot afford to do that all the time.

Sometimes I make a judgement call to spend more energy than usual. There are certain situations that warrant extra energy, including work crises, family sickness and pastoral needs at church. I deem those immediate needs outweigh my own.

And sometimes I just want to be playful and reckless. Life with chronic illness can get too serious. Quality of life is not just about being wise and conserving energy. Sometimes it is about spending all your spoons on something really worthwhile. That's what I do in worship ministry. But those are exceptions. Because I require extraordinary self-care afterwards.

So most days:

- I limit multitasking. When I multitask, the quality of my work suffers. If I am interrupted, I put down what I am doing.
- I triage constantly, ensuring I spend my precious spoons on what is most important.
- When undertaking a lengthy task, I take proper breaks in the middle. I do not work during what is supposed to be a break.
- I go outside. Getting outside the four walls helps.
- I allocate time to recuperate. It takes me longer than others to recover. There is nothing I can do to speed that up.
- My smoking colleagues take 'smokos'. As a non-smoker, I'm entitled to the same breaks, so I take 'smoko time'. I take a minute to stare out the window, grab a cuppa or stand in the sun.
- I remind myself no one is going to die if I take an extra minute.

Unless there is a genuine crisis—and they do happen, but not often—a short delay is not going to hurt anyone. It's OK to breathe, check in, digest, switch between tasks, allow my tired body to rest a little longer. It's not about dodging work. It's pacing. It means I will last the whole day.

- I choose how many medical appointments to slot into one week. I may have little control over my illness, but I retain control over my diary. Most appointments can wait.

Giving myself permission is key. If my brain is cluttered with 'Shoulds'—'I *should* get this done faster'—my pacing goes out the window. We are constantly invited into Shoulding. I see inspirational quotes on social media all the time: 'Live life to the full', 'Take hold of your dreams' and '*Carpe Diem*'. For some of us, these are unattainable. If I believe the Shoulds, I feel useless, lazy, demoralised, in every way inferior to society. But if I acknowledge my limitations it softens the guilt and pressure of Shoulds. Perhaps a more helpful Should is, 'I should pay attention to what my body is telling me.'

> I should pay attention to what my body is telling me.

It can be difficult for others to understand let alone respect our pacing. Well, I am tired of being judged for supposedly achieving less than anyone else. Our achievements just look different: getting out of bed, sending an email or being assertive with a doctor is just as significant as nailing a promotion or showing up to work.

We can let people know we are working with limited fuel. It might help them understand that while the spirit is willing, the flesh is profoundly uncooperative:

'I'm not 100%.'

'I'm not firing on all cylinders.'

'I'm operating at half speed.'

'My thoughts are half-formed right now.'

'I'm not quite myself.'

'This is taking longer than I originally planned.'

'I will get this to you, but later.'

'I'm a bit distracted/preoccupied.'

'I'm not all here!'

Communicating my limits allows others to be understanding. It means I don't have to 'fake good'. And often when they understand I am unwell, they offer to help.

Rest

Could rest be an act of defiance?

In Josh Garrels' song, *The Resistance*, he describes rest as a weapon against oppression and social control. He's right. Rest is distinctly countercultural in a society that values busyness, usefulness and productivity. In the eyes of society rest appears to produce nothing therefore has no value. We, however, know different. Holidays are socially reinforced: when we get tired or burned out, it is common for us to say, 'I need a holiday.' But do we have to wait for the yearly holiday before we rest?

> Rest is distinctly countercultural in a society that values busyness, usefulness and productivity.

Rest is not only delightful, it is vital. Without rest we do not survive. I'm not just talking about sleep, although sleep is certainly crucial. Rest is more than sleep. Rest encompasses all domains: physical, mental, emotional, social, spiritual. Is it any wonder we desire to 'switch off' at the end of the day? Is it surprising we need alone time after being around others? What about the relief we feel when gathering with God's family, or pausing to pray? Our minds and souls crave rest, just like our bodies. In fact, sleep can be seen as the perfect metaphor for other resting needs.

There is a concept amongst spoonies known as radical resting,[70] also called 'aggressively resting'. I think of it as preemptive resting. It is the conscious rest prior to doing something demanding, like doing nothing the day before I serve on the worship team. That is radical rest.

Rest is, unfortunately, not always restful for spoonies. We can rest but not feel rested. We can sleep but not feel refreshed. Sometimes this is because pain and other symptoms make it hard to relax. But often it is simply about our bodies' incapacity to recharge, like a worn-out battery. It feels like permanent low-power mode, sleep deprivation or jetlag—even after nine or ten hours' sleep. In spite of this, rest is essential. Because rest, while not always refreshing, prevents us from getting worse. And it is still countercultural. Even in the church.

If this resonates with you, feel free to engage in defiant resting. The idea of defiance might even spark something for you. Rest resists the temptation to find our identity in *doing* rather than *being*—something I can get better at.

> Even for God, who is immortal and eternal and has no need for sleep, rest is part of his rhythm.

Resting is something the Father does. When I rest, I am joining with the

Father's habits. The Father rested after creating the universe. Jesus took times of rest and retreat from the world. God has modelled a lifestyle characterised by both work and refreshment. Even for God, who is immortal and eternal and has no need for sleep, rest is part of his rhythm. That says something.

Psalm 61:3 says, 'You've always given me breathing room, a place to get away from it all...' (MSG) Not only does God want us to rest, he wants to *be* our rest. Psalm 62:2 echoes this: 'He's solid rock under my feet, breathing room for my soul...' Psalm 32:7: 'God's my island hideaway, keeps danger far from the shore, throws garlands of hosannas around my neck.' God invites us to retreat and rest in him. Matthew 11:28-29 (NIV):

> Come to me, all you who are weary and burdened,
> and I will give you rest. Take my yoke upon you
> and learn from me, for I am gentle and humble in
> heart, and you will find rest for your souls.

Good news indeed.

Rest is part of our relationship with God. The next time you have big plans, consider 'radically resting'.

Gratitude

There is a myth about gratitude. It says, 'Gratitude will fix all your problems. Ergo, if you are facing difficulty, you simply need more gratitude.'

Eeeep! Wrong! We will face difficulty no matter our level of gratitude.

Counsellors have recommended the whole gratitude thing to

me. 'Have you tried keeping a gratitude journal?' they probed. I groaned internally. Here we go.

No, I don't keep a gratitude journal.

Yes, I practise gratitude on a daily basis.

Yes, I still suffer with chronic illness despite my gratitude.

I will experience pain. I will hit walls of exhaustion. I will have flares and relapses and hospitalisations. All while experiencing a deep and abiding thankfulness. They coexist. Gratitude, while no panacea, does help though. It keeps me focused on what I have, rather than what I have lost. It reminds me of things I am looking forward to. It gives me enormous appreciation for what is good. It prompts me to thank those who support me. Gratitude can shift our perspective.

> Gratitude, while no panacea, does help though.

Brené Brown found the biggest factor in our day-to-day joy is gratitude.[71] Gratitude is not only good for our wellbeing, it helps us face anxiety-provoking and vulnerable-making situations. I try to practise gratitude, even or especially on bad days. After I have ugly-cried on someone's shoulder and covered them in snot and saltwater tears (it's called ugly for a reason), it helps to say, 'Thank you.' I appreciate their presence. Even if it was uncomfortable for them, and even if they couldn't fix my problem, it helped to have someone there. I tell them so.

Gratitude helps with God as well. There are times when I ugly-cry to him. Sometimes his meaningful silence infuriates me. There are moments of immense frustration when I just want to be healed already. But he is there. He is with me. He will never, ever leave me.

I know it, down in my bones. So after I have spilled my guts and sat in silence for a while, I tell him, 'Thank you.' It matters he still cares. It matters he stays up with me at midnight while the world sleeps. It matters he loves me unconditionally, even when I complain about not being healed. I am so glad he can handle my complaining.

Gratitude grounds me. After a bad day, I make space to remember the good bits from my day. It might only be fleeting. It might be a silent 'Thank you'. But the silent and fleeting moments matter.

'OK, today was hard, but I'm doing better than last week.'

'I may be out of sick leave—again—but my workplace is supportive.'

'I don't want to be in hospital, but on the plus side, this is the shortest hospital queue I have ever seen.'

'Thank God for friends who pray for me.'

I once complained of my legitimate struggles with going to work sick to a specialist who commented, 'How wonderful to have a job you love so much when you feel so bad!' I stopped mid-complaint. He was completely right. It threw my distress into sharp relief. It brought gratitude swiftly into focus. It has stayed with me.

Resilience

In the movie, *The Man from Snowy River*, there's a memorable scene where the horse-riding protagonist is thrown off a horse. His friend later urges him to get back on again. That is the perfect picture of resilience. Resilience is recovery muscle, built up by challenging and stressful experiences that force us to dig deep. Resilience does not mean we never get thrown by the horse. Resilience is about how we get back on afterwards.

So how is your resilience muscle?

Resilience, like gratitude, takes practice. None of us are born resilient. We develop it over years and still get knocked sideways. Resilience doesn't make us immune to difficulty. But it sure does help with bouncing back.

Everyone has bad days. On those days, resilience is not about smiling and faking it. It is about looking our monsters in the face and finding a thread of hope to cling to. That's real strength. Like a war wound, resilience tells stories of where we have been.

Unfortunately, in mental health services and other circles, 'resilience' can be used in a blaming way, AKA 'If you were more resilient, you wouldn't be struggling.' As though our problems would be more manageable if we could acquire this superpower from the resilience store.

Wrong!

There are extremely resilient people who feel like giving up. They have bad days of blinding pain and utter darkness. Their resilience is not based on mood. You can be in a rotten mood and still demonstrate resilience; good news for some of us! Resilience is how we recover more quickly than before. It's about progress. If you handle things slightly better than how you used to handle them—if you still react but your reactions are less intense and do not last as long—if you felt hopeless before but now you have a tiny sliver of hope—that's resilience.

I'm going to take a leap of faith here. The fact you are reading this book proves how resilient you are.

Before you toss this book across the room, hear me out. You

have waded through massive piles of mud and pulled yourself out of quicksand. You have been to hell and back with your illness. Maybe you have had some real scares. Maybe you have faced death or wanted to die. The fact you are here is a *huge* deal.

> The fact you are here is a huge deal.

Illness is a destroyer of lives and relationships. But you are still breathing. That's proof of your capacity to survive. Your body could have cashed it in, but it hasn't. It has carried you this far. As of today, you have come further than you ever have before. Our bodies, for all their flaws and foibles, are resilient.

Recognise those hard years. Acknowledge your survival. You have been through epic battles, my friend, and you are still here. That tells me something about you.

Bookmark this page. On your next bad day, remind yourself how far you have come. Tell yourself you can do hard things. Because you have. You are living proof.

Beauty

There is a lake near my house surrounded by trees and reeds and walkways. It has a bridge so you can walk over the water and watch the swallows diving. Fish and eels swim and ducks paddle calmly atop the water. Water birds teach their fluffy black chicks how to pull out the reeds for food. A pandemonium of parrots sings their unique songs. Ducks wash and nest along the shore. They emerge at dusk to feast on the insects congregating on the water's surface. There is a kids' playground nearby and a dog park. Most evenings people walk the loop around the lake, letting their dogs loose, jogging across the bridge or watching their kids run around.

The children take bikes and scooters and ride around for hours.

There is something about the sight of the lake, the rituals of the birds and the hollering of kids that does something for me. It's getting out of the house, especially after working from home. It's fresh air. It's physical movement, no doubt. (I hate exercise. But I must confess walking by the lake does feel good.) It's hearing human beings connecting with a simple 'Evening'. It's communing with birds and plants and living water.

We know from Chapter 9 that nature has tremendous healing capabilities. Personally, I feel a bit more human, more myself, in nature. It doesn't have to be the lake; It can be bushland, botanical gardens, the strip of green grass in my backyard. There is something beautiful, nurturing and sacred about nature. I don't want to over-spiritualise this, but I often meet God in nature. Sometimes the rhythm of prayer flows more effortlessly when I am walking among trees. I don't know what it is. I don't need to understand it. I only know it does me good.

Perhaps you have a 'beauty spot' that is special to you. Perhaps you like to frolic in the country among the cows. Perhaps you prefer the rustic beauty of camping. Perhaps it is the pungent saltiness of the beach that appeals to you. Think about the green and blue spaces in your world. Are there any special spots? Are there places where you feel inexplicably more yourself? Do you feel calmer, more awake, more alive? They might be good for your sanity.

Beauty can also be in sounds, smells, tastes and textures. For example, there are sensory gardens where you can touch herbs and smell them on your fingertips. I personally find staggering beauty in the strength and power of a storm. I can think of almost nothing better than standing on the front porch and watching a mighty storm roll overhead, lightning streaking across the sky as the wind howls and the rain pummels the earth. My skin shivers with every roll and clap of thunder, and I am awed into silent wonder. You can almost hear the earth sigh as it drinks in the moisture. The omnipotence of my illness doesn't have anything on storms.

When we are overawed by illness, let's be overawed by beauty too. I find beauty in the coziness of my cat sleeping, the sweet surprise of birdsong, the tenacity of garden weeds that simply won't die, the vintage colours of an op shop, the delicate curl of chocolate, balmy summer evenings when the whole world seems to take a breath. I find beauty in original songs, unusual movies and uplifting poems, like *If—* by Rudyard Kipling, *The Summer Day* by Mary Oliver, *The Thing Is* by Ellen Bass, *Resilience* by Jessica Kantrowitz and *Caged Bird* by Maya Angelou.

It's more than gratitude. It's ushering awe and wonder into our world. It's exoticising the domestic. It's refreshment for the soul.

> When we are overawed by illness, let's be overawed by beauty too.

Soft yet strong

Consider the woolly bush. This Australian native tree loves difficult climates and soils. I have a woolly bush in my front yard, and besides flooding, it seems able to cope with whatever the weather throws at it. The woolly bush differs from other Australian natives in an important respect: it does not respond to difficulty by developing defence mechanisms as other trees do, such as with spiky leaves or insect-repelling enzymes. The leaves of the woolly bush are marked by a curious softness. When woolly bushes are doing well, they sprout tiny bright red flowers at the utmost tips of their upward-reaching branches.

From an evolutionary perspective, this is unusual. Most plants and animals go on the offensive to survive. It's an instinctive response to threat and danger. But the woolly bush maintains its softness and beauty, while its taproot drives into the earth, strong and sure. I aspire to be soft yet strong like the woolly bush.

Chronic illness can change us. We can become bitter, angry, irritable, defensive—prickly. There's nothing inherently wrong with that. But it can twist and warp our true selves until we are no longer recognisable. I have prickly days. When illness flares out of control, it can be hard to keep one's softness. I zigzag in and out of prickliness.

But I want to be someone who returns to that home base of soft-yet-strong; not the fake-it-till-you-make-it kind of strong, but the genuine bravery of saying, 'Maybe I'll try getting out of bed today' or 'Maybe I'll call in sick' (that's courage) or 'Maybe God will help me'. I want the strength of being present with others, giving when I am exhausted and afraid I'll run out, telling someone when I am suicidal. It's a reclamation of the word bravery that isn't about toughing it out but giving up my fronts and being messy and not-all-there. It's about honesty, bouncing back to my true self.

> It's a reclamation of the word bravery that isn't about toughing it out but giving up my fronts and being messy and not-all-there.

Illness has already taken so much from me. I don't want it to take my disposition, personality and sense of joy too. Soft-yet-strong is something I can choose.

The dance of frustration

In 2018 a facebook video[72] captured a bad traffic jam. Cars stretched as far as the eye could see. One man got so frustrated he got out of his car. And started dancing in the street. In full view of a long line of cars and a woman with a phone camera, he wove up and down the road in a dance of frustration.

I would never have thought of that. But I love it.

Chronic illness is filled with frustration. It's part of the package deal. So I propose we dance. OK, some of our bodies will not let us do that. We might have to visualise the dance. But when the body permits, let's channel that frustration into a good ol' fashioned boogie.

It doesn't have to be public, like the traffic jam. You can be a closet dancer. Me, I'm a car dancer. I turn the music up *loud* and sing my heart out. I dance at traffic lights. I dance for joy. I dance for stress release. I dance for frustration and loss and rage bubbling just beneath the surface. And I don't care who sees me!

Dance is versatile. You can dance a dance of celebration, a dance of romance, a dance of grief. Dance can be moving, literally and figuratively. I'm no dancer—a frustrated dancer perhaps—but my body feels good when I try. There is something healing about movement. Why do we rock or sway when we're upset? Why do babies respond to the rhythm of a rocking cradle? Why is walking or exercising so grounding for us? Our bodies were made to move.

Yes, some days movement is limited. Sometimes pain overrules our mobility. Sometimes the fatigue is just too much. I understand how that feels. I also know how much better I feel when I put on a song, sit on the couch and dance with my hands. Swaying, jumping up and down, hand-dancing—all are valid forms of expression.

Dance that dance of frustration.

My body still breathes

It's a wonder I'm not dead yet. Seriously, how are some of us still alive?

I've had heart episodes, tumour scares, cancer scares, risks of blood clots. I've struggled to breathe. I've had a fracture falling from a standing height. I've had mental distress where I was on the cusp of losing my mind. I've fantasised about dying and ending it all. So how am I still here? How are *you* still here?

Even though there are times when I hate my body and feel thoroughly betrayed by it (apparently my relationship with my body needs work), it has carried me this far. Not well, true, but carried me nonetheless. I appreciate that, and in that sense I am still fearfully and wonderfully made. It has tried to warn me—albeit not always effectively—when something was wrong. It has done its best to look after me. Like a car, it has driven me from point A to point B, even though the suspension was shot and the ride was terrible. Like the Tardis from *Doctor Who*, it has not always taken me where I wanted to go but where I needed to be. I'm still here.

I'm not suggesting we should be grateful for being alive. For some of us, being alive with unending pain is worse than death itself. I'm simply noticing how remarkable it is that our bodies keep going. My body is still breathing.

When I had pericarditis, I couldn't breathe. Yet my body managed to take in enough air to keep me alive. I have had breathing complications that kept me housebound for months, left without answers or treatment and no end in sight, unable to talk or sing or walk for any decent length of time. Yet my body kept doing the breathing thing—even if it struggled to do so. I once fainted in public; when I came to, I couldn't move, so I just lay there and breathed. Air never tasted so good. I have had panic attacks where I struggled to breathe. I have lost the capacity to think clearly, to know my own mind, to stay in control of anxiety. Yet my body kept on breathing. I am still breathing today.

My body gets a lot of things wrong. But it gets the breathing thing right. Which is kind of important. It could have misread the breathing thing too. But it hasn't. With everything else going wrong, my body has kept me alive on this planet. I suppose I should (grudgingly) thank it for that.

Lately, I have developed a new nighttime habit of stillness inspired by Julia Baird's book, *Phosphorescence*, in the chapter entitled, 'Why we need silence'. It awakened a craving in me for silence and stillness. So I'm giving in to that craving. Before I sleep, I put all thoughts and music out of my mind and lie still, just listening. I listen to the crickets outside. I listen to the light fall of rain. I listen to the whispers of the Spirit. I feel my body breathing. I notice the gentle movement. I don't have to work on breathing; my body does it for me. It is effortless, natural, a gift. I know instinctively this will continue through the night while I sleep. Without me doing a thing, my body still breathes. It is a reminder of my body's capacity to take care of me.

> It is a reminder of my body's capacity to take care of me.

I have since learned this is a kind of 'centring prayer' that focuses on the body, on presence, on silence, rather than words. I didn't even know this was a thing. I just started doing it intuitively. Perhaps my body knew I needed it. Jessica Kantrowitz describes it thusly:

> It is a simple way of praying that does not involve speaking, but simply sitting in God's presence. You choose a word or phrase to help you focus, something simple like 'peace' or 'Jesus.' Then, sitting comfortably, you close your eyes, and say the word as you breathe. If you notice your attention wandering, you just gently bring it back.[73]

The word I use is 'stillness'. It helps me listen. It absolves me of the obligation to speak. It gives me permission to truly rest.

While I believe in the power of praying and complaining, I am coming to believe in the power of silence. When I lie down I imagine my pillow is God's chest, and I sink into it. I breathe. Sometimes I get the oddly comforting sensation of being gently rocked like a boat in a harbour. I bob on the water, free to drift, yet securely anchored. There are no wild waves to contend with, no stormy seas, no impending shipwreck. The Spirit reminds me, without words, that he is here. He is in the rocking, he is in the floating, he is the anchor. He stays with me until I drift to sleep. There is nothing quite like the sensation of 'bobbing' with God and not needing anything, knowing he needs nothing from me—just this moment.

Hope is in the breath.

Hope is in the breath. Despite brushes with death and death wishes, I am alive. I am still breathing. And each day I am alive is a chance to try again.

Glimpses of grace

Occasionally, glimpses of grace appear unbidden and intrude upon my misery. These are the weirdest, most surprising moments when I believe all is lost and want to give up, and something beautiful lands on my doorstep. Those startling moments—glimpses of grace—reconnect me with God in ways no prayer or scripture or worship song can.

These golden moments are more than silver linings, more than gratitude or resilience. They are, in fact, nothing to do with me. They are a pure gift, knocking me off my feet. They have shocked me into taking heart when I meant to sink into despair. They have ambushed me with delight.

It is worth dwelling on these glimpses a little longer, so we'll do that in the next chapter. We'll look at times when God has graced us with sheer kindness. We'll talk about how illness affects our faith, and how we hold on to it (faith, that is) despite the odds. Then we'll come back to grace; always to grace.

There's no take-home self-help tip here, except that good things can still happen. Even when our worlds are collapsing and our wells of optimism have run dry, strange and beautiful and unexpected things can happen.

Take heart.

Take a moment to notice how you are feeling after the chapter, and whether anything stood out for you or resonated with you. Time for some self-care.

*Amongst the forest rockery, I stumble upon
a huge boulder. It is bleeding down one side.
I don't know how a boulder can bleed,
but this one is.*

*I take a closer look. I feel an ache inside my
chest and tears well in my eyes. I stretch my arms
around the boulder, as far as they will reach, and
embrace it. I wrap my arms around the pain, around
the bleeding. I can feel the pain inside me.*

*Then God comes, wraps his arms around me,
swaddling me and my pain together. The pain
does not disappear; God envelopes all of it.
And he gently rocks me as I weep.*

12

FAITH

Ambushed by Kindness

I freaked out about writing this chapter.

What on earth do I know about faith?

How can I give advice when I am struggling daily to survive?

What insights can I offer when I still fall into despair and rage and wrestling with God?

I didn't know what to do. So I did the only thing I could think of. I took my imposter syndrome to God. 'God,' I groaned, 'I'm still in the middle of my illness mess. Why am I writing this? I don't have any solutions!'

I think I heard God snort. 'Thank goodness for that,' he replied. 'If you don't have the answers, you won't try to give them. Maybe just concentrate on asking the hard questions.'

A weight lifted. 'Yes, God,' I exhaled. 'Ask questions. I can do that!'

Therefore, no answers are forthcoming in this chapter. You may be disappointed. I know I am. But many of us have received pat answers in the past and found them profoundly unsatisfying. I know I have. Ten-step formulas tend to fall short. Heaven help me, I will not do that to you.

Instead, we are going to wrestle with hard questions and heavenly mysteries. I will share what I have with you, and hopefully it will help. Who knows? Together, we might find something valuable.

A glimpse of grace

I woke up from yet another night of bad sleep. I felt miserable. My head pounded, my stomach lurched, the room span dizzyingly around me. Every joint in my body ached. My glands felt swollen and I was too weak to stand. It felt like a bad flu. Without the actual flu.

I got up and did a few things—shower, breakfast—and returned to bed. Then I tried again, had lunch, tried to do a few things; and promptly returned to bed. As I lay there, useless, music began to form in my mind. I could hear chords playing over and over. That's nice, I thought. The music persisted. Then I got an idea for a theme for a song. Rest time was over.

Twenty minutes later, I had a song called *Hanging on to Jesus*. Because that's what I'm doing. No matter how bad I feel or what state my body is in, I am hanging on to Jesus. I wasn't looking for a song. I certainly had no creative ambitions when I retreated to bed. I was not praying or feeling especially spiritual. The song was a pure gift.

This glimpse of grace was unbidden and undeserved. I had done nothing to earn it. If anything, it was precisely the opposite: I was incapable of doing anything. God dropped a new song in my lap, just because he wanted to. He must like me or something. Such glimpses of grace are like a kiss on the forehead from my Father. It is like receiving a bunch of flowers 'just because'. It's pure kindness.

> Such glimpses of grace are like a kiss on the forehead from my Father.

God seems to be in the business of kindness. It's easy to forget that when illness is so cruel. But my being sick doesn't negate God's true character. As a perfectionist, I sometimes lose sight of God's kind nature and focus instead on beating myself up. (Maybe someday I'll write a book about surviving perfectionism.) Perfectionism is driven, whereas kindness just *is*. Kindness is a fruit of the Spirit, a sign of his residence in us, one of God's defining qualities.

I have seen God's kindness in hospital rooms and doctor's surgeries, watching other sick people being cared for by loved ones. Once a fellow patient even advocated for me in hospital—a complete stranger! Some of my most powerful encounters with God have been through other peoples' acts of kindness. God does not always heal us. But he is kind toward us, kinder than we think, kinder than we dare believe.

I was once disabled by illness with the threat of job and career loss looming. I lamented: what will become of me? What will I do with myself, with my life, if I lose everything? The very next day, a friend reached out and invited me to participate in a once-in-a-lifetime writing project. It brought tears to my eyes. God heard. God knew.

Glimpses of grace may be fleeting and easily forgotten, but they are also easily remembered, like a childhood photograph.

The upside-down kingdom

The last will be first. (Matthew 20:16)

Blessed are the poor in spirit. (Matthew 5:3)

Count it all joy when you suffer various trials. (James 1:2)

God often acts in surprising, unexpected and upside-down ways. This is true of suffering. You would think a loving God would stop pain and heal disease. But while God sometimes does, he often allows us to walk through them too. Isn't this the antithesis of a loving God? Well, no. Suffering is a part of being alive. For some reason, when we follow Christ, some of us suffer *more* instead of *less*.

> For some reason, when we follow Christ, some of us suffer more instead of less.

We take up our cross.

We follow the narrow path.

We lose our life so that, hopefully, we might find it.

We die to self, literally and spiritually.

God's upside-down kingdom means suffering is an honour, not a reproach. It is the Spirit working in us, stripping ourselves away until our true selves—and God in us—are revealed. I don't mean we should pursue unnecessary suffering, like self-flagellation or anything. But when suffering comes, maybe it's a compliment. When God allows pain in my life, maybe God is saying, 'I can trust Steph with this.'

If I can take the liberty of paraphrasing the opening story of Job:

God boasted about Job to Satan, saying proudly, 'Check out this guy! I love him like crazy!' Satan scoffed, saying, 'Um, no. He only serves you coz of all the blessings you've bribed him with. I can prove it.' God snorted. 'Go right ahead! He's got my complete confidence!' (Job 1:6-12 Steph's Contemporary Paraphrase)

I do not know if God actually snorts or if the story is literal or allegorical. I do not know if God goes around deliberately 'testing' people, as some Christians suppose. I do not think God gets any joy from our suffering. But boy, he loves it when we keep loving him, even in hardship.

A Christian friend of a friend of mine was arrested in China and thrown into prison without trial. She was doing fourteen hours of hard labour every day. My friend wrote her encouraging letters and prayed for her to be released. Her response astounded my friend—and me. She told him not to pray for her deliverance, because revival had broken out in the prison. She asked him to pray for strength to continue God's work.

Jaw drop

In a similar vein, pastors in China are apparently expected to serve three years in prison before they can become a leader. They consider it a crucial part of their pastoral training and spiritual maturity. In fact, they don't trust anyone who has not undergone significant suffering![74] We have this whole suffering thing upside down.

Paul asked God to remove his 'thorn' of suffering. God's answer? 'My grace is sufficient for you, for my power is made perfect in weakness.' (2 Corinthians 12:9) We might expect a loving God to remove Paul's torment, but he did the opposite: he left Paul in it. But he also provided grace, giving his own power for Paul's endurance. Upside down.

Jesus is our ultimate example. Not only did he endure the most horrific death imaginable, he went willingly. Well, 'willingly' might be a bit of a stretch, given how many times he begged for the cup, the impending crucifixion, to be taken away. God did not answer Jesus' prayer either. Jesus did not get what he asked for. But in the end, he surrendered. 'Not my will, but yours...' (Luke 22:39-42) That's true courage.

We don't want to suffer. We want this 'cup' taken away. And there's nothing wrong with that. Asking for deliverance does not make us bad Christians, or Jesus would be the worst 'Christian' of all. It is miraculous we can find a microbe of faith that says, 'Lord, not my will, but yours.' Courage is not never feeling afraid. It's trying to follow God in spite of it. As Mary Anne Radmacher says,

> Courage is not never feeling afraid. It's trying to follow God in spite of it.

> Courage doesn't always roar. Sometimes courage is the quiet voice at the end of the day saying, 'I will try again tomorrow.'[75]

Real courage includes fear, distress and vulnerability. Jesus, our example, prayed in anguish, repeatedly asking his disciples for support, sweated as heavily as one bleeds, and needed angels to strengthen him. And he surrendered. Real courage.

This is our King and his upside-down kingdom. Jesus was rejected, ridiculed, publicly shamed and finally crucified. The world did not recognise his kingship. They thought his suffering meant God had abandoned him.

In this paradoxical kingdom, what does it mean to take up our cross? For many of us, it means suffering rather than #bestlife. Maybe our cross is pain-shaped. Maybe isolation-shaped. If you're reading this book, illness is likely one of your crosses. Maybe mental distress is part of your cross. Jesus knows about carrying a cross. He wants to enter into your pain, your unique cross. Invite him into that painful, tender place. Let him care for you.

I am no walking advert for victorious living. I will never climb to the top of any spiritual mountain. My wounds are too profound. I may drag myself up to a little ledge where I can perch and encourage others who may join me there, similarly wounded. Perhaps I can help them catch their breath.

Following Jesus can mean non-stop cross-carrying where it can feel easier to die than to stay alive. Perhaps you know more about carrying a cross than most Christians. But suffering might be an honour, a compliment, a privilege in God's kingdom, not the other way around. Sometimes, as C.S. Lewis says, our reward for doing a good deed is being given something even harder and better to do.[76]

Jesus ultimately overcame the cross. Resurrected from the dead, he holds our ultimate hope. These hurting bodies and anguished souls we possess will one day see a resurrection of their own. On that day, we might see our suffering reflected in the jewels in our crowns.

> On that day, we might see our suffering reflected in the jewels in our crowns.

Sitting with mystery

Mystery is at the very heart of chronic illness—and faith.

My chronic illness is mysterious. 'Will I have another episode?' 'If I go out today, will it backfire?' 'If I stretch this way, will my back go into spasms again?' (This happens more often than I care to calculate.)

As I type this, I am in the middle of a highly mysterious flare. I am having trouble breathing on exertion. This makes walking, talking, singing—in fact, everything—difficult. At its worst, it feels like my airway is closing off and I can hardly breathe. It was triggered by a boring cold, not even COVID-19. I have been completely disabled by this, off work for over five months. This has never happened before.

Test results are normal. My heart rate is skyrocketing but no one can tell me why. The cardiologists do not think it is cardiac. The pulmonologists do not think it is respiratory. The immunologist does not think it is autoimmune. I have sought second and third opinions to no avail. It looks like Long Covid (gives me special empathy for those living with Long Covid) but it's not. There is no diagnosis and no treatment plan.

The great chameleon strikes again.

I am highly vulnerable. I am immunocompromised, meaning I catch every cold and flu going around. This effectively means I am sick with a fresh cold or flu almost every week. Every virus retriggers the severe breathing difficulties. I am exhausted. Without diagnosis, there is no end in sight.

Mystery makes me achingly vulnerable. I have wrestled with it for five months. I even wrestled with whether to share this with you. This story, as it currently stands, has no conclusion. How helpful is it to share a half-story, a half-testimony, when I know God is still good but there is no end? Is it helpful to share my stuckness and despair with you? Does it make your skin crawl, as it does mine? Does it resonate with you, or send you running for the hills? Does it reach out to you like a caring hand, letting you know you are not alone? Does it sing to you of hope, of God's goodness, of a better tomorrow?

I have wrestled with fear. I have confronted the terror of being permanently disabled, the horror of being medically retired in my early forties. I have faced my inability to prove myself, to people-please, to be perfect. I cannot meet anyone's approval, not even my own.

I have discovered, as perhaps you have, that there really are monsters under the bed, and they can take physical form and haunt your days and nights. My monster's name is Terror and he feeds on every cold, flu and flare. He only gets stronger with time and his grip tightens with every new health problem. I reach out for help, but no one can help me. I feel like I am calling the ambulance over and over but it never arrives. I am Terror's captive.

Despite this sensation of prison walls closing in, there is something sneaky and subtle here in the prison cell too: the promise of liberation. I am slowly, slowly, disentangling myself from others' expectations, from perfectionism, from even my own approval. Maybe God will use this for my emancipation.

God is with me in this prison cell. He is frustratingly silent at the moment, but he is undeniably here. He is present, attentively, compassionately, even if he does not answer my questions. I am discovering, like Frederick Buechner,

> I am discovering, like Frederick Buechner, that God does not always give us answers; he gives us himself.

that God does not always give us answers; he gives us himself.[77]

While God has been sitting in silence with me, he has been speaking to my friends about me, showing them visions, prompting them to pray for me. God has been speaking all along—just not directly to me. I forgot how much he works behind the scenes.

When doctors cannot give me answers—again—I come up against this mystery. It is the final frontier, the bit where we boldly (or not) go where we have never gone before. Mystery is both frustrating and freeing. Sure, it would be great to get answers. It would be great to have a plan for this flare, something more effective than 'Keep an eye on it'. But it also means I am fearfully and wonderfully made in ways only God understands. Doctors do not know me as completely as my Father.

Healing is uncertain. Answers are uncertain. Protection from harm is uncertain—we know that firsthand. We wrestle with uncertainty, resisting it, trying to provide certainty where there is none. 'God will look after you.' 'God will protect you.' 'God will not deny you.' How can anyone know that? No one can make promises on God's behalf, no matter how well-meaning. False promises can breed false hope, which can be even more harmful when God 'fails' to deliver on said promises.

I don't know if God will ever take lupus from me. I don't know if I'm destined to live with increasingly debilitating pain. I don't know if this current episode of breathlessness will get better. I'm asking God to either heal me or help me endure. Part of that is entering the mystery of not knowing, trusting him no matter the outcome. Isn't that the core of faith? To believe even though we cannot see?

Maybe not being able to see is the point. Maybe that's a beginning. The older I get, the more I recognise how little I know about God. Strange and terrible and wonderful things can happen when we follow God. Faith doesn't prevent bad things from happening, and it doesn't equate to certainty. Faith means sitting with mystery and following God anyway. It means driving blind. I can relate to that.

I have doubts and questions. I wrestle with God. I zigzag in my faith, now believing wholeheartedly, now quivering with fear, now worshiping God in reverence, now complaining bitterly. My faith legs are weak and shaky and sometimes require crutches. But there's a little room in my heart where the eight-year-old me whispers, 'Daddy, help me.' That's faith: trusting God when we have every reason not to.

> That's faith: trusting God when we have every reason not to.

Mystery means waiting. I am in a hurry, wanting to feel better *now*, get healed *now*, get back to normal *now*. That's understandable, especially when I am in pain. God, however, is not in a hurry. He took hundreds of years to rescue the Israelites from Egypt. Between the prophets of the Old Testament and the appearance of Jesus, there was a gap of four hundred years. When Jesus arrived, he didn't show up as a grown man, ready to jump into Saviourdom—he was born a baby and took thirty years to prepare for ministry. God does not live by time pressure.

This puts illness into perspective. While it would be great to find relief from today's symptoms, God takes time to do everything right. His work spans decades, even centuries. He occasionally does things instantly, but his character seems more about patience and gradual work. For some of us that means illness might be here a long time. Healing might be gradual, or never—at least, not in our lifetimes.

Perhaps one day God will reveal these mysteries to us.

Lament

My prayers often begin with, 'Dear God...I'm grieving.' Perhaps yours do too.

We have lost health, bodily functions, autonomy, future plans, identity, friendships, relationships, trust in others, jobs, careers, our sense of usefulness. Some of us have lost our faith or part of it. Being chronically ill is a permanent state of grief.

People try to cheer us up when we grieve. 'At least you're still alive.' Grief becomes disenfranchised and we struggle to grieve.[78] But we can. And we should.

Like mystery, lament can be hard to sit with. The church can struggle with lament. Many church songs focus on the blessings of God, which is right and proper, but what about those Sundays when we're not feeling so blessed? In fact, do we have any songs about lament? Lament is a gift to the church. It is time we made more room for it.

Perhaps we deny lament because we worry about failing God. Lament doesn't look 'victorious'. But denying lament does not make it go away. Only one thing heals grief, and that is grieving. Talking about grief in public spaces like church gives people permission to lament.

> Perhaps lament is a skill. Perhaps we can get better at it. Perhaps God is in our lament.

God is not averse to lament. In

fact, in his kindness, he joins in. Jesus lamented the fate of the cities of Chorazin, Bethsaida and Capernaum (Matthew 11:21-24). In Jeremiah 9:17-20 the Lord calls for the 'wailing women', those who are 'skilful' to mourn over Israel and teach younger women how to lament. (Thanks Marg Mowczko for her eye-opening article on wailing women.[79]) There are other examples of lament: the Psalms are full of loss and despair, the book of Job is a cracker, and have you ever read the book of Lamentations? Perhaps lament is a skill. Perhaps we can get better at it. Perhaps God is in our lament.

To lament is human. Those who live with chronic illness are exceptionally good at it. We eat lament for breakfast. Church, let us share this gift of lament with you. Give us space to remember what has been lost. Allow us to receive support from God's family. Lament is better when shared.

We are one body. If one is grieving, all are affected.

The unusual testimony

In Chapter 4 we saw how God once answered my prayer for healing:

'Your testimony will not be the usual testimony of getting healed. (Awesome.) Most testimonies feature someone who was sick and I heal them. But that is not your testimony. Your testimony will be you got sick, never got healed, and *continued to worship me anyway, even in the heights of illness*.'

His words floored me. I thought my sickness was pointless, futile, unnecessary. I never imagined God might use it to bring him glory. Apparently I can be wrong. Who knew?

Those words rang in my ears for days afterwards. They still

echo every now and again. I share this not because I feel amazingly uplifted by it—I don't—but because it might resonate with those who have not been healed and might never be healed.

Not being healed doesn't mean God doesn't care.

Not being healed doesn't mean God is not answering your prayers.

Not being healed doesn't mean your life is pointless.

Not being healed doesn't mean God can't show his glory through you.

Grrr, I hate double negatives. OK, let's turn these around. If God chooses not to heal you—my heartfelt sympathies—he still cares about you, he hears your prayers, and he plans to do beautiful things in and through your life. If you are not healed, God can give you an alternative testimony and make his glory shine through you. Even if you never get healed, you might be right on track, exactly where God means you to be.

> Even if you never get healed, you might be right on track, exactly where God means you to be.

It doesn't make chronic illness easier. It doesn't take the pain away. It simply reminds us God is constantly redeeming everything, even terrible suffering. Some redemption is instant, like being saved or miraculously healed on the spot. Other acts of redemption take years to work their way into the fibres of our being.

Think of the mango tree. It takes a long time—up to eight years, I am told—for a mango seed to grow into a tree and bear mangoes. A mango tree is an investment, requiring prolonged love and attention. It's worth it: fresh mangoes are amazing! As opposed to lettuces, which grow like weeds.

Not all of us can be lettuces. Our fruit may take years to materialise. And healing is not the only evidence of the Spirit within us. An absence of healing does not necessarily mean we are missing something. God may yet surprise us with healing, but in the meantime, there is other evidence or 'fruit' of the Spirit's work in us: patience, grit, fortitude, lovingkindness, long-suffering, endurance, gentleness (like the soft woolly bush), delight in the Lord—not in our circumstances, but him.

There is no sickness on the planet that can change God's faithfulness toward us. That's our testimony: not how good life is, but how good God is in the midst of it.

A better way

I wish God would heal me. I wish I did not have to live with illness. I wish I did not have to call on God for his help several times a day (or hour). Life would be much easier if I was simply made well.

However, if I had not grown up with back pain, I would not have learned good posture. Because of scoliosis, I learned stretches that are good for me. I attended Feldenkrais (movement) sessions and learned movement that is natural and good-fitting for my body. I discovered the life-restoring power of swimming. I value the ongoing input of professionals like massage therapists. Massage is good for both body and sanity.

Through joint pain, I have learned the benefits of turmeric and prescribed medication. I have been forced to pace myself, rather than running myself into the ground (or off a cliff). I have hired a cleaner.

Because of chronic fatigue and brain fog, I have learned self-kindness. When the fatigue really hits, there is nothing I can do. It's like having weights attached to every part of my body. There is no 'pushing through'. So I roll with it, even when I would prefer to ignore it and 'soldier on'. I no longer silence my body; I listen. I have been forced to rest, even when inconvenient or downright heartbreaking. I have been forced to trust God to meet me there, even when I was not sure he would. That's my body's wisdom.

> I no longer silence my body; I listen.

Remember the Enduring Somatic Threat from Chapter 6? I think I have acquired a kind of Enduring Somatic Wisdom. My body has gained wisdom and knowledge about itself over the years, and I am benefitting from that wisdom. It gives me intel about the illness and such knowledge is invaluable.

I have learned to be more assertive with others and my inner Perfectionist. I have learned, in some ways, to be selfish and put my body first instead of a thousand 'Shoulds'. My inner Perfectionist has mellowed as a result.

Living with a wildcard chameleon has been insanity-making. Because it is so mind-bendingly random, it has forced me to adapt at a moment's notice. I have learned in-situ flexibility, a mighty task for someone who prefers predictability. I have also stepped out of my people-pleasing persona because I simply cannot do all the things I and others expect of me.

It has forced me to accept help and smash that idol of independence. Perhaps that is a gift of emancipation from God. Joni Eareckson Tada, paralysed after a diving accident, once said,

'Maybe God's gift to me is dependence. I will never reach a place of self-sufficiency that crowds God out.'[80]

I have learned about autoimmune disease and medicine. A nurse once said to me, 'You have virtually earned a medical degree, haven't you?' She wasn't far wrong. I have wisdom to pass on to others.

I have dug deep into my professional repertoire for therapeutic ideas. Narrative Therapy has been particularly helpful, especially the idea of externalising illness. By viewing lupus as an external entity, I don't have to hate my body; I can hate lupus and what it does to my body. Me and my body are in this together.

I appreciate any form of wellness or respite that comes my way. I even appreciate the capacity to breathe. Every breath is a gift. And the next. And the next.

I am not claiming these are massive silver linings. I will not pretend illness is a 'gift'. Illness is both a blessing and a curse. The blessings do not outweigh the curse part, nor are they compensation for suffering. But they exist. They are gifts that accompany illness.

The same goes with God. If he had healed me, I would not have learned to find him in the heartache, in doctors' offices, in the throes of agony. I would not have recited the song, *In Christ Alone*, through frank weeping and blinding pain. I would not have clung to him alone in hospital, knowing he was the only one who could accompany me there. I would not have found his companionship in silence, in the absence of words and healing and answers. I would not have learned he was near, moment by unbearable moment, never abandoning me. I would never have learned it was possible to feel all the feels—anger, panic, doubt, despair—and still hang on to Jesus. I would not have realised that experiencing the effects of long-term illness do not make me a bad Christian, turn God off, or make me any less his child.

When we suffer, we join with Christ in his suffering. We become more like him. We are purified like gold, refined, made holy. We are pruned like the rosebush that otherwise fails to thrive. We are like pottery, crafted under his watchful eye with careful hands. Our Father loves us so much he wants to make us more like Jesus. Surely there is no higher honour in God's kingdom.

When Christ suffered, he joined with the whole of humanity in suffering. Our suffering joins us not only with Christ but with the whole of humanity. As Henri Nouwen says, 'Real healing comes from realising that your own particular pain is a share in humanity's pain.'[81] Perhaps illness makes us less alone than we realise.

> Had I been 'rich', I would not have experienced this intimacy with God; I would not have had the need.

Because of illness, I have learned fortitude the hard way (is there any other way?) and have held on to Jesus by my fingernails (which are brittle from autoimmune disease). I have learned the power of patience through gritted teeth and that God is always close to the poor in spirit. Had I been 'rich', I would not have experienced this intimacy with God; I would not have had the need. I can join with Monika Hellwig who says: 'The poor can wait, because they have acquired a kind of dogged patience born of acknowledged dependence.'[82] We know how to depend on God and others.

Some Christians believe God sends us trials to test our faith.

I don't know that God goes around 'testing' us like some kind of bullying authority figure (Miss Trunchbull from *Matilda* springs to mind); rather, trials prove God's faithfulness against all odds, and they prove where our faith really lies. As C.S. Lewis said,

> God has not been trying an experiment on my faith or love in order to find out their quality. He knew it already. It was I who didn't.[83]

I wish there was an easier way to learn this stuff. I wish you and I did not have to live through this suffering. Yet here we are, still breathing, still alive. We have learned about ourselves, illness, medicine, and God's matchless, unbroken companionship. He is with us on our productive days and non-productive ones.

Is illness worth it if it brings us closer to God? If it means we lean more on others, unlearning years of self-reliance? If we develop spiritual endurance? If it makes us more like Christ?

It's not an easy way. But perhaps it is a better way.

Spiritual healing

'God is trustworthy', many Christians say. Before my own trauma (illness-related and others), I would have agreed.

But here's the thing: trauma can crawl inside your soul and shred your most prized beliefs and sense of self. Like acid, it can burn your mind, eating away at your core being. It can affect your relationship with yourself and with God.

Spiritual healing is more than reconciling with God. It is reconciling with our faith. After my first traumatic experience in my twenties, I had to reconcile the fact that faith did not inoculate me against harm. As God and I tentatively reconnected, my trust in myself grew too. That was a big part of my spiritual healing. It took more than three years; trauma and grief are not quickly resolved. Thankfully, God was not in a hurry. God never judged the state of my heart. He redeemed it slowly, letting me know he could be trusted. He proved himself a healer. He was persistent—I knew he would not give up—but he was oh-so-gentle about it. He's got a great bedside manner.

At times, when I thought I was disappointed with God, I was really disappointed with myself: disappointed my faith was not stronger, disappointed at my apparent lack of resilience, disappointed that recovery was taking so long. But God never asked for perfect resilience, never expected superhero strength from me, never called me 'champion'. He called me 'child'. That's all he ever needed from me.

> God never asked for perfect resilience, never expected superhero strength from me, never called me 'champion'. He called me 'child'.

These days, my prayers are unfiltered and totally secure in the knowledge God will never leave me. I have been over the edge. I have rejected him outright. He never once rejected me. That kind of bottomless love boggles my mind. That's why I pray so frankly. That's why I'm so honest. It's not because I'm undisciplined or have no fear of God. Precisely the opposite: I know God is the only safe place.

While we crave the healing of our physical bodies, God craves oneness with us. He longs to bridge the gap that sickness and trauma have created between us like a bomb's crater. He wants you to know he cares about you and will never leave you. He wants us well, but more than that, he wants our souls secure in him, knowing there is nothing on this planet that can separate us from his love: not sickness, pain, running away, loss of faith, sleeplessness, trauma, or grief. There is nothing that can come between us and God. (Romans 8:38-39)

If you need spiritual healing, run to God.

Another in the fire

There's a song, *Another in the Fire* by Hillsong, that references the story of Shadrach, Meshach and Abednego in Daniel 3. These three men refused to bow down to the horrendous golden image of the king, even under threat of death. So the king had them bound and thrown into a furnace.

Lo and behold! They walked around freely in the raging fire, unfettered, and there was a fourth guy in the fire with them. Who was the mysterious fourth man? Well, we are not told, but apparently he looked like 'a son of the gods'. (Daniel 3:25) There was another in the fire.

It seems God was not content to leave his servants alone in the fire. He sent someone—maybe Jesus, maybe an angel—to be a companion in that terrifying place. God didn't quench the fire. He didn't stop the actions of the king. He didn't immediately deliver his servants. But he was with them, right in the middle of it.

> *God is our constant companion in the fire.*

Chronic illness feels like a fiery furnace. It's devastating, physically and mentally. It's all-consuming. There's the constant threat of death or harm. There's pain—which at times feels literally like fire. God is our constant companion in the fire. This truth is echoed in Isaiah 43:2: 'When you walk through the fire, you will not be burned; the flames will not set you ablaze.'

In every dark situation of my life, God has been there. He has never left me to my own devices. I have sometimes thought, in the silence, he might have stepped out for a quick breather. But even though he was quiet, he never left.

He's the friend who sits beside me on the kerbside, watching my life go down the gutter, his arm around my shoulder.

He sits beside me in hospital wards.

He's the nurse who changes my dressings, caring for my wounds.

He holds my hand for hours after we exhaust our words, his presence comfortable and familiar like an old winter blanket.

He's the light in the darkness, and the darkness yields to him.

He's the silent communer, reassuring me without a sound.

He's the only one who can be there for us.

I once had an experience where I felt like an angel had sat down beside me. (I'm not a big angel-seeking type, and I've never seen an angel, which made this experience all the more memorable.) I had lain down for the night, eyes closed, feeling like crap. I needed relief. I prayed something super profound like, 'God—help.'

As I lay there facing the wall, an image came to mind of an angel walking in and sitting on the floor against the wall, facing me. He didn't say anything. He just sat there. At first I thought it was the beginning of sleep seeping in. *It's a dream*. But the image persisted. The angel sat, calm yet alert, as though taking first watch. I didn't open my eyes, so I have no idea if it was a physical thing. But the image stayed with me as I slipped into the streams of dreaming. Whether it was real or a figment of my active imagination, it was a gift that night.

God can be present in ways no one else can. Friends and family can't always help. Spouses and carers can get sick themselves or be unavailable. But God is always with us, attentive, caring, watchful. Even when we feel alone, we are never alone.

I aspire to be like Shadrach, Meshach and Abednego, right before the king threw them into the furnace:

> If we are thrown into the blazing furnace, the God we serve is able to deliver us from it, and he will deliver us from Your Majesty's hand. But even if he does not, we want you to know, Your Majesty, that we will not serve your gods or worship the image of gold you have set up. (Daniel 3:17-18)

Mic drop

Let's substitute fire with illness. If I am thrown headlong into horrific illness, my God is able to deliver me from it...but *even if he does not*, I will not serve any other gods...

Trusting God can be scary. It's tempting to stay in worry-land. I have a few favourite fears I constantly revisit like reruns, like 'This is never going to get better' and 'I'm geriatric'. Trust means remembering God is in charge of my days and no illness can take me out before he takes me home. My days are numbered—not by lupus, but by God.

I cannot tell you what the future holds. I cannot say what will happen tomorrow. But today I make this choice: I will follow God with all my heart, even if he does not deliver me. Sometimes it's tempting to think God has walked out on us and we are fighting fire with a water pistol, but there is another in the fire. He is with us.

> There is another in the fire. He is with us.

He is with us.

Surrounded

I love rewatching the *Lord of the Rings* trilogy. What a cracker. Epic battle scenes with a stirring score and a heart-thumping climax. The good guys win, but what amazes me about those battle scenes is how often things look hopeless for our heroes. There are many opportunities to despair. There are times when they are hemmed in on all sides, pinned down, surrounded. Then something on the landscape changes. A new hero appears—Gandalf, the ghost army, the Ents—and anything seems possible.

I often feel 'surrounded' by illness. I am tempted to despair, waiting in futility for the landscape to change. But I am reminded (perhaps by the Holy Spirit?) of the prophet Elisha in 2 Kings 6:8-23. He was at home with his servant when the King of Aram's army completely surrounded Elisha's city. While the servant panicked, Elisha sat, cool as a cucumber.

Oh, that I would keep my head when I am surrounded.

Elisha prayed for his servant: 'Open his eyes, Lord, so that he may see.' The Lord opened the servant's eyes and he saw: the hills around Elisha were filled with God's heavenly horses and chariots of fire. It looked like they were

> It looked like they were surrounded. And they were. By God.

surrounded. And they were. By God.

When I am surrounded by the armies of illness and battle cries fill my ears, may the Lord remind me I am surrounded by him. May the Lord open our eyes so we can see. May we remember not only that the Lord is with us, he sends angels to strengthen us, he guards and protects and fight for us, and a great cloud of witnesses watches over us.

We are surrounded.

Killing me softly

Illness has a way of bringing us to the end of ourselves. I am rapidly running out of ideas for survival. I am at the point where any survival on my part has nothing to do with me. It is entirely Jesus, and his grace, seeing me through. Maybe this is what Jesus meant about dying to self.

'For to me, to live is Christ and to die is gain', Paul famously said. (Philippians 1:21) Amen, brother. The goal of the Christian is to die to self. Less is more: the less there is of us, the more of Christ there is in us. The theory, however, is easier than the practice.

I would love if the 'dying to self' process was instantaneous. That would be way simpler, thanks very much. Unfortunately, dying to self seems lifelong and agonising.

What if physical pain and chronic illness are part of this process?

What if sickness is stripping away ourselves, making more room for Christ?

What if God allows illness—not causing but utilising it—to help us die to ourselves?

Fire helps the impurities in gold to rise to the surface. The fire of chronic illness has certainly brought my impurities to the surface: irritability, complaining, rage, doubt, depression, ugly crying, bitterness, disappointment. What if that was the point? What if that was God's purpose all along: to reveal my true fallen self to me, so I knew what must be put to death? What if fire helps us become holy?

Alia Joy understands the brutality of chronic weakness but also the potential for God to fill such cavernous weakness with himself:

> I didn't know my dry and weary bones were kindling for a spirit ablaze with the weight of God's glory...My deficiency was the strongest thing about me because God was fully present in my lack.[84]

When our bones wear out, perhaps God is gathering kindling for his holy bonfire.

I don't know why some of us suffer way more sickness than others. But I know God cares about our holiness—to the degree he will allow fire in our lives if it has a chance of making us holy.

> When our bones wear out, perhaps God is gathering kindling for his holy bonfire.

Putting myself to death does not look pretty. I have had some strongly worded conversations with God on the subject. But what can I say to God? You don't know what you're doing? You don't care? I would never buy that. I know in my bones he cares about me madly. Where can I run from God's presence? How can I possibly dodge his fire? I may resist—I've had enough fire to last me a lifetime—but I will ultimately surrender to his will because I love him and he loves me. I will surrender to the fire, not because I enjoy it (I'd rather have a root canal) but I know what awaits me on the other side. I will join with the penitent prayer of John Donne: 'My God, thou hast made this sick bed thine altar, and I have no other sacrifice to offer but myself.'[85]

I know the value of refined gold. I know God's heart for holiness. And I know, no matter what fire surrounds me, he is with me, watching, waiting, purifying.

My redeemer lives

God has a way of redeeming stuff I thought was dead and buried.

He has dropped new songs in the heights of unwellness. He has reminded me of his promises while I'm lying in hospital. He has moved others to show me incredible kindness. He has reminded me his angels and the cloud of witnesses are still looking out for me. Little old me.

There have been stretches of non-healing when I have begged him to intervene and he hasn't, followed by unexpected glimpses of kindness. He has not healed the illness in question, but slowly and gently redeemed what was lost. This is more than a 'silver lining' or 'count your blessings' sermon. (We've heard enough of those, am I right?) This is about God showing his love for us in surprising ways, especially when all hope seems lost.

I once had a stunningly clear dream about heaven. (Caveat: I am not claiming to have seen heaven. I only know what I dreamed—which may be entirely fictional.) I spent the dream roaming around a beautiful country campsite and awoke feeling like I had been on retreat. I had not asked God for a dream about heaven. I didn't know I needed that. But he ambushed me with a gift, totally unbidden and uninvited, just because he loves me. Moments like that can redeem dark days.

This is not about being grateful. This is about God being present in spite of our trials, seeing him in the middle of them as he really is. This is about the gentle and gradual ways God rebuilds us after the bushfire has devastated everything.

John the Baptist experienced the redemptive compassion of Jesus. His whole life was dedicated to pointing to Jesus. He knew who Jesus was. He even recognised Jesus while still in his mother's womb! (Luke 1:39-45)

Plot twist: John had severe doubts about Jesus. In Matthew 11, sitting in jail, John gave voice to his doubts: 'Are you the One we've been expecting, or are we still waiting?'

Notice what Jesus did not say in reply. He did not tick John off for lacking faith. He did not accuse him of being a bad prophet. He did not get offended by John's doubts. Instead, he gave this stunning response:

> Go back and tell John what's going on: the blind see, the lame walk, lepers are cleansed, the deaf hear, the dead are raised, the wretched of the earth learn that God is on their side. Is this what you were expecting? Then count yourselves most blessed! (Matthew 11: 2-6 MSG)

Jesus reminded John, gently but firmly, he was doing God's work. He said he came for the wretched of the earth—including John. He confirmed John would be blessed if he believed and trusted Jesus. He redeemed John's faith.

It can be hard to trust Jesus when everything goes wrong. Like John, we can feel like neglected prisoners where hope is not merely endangered but extinct. We can question things we never thought we would: God, do you care? Are you listening? Are you still good, even now? And Jesus says: 'I am the Christ. I am doing good things in the earth. I will do good things in you. Trust me. Even in prison, trust.' I'm hanging on to that.

Did you notice Jesus did not deliver John from jail? He left him there. He didn't physically redeem him. John still lost his head. Nothing Jesus said changed that outcome. But Jesus redeemed John from the inside out.

Jesus redeemed Peter too. Peter did one of the most unforgivable things: denying Jesus. Three times. Kinda throws our doubts into sharp relief, doesn't it? And Jesus redeemed Peter. This is our redeemer. There is nothing on earth he cannot redeem. There is still time. It is not too late. While we are still breathing, this story is not finished. God, the redeemer, is at work.

> While we are still breathing, this story is not finished. God, the redeemer, is at work.

There have been times when God has healed me, not of lupus but specific symptoms and injuries. He has brought instant pain relief or restored movement when everything was completely frozen. He has made colds and flus disappear. He has brought the sweetness of sleep. He has brought caring people when I needed them. Even though lupus remains, God has redeemed my wellbeing.

In my mind, redemption looks like God and I sitting together on a deck, sharing a pot of tea, watching the sun go down. In a space where we can breathe, we talk about everything: fear, courage, pain, depression, progress, beauty, weakness and gratitude. I speak in bursts, spewing ideas and reflections as they come to me, and he does not interrupt. We lapse into silence between speaking and wondering. We are not frantically searching for answers. We are in the not-knowing together; even though he is all-knowing, he doesn't rescue me from not-knowing. I find his quietness oddly comforting. There is no pressure for me to be or do or solve. And there, in the middle of many unknowns, I begin to feel OK again.

Breathing space is a form of redemption. So is a friend inviting me to coffee. A bird suddenly landing next to me. A kiss from my cat. An out-of-the-blue compliment. An old song springing back into consciousness. A storm breaking overhead on a weepy kind of day.

These are things I cannot control or conjure. These are moments of redemption, awakening the hope I thought was dead and buried. They say, 'Maybe things will get better'. They give me glimpses of joy—yes, God can redeem joy! My body may be sick, but God is redeeming my heart and mind and spiritual health. I'm so glad God is passionate about redemption.

My redeemer lives.

Take a moment to notice how you are feeling after the chapter, and whether anything stood out for you or resonated with you. Time for some self-care.

I found treasures in the back of the cave.

I found freedom from proving myself and earning approval. I found liberty in relenting and relying on God's pace rather than my own. I have been slowly and painfully emancipated from the clutches of the Perfectionist. Life can look different, I can be different, from how I am 'supposed' to be.

These treasures I found in the dark, sifting the dirt, inch by inch, moment by moment, without light.

13

INCONCLUSIONS

How Shall We Live?

So how do we ride the rollercoaster of chronic illness?

How shall we follow God through the fog of mystery?

How shall we respond when let down by our bodies?

I don't have ready answers for you. (The chapter title probably gave that away.) There's no formula, no promise of breakthrough, no seven steps for 'claiming' your healing. But I have some final thoughts to share. I will not dispense false hope or guarantees. But I do want to impart genuine hope that things may one day get better, and that Christ's redemption is chasing us down.

Relentless illness, relentless God

As relentless as illness is, God's love is even more relentless.

God has ambushed me with kindness and sprinkled droplets of goodness over my days. He has appeared unbidden in the night, visiting me in songs, visions, dreams, the caring words of others, the wide rolling thunder and the kiss of rain. He has persistently loved me without regard for my mood or subjective sense of spirituality. He has loved me without restraint, without guardedness, with compassion and vulnerability. He has loved me stronger than an ancient tree and gentler than a flower's petal.

This is my confidence: God's love will pursue me even more relentlessly than illness. My faith can be shaken and shattered, but Christ cannot be shaken. He is the rock of salvation and I build my life upon that rock—not my own strength. Coz I don't have any left. Christ endures. His love endures. That's the alternative to the dominant story of chronic illness. God chronically loves us, he is chronically near in suffering, and he brings chronic light to a chronically dark world.

In John 9:1-41, Jesus heals a blind man who then gets interrogated by the Pharisees and thrown out of the synagogue. He doesn't know what Jesus looks like or how to find him. So Jesus takes the initiative, seeks him out and reveals himself as the Messiah. Sometimes my faith is so blinded I no longer know how to find Jesus. Good news: Jesus seeks us out. It's not all up to us. When we are lost, he finds us.

> When we are lost, he finds us.

When I am trapped in a dark cave looking for a way out, I

hold on to that thread of hope that God's love will find me. When immersed in deep water, I trust God's love will meet me underwater. When I am lost, overwrought, surrounded by fire, I hope and pray God's love will be the single common plotline in these stories—his story. Through many dangers, toils and snares, God's love has pursued and hunted me down. Nothing can separate me from his love. The great magnitude of his grace which brought me thus far will lead me home.

'Surely your goodness and love will follow me all the days of my life, and I will dwell in the house of the Lord forever.' (Psalm 23:6) I couldn't have said it better.

Resurrection

I have glimpsed resurrection in this life.

Every time I've had vocal nodules, God has healed me. He has given my voice something new each time, a new quality or greater range. I never would have gained that without the nodules. God can redeem anything.

I will get a new body one day. This body is a daily reminder of the impermanence of life and the part of me that is eternal. The resurrection holds a great promise for all of us: deliverance from sin and pain. For those of us with bodies that are particularly broken, the notion of resurrection holds special hope. Romans 8:23 says,

> We ourselves, who have the firstfruits of the Spirit, groan inwardly as we wait eagerly for our adoption to sonship, the redemption of our bodies.

I've certainly done my share of groaning, waiting for that redemption.

When I think of resurrection, I think of *The Last Battle* by C.S. Lewis.[86] (Yes, you are reading a book written by a Narnia fan. Come at me.) When the characters arrive in Aslan's country (spoilers), they look like their normal selves except they are dressed in their nicest and most comfortable clothes. The dirt of battle is gone. Their injuries no longer hurt. The older ones feel 'unstiffened'.

In the resurrection we may not get a complete overhaul like selecting a new body from a buffet, but a refreshed version of our true selves—without the suffering that marks our current lived experience. Some say our heavenly bodies will carry our scars and disabilities, in the same way Jesus still bears his crucifixion scars. This poses some interesting questions: will we retain surgical scars, burns, deformities? Will I take my twisted spine into heaven? What about those with amputated limbs? Maybe some of these 'disabilities' will turn up in heaven. And maybe that's OK. As one deaf lady puts it: 'I look forward to signing with Jesus in heaven.'[87] There will be no pain in heaven and no reason to cry (Revelation 21:4); what form that takes is God's business, but I know he delights in making all things new.

Our bodies and brokenness remind us this life is temporary. The groaning of our bodies mirrors the yearning of this earth for resurrection, and God's nearness in the midst of illness mirrors the nearing restoration of this world, his impending plan to make all things new. In the meantime, my body still breathes. Every breath is God's life-giving

> *The groaning of our bodies mirrors the yearning of this earth for resurrection.*

power keeping me alive, keeping me here.

I don't know how long this temporary resurrection will continue until the lasting one hits. But I know God can, and probably will, continue redeeming me till then.

The ongoing wrestle

Surprisingly, I don't know everything.

This book was never supposed to be a 'healing action plan' or anything so trite. (Not that healing is trite. But formularised healing might be.) This book was intended to explore and ask hard questions without necessarily answering them. Including questions about God and faith.

It is tricky to ask such questions, partly because it is countercultural (you are supposed to 'just believe', aren't you?) and partly because it can give rise to attachment concerns. Will God get angry or impatient with us for doubting? Will he walk away? Will he punish us? Faith, for most of us, is not a straight road from A to B. Instead, it resembles a zigzag road, or a roundabout, or a rollercoaster. The older I get, the more I think the zigzag is the norm rather than the exception. *Breathes audible sigh of relief*

While I generally remain confident in God's love and steadfastness, the rest of me waxes and wanes according to circumstances, flares, mood and spiritual temperature. I have moments of sweet

> *I may continue to wrestle with God. And myself. And illness.*

closeness with God, and times I can hardly bear to face him. I have ongoing questions that refuse to resolve themselves. I struggle to comprehend my illness and keep the faith. I may continue to wrestle with God. And myself. And illness.

There will be mental gymnastics around taking up my cross and following a God whose 'yoke is easy'. (Matthew 11:30) I will wrestle with the notion that while God does not heal, he promises his strength in our weaknesses (2 Corinthians 12:9), not 'brute strength but a glorious inner strength'. (Ephesians 3:16 MSG) I will rest and revel in the strengthening of his Spirit. Some days I will resist him; others, I will embrace his invitation in Matthew 11:28: 'Come to me, all you who are weary and burdened, and I will give you rest.'

Wrestling is not inherently bad. Jacob wrestled with God in Genesis 32:24-31 and his hip was permanently thrown out—but God blessed him there. It takes great courage to wrestle, especially out loud. Beautiful things can come from wrestling: we can discover solidarity with others, friends willing to journey with us; we can remember our faith is built on Christ who can never be shaken; we can be surprised by kindness from God.

Times of wrestling can be interspersed with times of nestling (thanks to Brent Christianson[88] for the idea). Just like a baby bird nestles in the nest in between times of being forcibly kicked out to learn to fly, so we may experience times of comfort between the challenges. We may wrestle with God but we can nestle with him too. When we are worn out, exhausted from the physical and mental gymnastics of chronic illness, we can climb into God's lap and say, 'I can't do it anymore, God. I'm out. I'm done.' At times, he waits for us to reach the end of our tether so he can step in.

Like the prodigal son, sometimes we must come to the end of ourselves to rediscover our home in him. And he welcomes us like the father welcomed the prodigal son (Luke 15:20), not reluctantly or with a sigh but madly running out to meet us and throwing his arms around us.

Making meaning, glimpsing joy

> There may not be profound spiritual meaning behind our illness. But we can make meaning of it—or search for meaning.

There may not be profound spiritual meaning behind our illness. But we can make meaning of it—or search for meaning, as Viktor Frankl did in his concentration camp (see Chapter 4). Or perhaps we may break in interesting ways. Or fill the cracks with gold.

Some find meaning in helping fellow sufferers, perhaps through sharing information or offering emotional support. I have recommended good doctors to friends with autoimmune diseases, because good autoimmune specialists are rarer than cures for lupus. It feels good to use my hard-earned wisdom for others. Some find meaning in sharing their faith. Friends of mine have talked about Jesus with other patients in hospital and with staff. You never know who God might bring across your path.

I have received unquestionable kindness from others. Doctors, nurses and even fellow patients have gone out of their way to show me they care. Once a patient saw me sobbing in the doctor's waiting room and insisted I jump the queue ahead of her. 'I can wait, but you can't', she said emphatically. I was beyond grateful. It restores my faith in humanity. And it feels like an encounter with God.

Others find meaning in becoming fierce advocates for change or champions for a cure. Some participate in clinical trials. Some fight for funding, because some diseases are poorly funded. Common diseases typically receive more funding because they impact more of the population. While this makes sense, it means rare illnesses like lupus are neglected.

Other ways of helping fellow illness-livers (sounds like a liver disease, doesn't it?) include joining support groups or online forums. I derive immense satisfaction in exploiting my illness (sucks to be you, lupus), using my lived experience to write passionate messages of support to others. I can't live the life I want, but I can still write about it. I have something to offer. I am more than lupus, more than limitations, more than loss. Plus, my writing might help others. That's meaningful.

We can find meaning in digging deep in our faith. We can hijack what illness meant for evil and channel it into worshiping God. That is not always easy—the zigzag road leaps to mind—but if we do find richer and more durable faith in the process, that's meaningful. It holds meaning when we join with Christ in his suffering—perhaps the highest honour in the kingdom. Our surrender in the midst of great pain links us to Christ's surrender on the cross. It gives life meaning when we discover God's presence and joy in our mess.

Speaking of joy, nothing adds purpose to our days like joy. Joy does not remove the impact of illness—but neither does illness completely remove our joy. I have experienced the sweetness of God's presence, the sweetness of sincere friendship, sweet acts of mercy from others, and the sweet taste of exquisite chocolate in the midst of horrible illness. Sweetness alongside the bitterness.

I find joy in simple things: reconnecting with a friend, being in nature, having a belly laugh, indulging in silliness (especially the overtired kind), being playful, throwing myself into something even though I'll pay for it later, doing things I loved as a kid, enjoying the little things, being grateful, lingering with enjoyment, noticing fun moments, exoticising the domestic. None of these things sound super spiritual, and they don't have to be. Sometimes reconnecting with joy helps. And sometimes God meets us in those spaces.

If we do not find deeper faith or sweetness in this life, we may find value in thinking of the next life. The bible refers to receiving crowns in heaven, and some believe the hardships of this world will turn into jewels in our heavenly crowns. It might help to think of every illness, every flare, every rough day as another jewel in your crown. I can't promise you jewels or crowns—that is God's business—but God certainly sees everything we go through and will not forget it.

Finding meaning does not necessarily take away the sting of illness. It does not make it easier to bear. But it might help us hold on, especially on the bad days. Anything that keeps us holding on is worth it.

> It might help to think of every illness, every flare, every rough day as another jewel in your crown.

How can she sing anyway?

In a world and body gone mad, it can be tempting to question God's goodness. 'How can God still be good?' we cry.

Look at a flower. It may be beautiful in colour and form and give off a stunning fragrance, but eventually it withers. The flower might be picked to pieces by birds or shredded by storms. Does that make the flower any less beautiful? Does it make God any less good? Of course not. The flower retains its inherent beauty as a creation of the Creator, despite the ills that befall it. Same with us.

This world contains brokenness as well as beauty. I hold great admiration for God's creation. I am in awe of his giant mountains and tiny ladybugs. I see his splendour spelled out in the world—and worship him. Our bodies are part of his creation, like those ladybugs. Our bodies, luminescent though ravaged by disease, are just as fearfully and wonderfully made. It's taken me a while to see that. I thought my body was trash because it refused to work properly. But I love his creation—and I'm part of that.

It may take time before I see the extent of beauty in this body that I currently see in a flower. But God is gently helping me see he takes just as much delight in me, whom he created, as he takes in magnificent gardens and stunning alpine ranges. It all comes from him, and it all points back to him. God is showing me he is still good, even when I can only see the bad.

So how do I respond to God's goodness when everything looks dreadful? How do I respond when the great chameleon strikes again, when my wellbeing, hope and voice are taken from me? I go back to what God told me: 'Your testimony will be that you worshiped me *in the middle of your illness*.'

> When people look at me I hope they no longer ask, 'How can God be good when she is so sick?', but rather, 'How can she sing anyway?'

I will sing anyway. Even in a faltering voice, even in a whisper, even with half my vocal range gone, I will sing. While I have breath in my lungs, I will sing, even breathlessly. I don't know how long I have, but my time and health are God's. And while I can still draw breath, every breath will be a monument to his kindness.

When people look at me I hope they no longer ask, 'How can God be good when she is so sick?', but rather, 'How can she sing anyway?' Let that be my testimony. Let that be a spectacle of grace. Let that simple act of resistance show God's splendour. Let my song bring him glory—more than physical healing ever could.

Grace awaits us

God hasn't healed me. But he has been near in every painful flare, every trip to hospital, every silent night. He has engraved me on the palms of his hands. (Isaiah 49:16) He cares deeply about the things that affect me. He is with me in the fire. He surrounds me. I can join with King David saying, 'Oh, blessed be God! He didn't go off and leave us.' (Psalm 124:6 MSG) I may be in troubled waters, up a certain creek without a paddle, but God has not abandoned me there. Which is great, because I need God's presence way more than physical healing.

What difference does it make, knowing God's grace is near? All the difference. We can lean on the grace of the God who gives us himself rather than answers, who speaks in storms and whispers rather than words, who names us and has sworn himself to us, who will not and cannot abandon us, who joins us in fires and deep waters and prison cells, who weeps and improvises alongside us, who empathises out of his own human experience, who promises us not deliverance but his Spirit, who ambushes us with kindness and surprises us with hope.

Grace awaits us in every difficulty, every depressed day, every diagnosis. Grace awaits us in hospital beds and MRI machines.

Grace awaits us in sleep and sleepless nights. Grace awaits us in misery and mystery.

When we have questions, grace waits for us there.

When we are filled with faith and joy, grace meets us there.

When we are at the end of our rope, grace is waiting right there.

That grace is enough to hold me. Within myself, I am not enough. My resilience has gone, worn out like pages of a book read too many times, my faith brittle as nails, my hope eaten away like my bones. By God's grace alone I can stand. I am held by that grace, steadied by it, swaddled by it. Through many dangers, toils and snares, we have come. Grace will lead us home.[89]

Let grace hold you. When nothing else works, when weariness seeps into your bone marrow, when you can scarcely speak, let grace hold you. When no one understands and God himself seems silent, let grace hold you. When it takes all your energy to pass air in and out your lungs, let grace hold you. I have nothing else to offer—only empathy, the assurance you are not alone, and a glimpse of God's grace in the apocalypse.

> When it takes all your energy to pass air in and out your lungs, let grace hold you.

Let grace hold you.

Benediction

This is my prayer for you:

> The Lord bless you and keep you;
> The Lord make his face shine on you and be gracious to you;

> The Lord turn his face toward you and give you
> peace. (Numbers 6:24-26)

I pray for Emmanuel to be with you.

I pray Christ will be before you and behind you, on your left and right. May Christ be all around you and within you, bathing you in peace, soaking you in love.

I pray for God's courage to accompany you and his non-anxious presence to reside in you.

I pray for the quiet assurance of the Spirit to rest upon you.

I pray for wholeness throughout your entire being, inside and out.

I pray for God's spectacle of grace to be displayed in you.

I pray you will hold on to Jesus when you have nothing and no one else.

I pray, whenever your path diverts down strange and shadowy roads, you will find grace waiting for you there.

I pray for grace to hold you in the face of horrific pain, catastrophic medical appointments, devastating diagnoses, regressive narratives, crippling fatigue, crises of faith, the abyss of grief, seasons of doubt, depths of despair and hints of hope.

And I pray it won't be long before we meet Jesus face to face, fully redeemed and resurrected, and he wipes every last tear from our eyes.

Take a moment to notice how you are feeling after the chapter, and whether anything stood out for you or resonated with you. Time for some self-care.

*There is a light on the water.
I can't see where it's coming from.*

It shines like a beacon, a long line of white against the night. It flashes in my face, leaving me momentarily blinded. I shake my head and squint into the distance. There's someone there. They're coming this way.

I try to move my arms and legs, but they are stiff and cold from the water. Feebly I begin splashing and thrashing about to get my muscles moving. Slowly I inch my way toward the approaching light. Hands grab me. They lift me up. My teeth chatter. Tears escape from my eyes.

*I am cold, exhausted and wet
through—but I'm home.*

HELPFUL RESOURCES

13YARN: 13 92 76. https://www.13yarn.org.au/
1800RESPECT (DV/Sexual Assault helpline): 1800 737 732. https://www.1800respect.org.au/
Arthritis Australia: 1800 011 041. https://arthritisaustralia.com.au/
Beyond Blue: 1300 224 636. https://www.beyondblue.org.au/
Beyond Now: suicide prevention app from Beyond Blue, available to download from the Apple Store and Google Play. https://www.beyondblue.org.au/get-support/beyondnow-suicide-safety-planning
Carer Gateway: 1800 422 737. https://www.carergateway.gov.au/
Carers NSW: (02) 9280 4744. https://www.carersnsw.org.au/
Dulwich Centre: (08) 8223 3966. https://dulwichcentre.com.au/
DV Connect: 1800 811 811. https://www.dvconnect.org/
DV Line: 1800 65 64 63.
Emerge Australia: support for those living with Myalgic Encephalomyelitis (ME) or Chronic Fatigue Syndrome (CFS), as well as Long Covid. 1800 865 321. https://www.emerge.org.au/
Endometriosis Australia: https://endometriosisaustralia.org/
Haven (Steph Penny's song): https://youtu.be/QixVwc7qnwI?si=PSdo5DGhlmlNP5Ug
Headstart (searchable mental health service website): https://headstart.org.au/
Lifeline: 13 1114. Text: 0477 13 11 14. https://www.lifeline.org.au/
LivingWorks (suicide first aid training): https://livingworks.com.au/
Lupus Association of NSW Inc.: 1800 80 20 88. https://lupusnsw.org.au/

MensLine Australia: 1300 79 88 79. https://mensline.org.au/
Mental Health Line: 1800 011 511. https://www.health.nsw.gov.au/mentalhealth/Pages/mental-health-line.aspx
National Domestic Violence Hotline (U.S.): https://www.thehotline.org/resources/healthy-relationships/
National Organisation for Rare Diseases (NORD): https://rarediseases.org/
NDIS: 1800 800 110. https://www.ndis.gov.au/
Suicide Call Back Service: 1300 659 467. https://www.suicidecallbackservice.org.au/
Wilderness to WILD: https://www.wildernesstowild.com/

ABOUT THE AUTHOR

STEPH PENNY is an author, blogger and songwriter who is passionate about using her lived experience to help others. *Surviving Chronic Illness* is the third book in the *Survival* series, following *Surviving Childlessness* and *Surviving Singledom*.

Steph blogs weekly about chronic illness, childlessness, singledom, creativity and countercultural Christian living. You can subscribe to her blog here: **www.stephpenny.com.au**.

Steph's songs can be found at her website and on YouTube (just search for Steph Penny) and don't forget to subscribe to her YouTube channel!

Connect with Steph on [f] and [y] for the latest on her books, blogs and songs.

> *Like Steph's writing?*
> *She would love to hear from you!*
> *Contact Steph direct via social media*
> *or her website, or email her at*
> *steph@stephpenny.com.au.*

REFERENCES

1. Newton, J 1772, Amazing grace, public domain, Great Britain.

2. Burke Harris, N 2014, *How childhood trauma affects health across a lifetime*, online video, September 2014, viewed 27 May 2022, https://www.ted.com/talks/nadine_burke_harris_how_childhood_trauma_affects_health_across_a_lifetime?language=en

3. Apostolopoulos, D & Hoi, AY 2013, 'Systemic lupus erythmatosus', in *Australian Family Physician*, Volume 42, Issue *10*, viewed 18 February 2023, https://www.racgp.org.au/afp/2013/october/systemic-lupus-erythmatosus/

4. Benness, B 2020, 'Brianne's TEDx talk: Disease begins before diagnosis', *No end in sight blog*, online video, 10 September, viewed 18 February 2023, https://noendinsight.co/briannes-tedx-talk-disease-begins-before-diagnosis/

5. Hagenbach, AJ 2019, *Glorious weakness*, Baker Books, Grand Rapids, Michigan, United States of America.

6. Miserandino, C 2019, 'The spoon theory written by Christine Miserandino', *But you don't look sick blog*, web log post, viewed 18 February 2023, https://butyoudontlooksick.com/articles/written-by-christine/the-spoon-theory/

7   Morgan, A 2000, *What is Narrative Therapy?*, Dulwich Centre Publications, Adelaide, South Australia, Australia, viewed 17 July 2023, https://dulwichcentre.com.au/what-is-narrative-therapy/

8   Weingarten, K 2001, *Making sense of illness narratives: Braiding theory, practice and the embodied life*, Dulwich Centre, viewed 18 February 2023, https://dulwichcentre.com.au/articles-about-narrative-therapy/illness-narratives/

9   Brock, B 2021, *Disability*, Baker Publishing Group, Grand Rapids, Michigan, United States of America.

10 Fossella, T 2011, 'Human nature, buddha nature: An interview with John Welwood', *Tricycle: The Buddhist review*, viewed 01 December 2023, https://tricycle.org/magazine/human-nature-buddha-nature/

11 Anthony, I 2019, *The steadiness of improvising*, Reservoir Church, 09 June, viewed 18 February 2023, https://www.reservoirchurch.org/sermon/the-steadiness-of-improvising/

12 McKibben Dana, M 2018, *God, improv, and the art of living*, Eerdmans Publishing Co., Grand Rapids, Michigan, United States of America.

13 Frankl, VE 1959, *Man's search for meaning*, Random House Group, United Kingdom.

14 Frankl, VE 1959, *Man's search for meaning*, Random House

Group, United Kingdom.

15 Peterson, E 2000, *A long obedience in the same direction*, InterVarsity Press, Downers Grove, Illinois, United States of America.

16 Clifton, S & Wells, GEC 2020, 'Theology of disability: The Spirit and disabled empowerment', in Wolfgang Vondey (Ed.) *The Routledge handbook of Pentecostal theology*, Routledge, Oxford, United Kingdom, and New York, United States of America.

17 St Andrew's Cathedral Sydney, 2023, *Disability and the church*, online video, 26 May, viewed 21 July 2023, https://www.youtube.com/live/Ssm8qz2S0oo?feature=share

18 Lewis, C S 1955, *The magician's nephew*, The Bodley Head, London, United Kingdom.

19 O'Rourke, M 2013, 'What's wrong with me?', *The New Yorker*, 19 August, viewed 18 February 2023, https://www.newyorker.com/magazine/2013/08/26/whats-wrong-with-me?utm_source=onsite-share&utm_medium=email&utm_campaign=onsite-share&utm_brand=the-new-yorker

20 O'Rourke, M 2013, 'What's wrong with me?', *The New Yorker*, 19 August, viewed 18 February 2023, https://www.newyorker.com/magazine/2013/08/26/whats-wrong-with-me?utm_source=onsite-share&utm_medium=email&utm_campaign=onsite-share&utm_brand=the-new-yorker

21 Krznaric, R 2012, 'Ready for a vulnerability hangover? Five ideas from Brené Brown', *Roman Krznaric blog*, viewed 14 January 2023, https://www.romankrznaric.com/outrospection/2012/10/16/1729

22 Schramer, M H 2018, *Has serious or chronic illness got you depressed?*, Edward-Elmhurst Health, viewed 14 January 2023, https://www.eehealth.org/blog/2018/03/chronic-illness-depression/

23 ABS (Australian Bureau of Statistics) 2020-2022a, *National Study of Mental Health and Wellbeing (https://www.abs.gov.au/statistics/health/mental-health/national-study-mental-health-and-wellbeing/2020-2022#comorbidity-of-mental-disorders-and-physical-conditions)*, viewed 01 December 2023.

24 Doka, KJ 2008, 'Disenfranchised grief in historical and cultural perspective', in Stroebe, MS, Hansson, RO, Schut, H & Stroebe, W (Eds.), *Handbook of bereavement research and practice: Advances in theory and intervention*, pp. 223–240, viewed 3 February 2023, https://psycnet.apa.org/record/2008-09330-011

25 Brown, B 2013, *Brené Brown on empathy*, online video, 10 December, viewed 18 January 2023, https://youtu.be/1Evwgu369Jw

26 Lewis, CS 1961, *A Grief Observed*, Faber and Faber Ltd, London, United Kingdom.

27 Storment, J 2016, 'Bono and Eugene Peterson on the Psalms', *Patheos*, 26 May, viewed 18 February 2023, https://www.patheos.com/blogs/jonathanstorment/2016/05/bono-and-eugene-peterson-on-the-psalms/

28 Smith, K 2021, *Chronic pain and anxiety: How to cope*, Psycom, viewed 15 January 2023, https://www.psycom.net/chronic-pain-illness-anxiety

29 Tjornehoj, T 2023, *The relationship between anxiety and depression*, Hartgrove Behavioural Health System, viewed 15 January 2023, https://www.hartgrovehospital.com/relationship-anxiety-depression/

30 Rokach, A 2016, *Psychological, emotional and physical experiences of hospitalized children*, Open Access Text, viewed 16 January 2023, https://www.oatext.com/Psychological-emotional-and-physical-experiences-of-hospitalized-children.php

31 Owens, B 2023, *Cumulative stress and PTSD*, Black Bear Lodge, Georgia, United States of America, viewed 16 January 2023, https://blackbearrehab.com/mental-health/ptsd/cumulative-stress-and-ptsd/

32 Fabian, R 2019, 'What you should know about chronic illness-induced PTSD', *The Mighty*, 29 August, viewed 16 January 2023, https://themighty.com/topic/chronic-illness/chronic-illness-induced-ptsd-trauma/

33 American Psychiatric Association 2023, *What is Posttraumatic Stress Disorder (PTSD)?*, American Psychiatric Association, Washington, D.C., United States of America, viewed 27 October 2023, https://www.psychiatry.org/patients-families/ptsd/what-is-ptsd

34 King, P 2004, *Your life matters*, Random House Australia, North Sydney, New South Wales, Australia.

35 Family Planning Australia, *All about sex*, Family Planning Australia, viewed 20 January 2023, https://www.fpnsw.org.au/factsheets/individuals/disability/all-about-sex

36 Better Health Channel, 2021, *Disability and sexuality*, Better Health Channel, viewed 20 January 2023, https://www.betterhealth.vic.gov.au/health/servicesandsupport/disability-and-sexuality

37 Aruma, 2019, *Sex and disability: The facts*, Aruma, viewed 20 January 2023, https://www.aruma.com.au/about-us/blog/sex-and-disability-the-facts/

38 Shine SA, 2023, *Sexual health and people living with a disability*, Shine SA, viewed 20 January 2023, https://shinesa.org.au/community-information/disability-sexuality/sexual-health-living-with-disability/

39 Penny, S 2016, *Surviving singledom: Or hang in there!*, Christianity Works, India.

40 Penny, S 2021, *Surviving childlessness: Faith and Furbabies*, SOS Print and Media, Sydney, New South Wales, Australia.

41 1800RESPECT, 2022, *Domestic, family and sexual violence experienced by people with disability*, 1800RESPECT, viewed 20 January 2023, https://www.1800respect.org.au/inclusive-practice/supporting-people-with-disability

42 DVConnect, 2023, *What is domestic violence?*, DVConnect, viewed 20 January 2023, https://www.dvconnect.org/womensline/what-is-domestic-violence/

43 Dugal, S & Wise-Mays, B 2023, *Wilderness to WILD*, viewed 08 December 2023, https://www.wildernesstowild.com/

44 National Domestic Violence Hotline, 2023, *Healthy relationships*, U.S. Department of Justice, Texas, United States of America, viewed 08 December 2023, https://www.thehotline.org/resources/healthy-relationships/

45 Peterson, E 2000, *A long obedience in the same direction*, InterVarsity Press, Downers Grove, Illinois, United States of America.

46 Plass, A 2018, 'Jesus—safe, tender, extreme', *Adrian Plass blog*, viewed 21 January 2023, https://adrianplass.com/product/jesus-safe-tender-extreme/

47 Mayfield, K 2022, *Attached to God*, Zondervan, Grand Rapids, Michigan, United States of America.

48 Kirkpatrick, LA & Shaver, PR 1990, 'Attachment theory and religion: Childhood attachments, religious beliefs, and conversion', in *Journal for the Scientific Study of Religion*, Volume 29, No 3 (Sept 1990), pp. 315-334, viewed 30 June 2023, https://www.jstor.org/stable/1386461?origin=crossref

49 Burke Harris, N 2014, *How childhood trauma affects health across a lifetime*, online video, viewed 21 January 2023, https://www.ted.com/talks/nadine_burke_harris_how_childhood_trauma_affects_health_across_a_lifetime?language=en

50 Lewis, CS 1961, *A Grief Observed*, Faber and Faber Ltd, London, United Kingdom.

51 Van Biema, D 2007, 'Mother Theresa's crisis of faith', *Time*, 23 August, viewed 18 February 2023, https://time.com/4126238/mother-teresas-crisis-of-faith/

52 Rilke, RM 2011, *Letters to a young poet*, Penguin Classics, St Ives, United Kingdom.

53 Donne, J 1959, *Devotions/Death's Duel*, Christian Classics Ethereal Library, Grand Rapids, Michigan, United States of America.

54 Lewis, CS 1954, *The horse and his boy*, Geoffrey Bles, London, United Kingdom.

55 Reinke, T 2015, *Newton on the Christian life: To live is Christ*,

Crossway, Wheaton, Illinois, United States of America.

56 Penny, S 2017, *Haven*, online video, 20 April, viewed 18 February 2023, https://www.youtube.com/watch?v=QixVwc7qnwl

57 Baird, J 2020, *Phosphorescence*, HarperCollins, Sydney, New South Wales, Australia.

58 Kobayashi, M, Kikuchi, D & Okamura, H 2009, 'Imaging of ultraweak spontaneous photon emission from human body displaying diurnal rhythm', in *PLoS ONE*, Volume 4, Issue 7, 16 July, viewed 18 February 2023, https://journals.plos.org/plosone/article?id=10.1371/journal.pone.0006256

59 Ulrich, R 1984, 'View through a window may influence recovery from surgery', in *Science*, New Series, Volume 224, Issue 4647, pp. 420-421, viewed 25 January 2023, https://www.researchgate.net/publication/17043718_View_Through_a_Window_May_Influence_Recovery_from_Surgery

60 Barton, J & Pretty, J 2010, 'What is the best dose of nature and green exercise for improving mental health? A multistudy analysis', in *Environmental Science & Technology*, Volume 44, Issue 10, pp. 3947-3955, viewed 25 January 2023, https://www.researchgate.net/publication/42587600_What_is_the_Best_Dose_of_Nature_and_Green_Exercise_for_Improving_Mental_Health_A_Multi-Study_Analysis

61 BBC Television, 2016, *Life that glows*, BBC Natural History

Unit, Bristol, United Kingdom.

62 Hemingway, E 1929, *A farewell to arms*, Charles Scribner's Sons, New York, United States of America.

63 Goodnet, 2020, *Head, heart, and gut: How to use the 3 brains*, Goodnet, 20 August, viewed 18 February 2023, https://www.goodnet.org/articles/head-heart-gut-how-to-use-3-brains

64 Hernandez, P, Gangsei, D & Engstrom, D 2007, 'Vicarious resilience: A new concept in work with those who survive trauma', in *Family Process*, Volume 46, Issue 2, pp. 229-241, viewed 27 January 2023, https://pubmed.ncbi.nlm.nih.gov/17593887/

65 Carey, M & Russell, S 2002, 'Externalising—Commonly-asked questions', in *International Journal of Narrative Therapy and Community Work*, Issue 2, No. 2, viewed 27 January 2023, https://dulwichcentre.com.au/articles-about-narrative-therapy/externalising/

66 Dulwich Centre, 2020, *Exoticising the domestic*, Dulwich Centre, viewed 28 January 2023, https://dulwichcentre.com.au/exoticising-the-domestic/

67 Ayres, E 2021, *Whole Notes*, ABC Books, Sydney, New South Wales, Australia.

68 Lewis, CS 1940, *The Problem of Pain*, Collins Clear-Type

Press, London and Glasgow, Great Britain.

69 Dulwich Centre, 2021, *Part one: Developing team sheets*, Dulwich Centre, viewed 18 February 2023, https://dulwichcentre.com.au/team-of-life/part-one-developing-team-sheets/

70 Seltzer, J 2023, *Pacing and management guide for ME/CFS*, The Myalgic Encephalomyelitis Action Network, viewed 18 February 2023, http://www.meaction.net/wp-content/uploads/2021/02/Pacing-and-Management-Guide-for-ME_CFS-9.pdf

71 The Editors of goop, 2019, *Brené Brown's simple gratitude practice*, GOOP, 28 November, viewed 29 January 2023, https://goop.com/wellness/mindfulness/brene-brown-gratitude-practice/

72 Mandras, EK 2018, *No title—Facebook update*, online video, 19 December, viewed 18 February 2023, https://www.facebook.com/ekonheim/videos/10216578473188440/

73 Kantrowitz, J 2020, *The long night: Readings and stories to help you through depression*, Fortress Press, Minneapolis, United States of America.

74 Ripken, N 2013, *The insanity of God*, B&H Publishing Group, Nashville, Tennessee, United States of America.

75 Radmacher, MA 2009, *Courage doesn't always roar*, Conari Press, San Francisco, California, United States of America.

76. Lewis, CS 1954, *The horse and his boy*, Geoffrey Bles/HarperCollins, London, United Kingdom.

77. Buechner, F 2009, *Listening to your life: Daily meditations with Frederick Buechner*, HarperOne, New York, United States of America.

78. Doka, KJ 2008, 'Disenfranchised grief in historical and cultural perspective', in Stroebe, MS, Hansson, RO, Schut, H & Stroebe, W (Eds.), *Handbook of bereavement research and practice: Advances in theory and intervention*, pp. 223–240, viewed 03 February 2023, https://psycnet.apa.org/record/2008-09330-011

79. Mowczko, M 2013, 'Biblical Women Who Led Celebrations and Lamentations', *Marg Mowczko blog*, web log post, 01 August, viewed 09 December 2022, https://margmowczko.com/bible-women-who-led-celebrations-and-lamentations/

80. Quoted in Yancey, P 1990, *Where is God when it hurts?* Zondervan, Grand Rapids, Michigan, United States of America.

81. Nouwen, HJM 1996, *The inner voice of love*, Random House, Inc., New York, New York, United States of America.

82. Hellwig, M 1983, 'Good news to the poor: Do they understand it better?' In *Tracing the Spirit*, James E Hug (ed.), Paulist Press, Mahwah, New Jersey, United States of America.

83. Lewis, CS 1961, *A Grief Observed*, Faber and Faber Ltd,

London, United Kingdom.

84 Hagenbach, AJ 2019, *Glorious weakness*, Baker Books, Grand Rapids, Michigan, United States of America.

85 Donne, J 1959, *Devotions/Death's Duel*, Christian Classics Ethereal Library, Grand Rapids, Michigan, United States of America.

86 Lewis, CS 1956, *The last battle*, The Bodley Head, London, United Kingdom.

87 St Andrew's Cathedral Sydney, 2023, *Disability and the church*, online video, 26 May, viewed 21 July 2023, https://www.youtube.com/live/Ssm8qz2S0oo?feature=share

88 Christianson, B 2019, *The good grief devotional: 52 weeks toward hope*, Fortress Press, Minneapolis, Minnesota, United States of America.

89 Newton, J 1772, *Amazing grace*, public domain, Great Britain.

www.ingramcontent.com/pod-product-compliance
Lightning Source LLC
Chambersburg PA
CBHW022031290426
44109CB00014B/816